THEY SAW IT HAPPEN

TO

D.W.M.P.

AND

IN MEMORY OF

V.P.N.

THEY SAW IT HAPPEN

*An Anthology
of Eyewitness's Accounts of
Events in British History
1689—1897*

By

T. CHARLES-EDWARDS

AND

B. RICHARDSON

ASSISTANT MASTERS, AMPLEFORTH COLLEGE

with a foreword by

DAVID MATHEW

OXFORD
BASIL BLACKWELL

© *Basil Blackwell & Mott, Ltd.*, 1958

0 631 05230 5

First Printed January, 1958
Second impression November, 1958
Third impression April, 1962
Reprinted 1965
,,   1970

PRINTED IN GREAT BRITAIN
BY A. T. BROOME AND SON, 18 ST. CLEMENT'S, OXFORD
AND BOUND BY THE KEMP HALL BINDERY, OXFORD

FOREWORD

We all need to study the materials for History and in this volume a selection of the sources of a prolonged and changing period is set out for us. Much of the detail is military and a certain unity links together the Duke of Marlborough's victories with the battles fought in the Crimea. On the naval side we deal with the shorter span between Admiral Vernon's attack on Cartagena and Lord Exmouth's bombardment of Algiers. It is inevitable that the bulk of these accounts should deal with fighting.

I have always thought that in regard to the Royal Navy two accounts in particular give us the feel of the period between the wars and, perhaps still better, of those years of blockade between the battles. There are first the incomparable *Recollections of James Anthony Gardner*, which provide in this volume an account of smugglers in the Channel. In these Recollections the life of the eighteenth century gunroom is faithfully recorded in tranquillity. He looks back on his years in the *Salisbury*, ' this[1] old devil of a ship, properly called the Hell Afloat '; on all the tribulations of a fourteen year old boy, and with these the occasional excitements like finding ' a vessel[2] from the coast of Africa in want of provisions, the crew living on parrots and monkeys and in great distress.' We see the generous reckless companions; the background of capillair and brandy. Lieutenant Field in the *Brunswick* is, perhaps, the prime example. ' He was,' wrote Gardner,[3] ' a very good fellow in many respects, but he drew a long bow and kept it up too much. He . . . could trace his genealogy to Henry II. Our ship was full of rats and one morning he caught four which he had baked in a pie with some pork chops.' Another companion Lieutenant Wangford of the *Edgar* roared[4] out " I am going to hell before the wind ".'

At the polite end of the scale of naval life is the delightful series of letters written by Captain Thomas Fremantle to his wife and printed in the Wynne Diaries. He was aboard the *Neptune*

[1] Printed for the Navy Records Society in 1906, p. 41.
[2] *Ibid*, p. 42.   [3] *Ibid*, p. 244.
[4] *Ibid*, p. 75.

off Cadiz before Trafalgar. 'These cabins,' he writes,[1] 'are so large that two wax candles are not perceived in them.' And again, 'I am[2] at the time living entirely in my upper cabin, the lower one painting, but what is the use of large apartments and neat without society.' His comments on those he met with on his travels reflect the self-confident insularity of many of those whose letters are printed in this volume. At Berehaven[3] 'there are two famous priests, father O'Flarty and father Mullahoon. . . . Father Mullahoon is of the social sort but much more the manners of the world, and more the conduct of a gentleman.' Some years later Freemantle is in the *Milford* lying off Lissa. 'I have[4] lately been paying a visit to the Pasha of Scutari, who made me a present of a fine Arabian horse which I mean to bring home with me. The Pasha is sixteen, married eighteen months ago. He had completely the manners of a gentleman, tho' he seemed diffident as it was the first visit ever made him by one of my rank. . . . This war in the Adriatic is a war of pots de chambres.' There is much that is typical of Fremantle's class and period in this calm assessment of a Turkish pasha and the Popish clergy.

Although there are different opinions on this subject, it seems to me that the real division in this period comes in 1815 with Waterloo. In the previous century there is still at times in evidence that impression which is first seen clearly at the Restoration, of the King-and-Court as managers. The notion is well conveyed in the words of Sir John Reresby, a wealthy country gentleman in politics, writing about the position of the Marquess of Halifax in the early years of William III. A fairly lengthy quotation is necessary. The conversation reported took place with a lady who acted as an agent on Halifax's behalf. 'She said[5] his lordship knew that herself was privy to his being often invited to Court, and that he might have had his own terms long before, but held off: but though he had now embarked so deep in another interest it became him to be aware, for the Earl of Danby would certainly gett before him and play the same part with him in this Court that Lord Sunderland had acted in the other: that all that

---

[1] *The Wynne Diaries*, ed. Anne Fremantle, vol. iii, p. 174.
[2] *Ibid*, iii, p. 209.   [3] *Ibid*, iii, p. 100.
[4] *Ibid*, iii, p. 364.
[5] *Memoirs of Sir John Reresby*, ed. Andrew Browning, pp. 552–3.

was doeing was upon sandy foundations.' It seems to me that
these phrases set the tone for political comment from close-at-
hand for almost a hundred years. This was the course that Lord
Hervey steered.

The most intimate account of the Hanoverian royal family is
that left by Lord Hervey. It begins at the time when, as the
memoirs writer[1] expresses it, ' the late King died on the road to
Hanover, on the 11th of June, 1727, at Osnaburg, in the very
same room where he was born.' The analysis of the outlook of
George II upon his native country gives in a little space the whole
complaint of the English courtiers against the House of Brunswick. 'After this[2] last journey Hanover had so completed the
conquest of his (the King's) affections that there was nothing
English ever commended in his presence that he did not always
show, or pretend to show, was surpassed by something of the
same kind in Germany. No English or even French cook could
dress a dinner; no English confectioner set out a dessert; no
English player could act; no English coachman could drive, or
English jockey ride, nor were any English horses fit to be drove
or fit to be ridden; no Englishman knew how to come into a room,
nor any Englishwoman how to dress herself, nor were there any
diversions in England, public or private, nor any man or woman
in England whose conversation was to be borne—the one, as he
said, talking of nothing but their dull politics, and the others of
nothing but their ugly clothes. Whereas at Hanover all these
things were in the utmost perfection.' This is a passage which
should be studied in depth; it makes so very plain what were the
contemporary preoccupations.

A companion piece[3] deals with the conversation at Court.
' His Majesty stayed about five minutes in the gallery; snubbed
the Queen, who was drinking chocolate, for being always stuffing,
the Princess Emily for not hearing him, the Princess Caroline for
being grown fat, the Duke (of Newcastle) for standing awkwardly,
Lord Hervey for not knowing what relation the Prince of Sultzbach was to the Elector Palatine.' This last query was typical
of a long interest at the British Court. It may be held to have

---

[1] Lord Hervey's *Memoirs*, ed. Romney Sedgwick, vol. i, p. 22.
[2] *Ibid*, ii, p. 485   [3] *Ibid*, ii, p. 490

continued until Lord Acton, as a lord-in-waiting, satisfied the ageing Queen Victoria on the intricacies of German royal genealogies. This chimes with one of the King's comments when he was lamenting the restricted choice of brides for his son Frederick. 'Besides,[1] for Protestant princesses there is not a great choice of matches. The Princess of Denmark he would not have. The Princesses of Prussia have a madman for their father, and I did not think ingrafting my half-witted coxcomb upon a madwoman would mend the breed.'

A problem for the student is the need to attempt a correct assessment. Thus whatever Queen Anne's qualities, it is beyond dispute that the Duchess of Marlborough's account printed in this volume is a piece of calculated invective composed in a flaming temper by a woman enraged by her husband's dismissal. Another example is that of Mrs. Arbuthnot. She was a woman of charm, who managed her own life with discretion. An element of venom is apparent in her account of the uninhibited manners of George IV at his coronation. A tribute from the same source is paid to Castlereagh. This errs in the other direction. There is no reference here to his formidable character; to the moneyed Ulster stock from which he sprang; to his capacity to arrange with so many Anglo-Irish gentlemen about the terms on which they would support the Government. There is no suggestion that he was in fact marmoreal and implacable. Primary sources are of great significance; it is an interesting work trying to evaluate them.

The period after Waterloo is very skilfully presented. The entertainment of tenants at Petworth and at Belvoir are nicely contrasted pieces. The increasing element of the popular choice is carefully indicated in the successive accounts of the Westminster Elections. There is a remarkable account of Peterloo. The stage coach journeys and the coming of the railways are both clearly set down. The description of the House of Commons as it appeared to Prince von Puckler-Muskau is most illuminating. A whole passing generation is summed up in the interview with Dr. J. M. Routh, who was president of Magdalen from 1791 until 1854.

[1] *Ibid*, iii, p. 814.

The last section of the volume deals with the reign of Queen Victoria and opens suitably with the account of her accession and coronation from her private journals. The spirit of the Factory Acts is set out plainly. Disraeli and Gladstone are treated in detail. This is a period which is now becoming far enough away for us to visualise. There is a note of self-righteousness which, to me, is repellent. The Empire was constantly increasing. The middle class was building up its new position. It is worth noting how many of the extracts from this time bear the mark of the self-confidence of an expanding economy.

It is appropriate that the last entry should deal with the Diamond Jubilee celebrations as the old Queen saw them. She was the last sovereign of the House of Brunswick; the last English monarch to think in terms of the German royal houses and to feel most at ease with the German domestic scene and virtues. This is perhaps the one continuous thread in all these changing years since William III signed the Act of Settlement which made the Electress of Hanover the second heiress to the English Throne. George I and his descendants were a military race; they went out to the sound of bugles. ' Had a quiet luncheon ', the Queen wrote in 1897, ' with Vicky, Beatrice, and her three children. Troops continually passing by.'

DAVID MATHEW.

CONTENTS

B

INTRODUCTION

' To converse with historians is to keep good company,'
wrote Bolingbroke. If mixed company be good company, and
if good company be entertaining company, there is some substance in Bolingbroke's claim. And this is particularly so of the
eye-witness, for what he has to say has a vivid actuality which
pierces like a searchlight into the past. Like the searchlight,
however, he may distort the situation while he illuminates the
object. For the story of the eye-witness is not history, but a part
of the material of history. It seemed wiser, therefore, in dealing
with the crowded events of the eighteenth and nineteenth
centuries, to help the reader by providing him in places with a
cluster of eye-witness accounts converging upon one event.
The Charge of the Light Brigade, for instance, is more easily
appreciated if it is seen both from the point of view of the young
officer on the hill and from that of the trooper galloping towards
the Russian guns; and the many-sided personality of Wellington
needs to be seen from a variety of viewpoints. The extent to
which this treatment is possible is clearly limited by the demands
of space, but the experiment seemed worth making. A group of
eye-witnesses makes, in fact, more informative and, therefore,
better company.

' It is the reproach of historians,' wrote J. R. Green, ' that
they have too often turned history into a mere record of the
butchery of men by their fellow-men. But war plays a small part
in the real history of European nations, and in that of England
its part is smaller than in any '. Born and bred in Victorian
Oxford, in the Antonine peace of the nineteenth century, he had
excuses for this remarkable opinion which we, who live in more
normal because more dangerous times, cannot put forward.
' Place History on her rightful throne, and at the sides of her
Eloquence and War '. The century of Stalin, of Hitler and of
Sir Winston Churchill is closer to Landor than to Green. If eye-
witness accounts of deeds of arms can help to destroy the twin
romanticisms of militarism and pacifism, while maintaining the
memory of the men who brought victory to England, the authors
of this book will accept with equanimity the strictures of the
romantics.

There remains the problem of edification. In the past the historian was urged to pass over in silence the misdeeds of ecclesiastics: episcopal gallantries or archidiaconal homicides were unedifying. Raleigh's *History of the World* was condemned by James I for being ' too saucy in censuring the acts of princes ' in an England in which the dogma of the Divine Right of Kings was fashionable. To-day it is fashionable to consider physical pain and death as the supreme evils, and the historian and the schoolmaster are under pressure to present history in such a way that the unedifying fact of their existence may at least be blurred. History, however, is concerned with men and women as they are; and, therefore, with sin and sanctity, folly and wisdom, and their consequences. The diabolical cruelty of the slave-trader and the dedicated holiness of John Woolman are equally its concern; and, if it is rightly read, a generation which has learnt to prefer a cup-tie to a public execution as a means of relaxation will be grateful rather than complacent.

Our thanks are due to Mrs. Gell for her patience and skill in typing the materials for this book; to Mr. T. B. Hansen of the York Public Library for his invaluable and cheerful assistance; to Mr. R. H. Taylor, the secretary of the Blackburn Rovers, and to the Editor of the *Blackburn Times* for helping us to secure the account of the Cup Final of 1882; to Mr. Geoffrey Green of *The Times* and to Major the Lord Wynford for so readily answering questions; to Mr. Peter Burns for his encouragement and advice; and to a number of our colleagues at Ampleforth for their accurate information and their astringent criticism.

In the extracts the spelling and punctuation have been generally modernised for the convenience of the reader. Dates have been left in the Old Style in the extracts, while in the comments and notes they have been put in the New Style. In conclusion, it may not be out of place to call the attention of the reader to the ' Britain in Pictures ' Series of illustrated essays (published by Messrs. Collins); in particular to Sir Ernest Barker's essay, *British Statesmen* and to Dame Rose Macaulay's *Life Among the English*.

T. C-E.
B. R.

ACKNOWLEDGEMENTS

The compilers and the publisher wish to thank the following for permission to reproduce copyright material:

George Allen and Unwin, Ltd., for an extract from *Life of Francis Place*, by G. Wallas.

Wm. Blackwood and Sons, Ltd., for a passage from Mercer's *Journal of the Waterloo Campaign*.

University Press, Cambridge, for an extract from Gunning's *Reminiscences of Cambridge*, Selected by D. A. Winstanley.

Jonathan Cape, Ltd., for extracts from *The Journal of Nicholas Cresswell*.

The Champlain Society, Toronto, for an extract from *The Journal of Captain J. Knox*, Volume II.

Chapman and Hall, Ltd., for passages from *Letters of the English Seamen*, by Hallam Moorhouse.

The Chetham Society, for an extract from the *Private Journal and Literary Remains of John Byrom*.

Eyre and Spottiswoode, Ltd., for extracts from *English Historical Documents*, Volumes VIII, and IX, *George Canning* by Sir Charles Petrie, and *Britain at Arms*, by T. Gilby.

Faber and Faber, Ltd., for a passage from *London in* 1710 by Von Uffenbach.

George G. Harrap and Co., Ltd., for two extracts from *Marlborough*; *His Life and Times*, by Sir Winston Churchill.

Rupert Hart-Davis, Ltd., for an extract from *Landsman Hay*, Edited by M. D. Hay.

Hutchinson and Co., Ltd., for an extract from *The Farington Diary*, Edited Greig.

Michael Joseph, Ltd., for an extract from *Henry Clifford*, V.C.

The King's Own Yorkshire Light Infantry for part of a letter by Lieut. H. Montgomery which appeared in Volume I of *The History of the K.O.Y.L.I.*, by Col. H. C. Wylly.

Longmans Green and Co., Ltd., for extracts from *Strange Island*; *Life and Letters of Lord Macaulay*, and *Short Stories on General Subjects*.

Longmans Green and Co., Ltd., London, and New York, for an extract from E. F. Benson: *As We Were*.

Longmans Green and Co., Ltd., and Lieut.-Commander C. F. Walker for an extract from *Young Gentlemen*.

Macdonald and Co., Ltd., for an extract from the Macdonald Illustrated Classics edition of *Autobiography and Journals of B. R. Haydon*.

Macmillan and Co., Ltd., for extracts from *Life of Charles Napier*, by Sir William Butler, and *Gladstone* by J. Morley.

Massachusetts Historical Society for an extract from *The Letters of John Andrews, Esquire*, 1772–76, edited by Winthrop Sargeant.

Methuen and Co., Ltd., for extracts from Fraser: *Sailors Whom Nelson Led* and *More English Diaries*.

John Murray, Ltd., for extracts from de Saussure: *A Foreign View of England*: Mahon: *History of England*; Sturgis *A Boy in the Peninsular War*; *Creevey's Life and Times*; Benson: *Letters of Queen Victoria*; Monypenny and Buckle, *Life of George Bentwick* and *Life of Benjamin Disraeli*; Bessborough: *Diaries of Lady Charlotte Guest*; *Sixty Years in the Wilderness*; *Parliamentary Reminiscences*; *Chronicles of an Old Campaigner* and Buckle *Letters of Queen Victoria*.

The Navy Record Society for extracts from their publications.

Thomas Nelson and Sons, Ltd., for extracts from *1745 and After* by A. and H. Tayler.

Clarendon Press for extracts from Burnet *History of my Own Time* and Moritz *Travels of Carl Philipp Moritz in 1782*.

Penguin Books, Ltd., for an extract from their edition of *Anson's Voyage Round the World*.

Routledge and Kegan Paul for extracts from Russell *The Crimean War*.

Mr. Russell Thorndike for an extract from *Children of the Garter*.

A. P. Watt and Son, and Mrs. J. B. Beresford for extracts from *The Diary of a Country Parson*.

The Duke of Wellington for extracts from *The Journal of Mrs. Arbuthnot*.

Sir Gerald Trevor for the letter of Edward Trevor: describing the attack on Algiers.

Mrs. Leighton for the letter from the *Commonplace Book of T. N. Parker*, of Sweeney Hall, Oswestry.

We have tried to trace the owners of all copyright material, but in certain cases it has proved impossible to trace the probable owners of the copyright and in the event of this book reaching them we should be glad if they would let us know of any omissions so that we may make proper acknowledgement in future editions.

WILLIAM III

William III was the son of William II, Prince of Orange, and Mary, daughter of Charles I of England. In 1677 he had married Mary, daughter of James II and Anne Hyde.

Source : Supplement to Burnet's *History of My Own Time*, H. C. Foxcroft, Oxford, 1902, pp. 190–3.

Further Reading : David Ogg: *William III*, Collins, 1956.

The prince has showed by his conduct and action that notwithstanding all the defects of his education, and his total want of literature, nature is capable of producing great matters, even when she is not at all assisted by art. He has a great application to affairs, and turns them much in his thoughts; and indeed perhaps too much, for his slowness in coming to a resolution is much complained of. But if he is slow in taking up a resolution he is as firm in adhering to it. He has a vast memory, and a true judgement, for he sees presently the critical point of any matter that is proposed to him. He is the closest man in the world, so that it is not possible so much as to guess at his intentions till he declares them. He is extreme calm both in council and actions, and hears very gently things that are said to him, even when he is not pleased with them. . . .

His courage is indeed greater than it ought to be; and though it was very fit for one that had the ambition of arriving at the reputation of his ancestors to hazard his person sometimes, that so it might appear that he was a soldier as well as a general, yet his great carelessness of all personal danger both in time of peace and war has been censured as excessive, for to see him go about with a footman or two when so much depends on his life has been called rather a tempting of providence than a trusting to it. . . . This is . . . the nature of his courage that it does not sink with misfortunes, for when things have miscarried in his hands he has been observed to have the same calm equality that he had upon happier occasions.

. . . He has a coldness in his way that damps a modest man extremely, for he hears things with a dry silence that shows too much of distrust of those to whom he speaks. . . . If the prince does not in many things change his way he will hardly gain the hearts of the nation. His coldness will look like contempt, and that the English cannot bear; and they are too impatient to digest that slowness that is almost become natural to him in the most inconsiderable things, and his silent way will pass for superciliousness.

THE SIEGE OF LONDONDERRY

Source : Letter from George Holmes to William Fleming. Historical Manuscripts Commission, Twelfth Report, App. VII, pp. 264–280 quoted in *English Historical Documents* vol. viii, ed. Browning, Eyre and Spottiswoode, 1953, pp. 753–4.

Further Reading : Macaulay: *History of England,* ch. xii.

Strabane, 16 November, 1689.

. . . on the 12th of April last the Irish army appeared before our city, but at that distance that one of our cannons had enough to do to reach them; but in short time they approached nearer to our walls. In the first place we burned all our suburbs and hewed down all our brave orchards, making all about us as plain as a bowling-green. About the 18th of April King James came within a mile of our walls, but had no better entertainment than bullets of 14, 16 and 22 pounds weight. He sent us a letter under his own hand, sealed with his own seal, to desire us to surrender, and we should have our own conditions. The messenger was a lord with a trumpet, and out of grand civility we sent three messengers, all gentlemen; but two of them ran away from us, and the other came again. In short, we would not yield.

Then we proceeded, and chose captains and completed regiments, made two governors. We had 116 companies in the city. All our officers fled away, so we made officers of those that did deserve to be officers. I was made captain. And then we began to sally out, and the first sally that we made we slew their French general and several of their men with the loss of nine or ten of our men, which was the greatest loss that ever we lost in the field. Every day afterward we sallied out and daily killed our enemies, which put us in great heart; but it being so soon of the year, and we having no forage for our horses, we was forced to let them out, and the enemy got many. The rest of them died for hunger.

About the 20th of May the enemy gave us a general onset on all sides, but was so defeated that we were not troubled with them again for a week. . . . Ten days after that battle they came again very boldly, but in half an hour's time returned with greater loss than before. They began to run their approaches near us on one side. They came within 100 yards of us, and one night they attempted so near that one of them knocked at our gate and called for faggots to burn it with. This being in the dead of the night and our men being gone off their posts we were in some danger. The drums beat alarm, and we got a party together and sallied out at another gate, fell upon them and put them to the rout and recovered our own ground again, came so near them that we might have taken them alive, but we gave them old quarter. This night our great guns did execution with case-shot off the walls; that's musket bullets.

At this time they played abundance of bombs (the weight of many of them was near three hundredweight), which killed many people. One bomb slew seventeen persons. I was in the next room one night at my supper (which was but mean), and seven men were thrown out of the third room next to that we were in, all killed, and some of them in pieces. Into this city they played 596 bombs, which destroyed many of our people and demolished many of our houses. Cannon bullets flew as fast as you could count them, and as soon as we took up their bullets we sent them back again post paid. Thus men, horses, and all went to destruction.

But at last our provision grew scant and our allowance small. One pound of oatmeal and one pound of tallow served a man a week; sometimes salt hides. It was as bad as Samaria, only we had no pigeon's dung.[1] I saw 2s. a quarter given for a little dog, horse blood at 4d. per pint; all the starch was eaten . . . horse flesh was a rarity, and still we resolved to hold out.

Four days before we got relief from England we saw a great drove of cows very near us, and we were very weak, but we resolved to sally out, and in order thereto we played our great guns off the walls and sallied out on our enemy. I led the forlorn hope, which was about 100 men of the best we had, with which I

[1] 2 Kings, vi, 25

ran full tilt into their trenches; and before our body came up we had slain 80 men, put many to the rout. We got arms enough and some beef, but durst not stay long, not above half an hour. This vexed our enemies much; they said we took them asleep. I praise God I had still my health, and has yet.

After the ships came in with provision to us our enemies thought it was in vain to stay any longer, so on Lammas day they left us the wide fields to walk in. In the siege we had not above 60 men killed, except with the bombs killed. But I believe there died 15,000 men, women and children, many of which died for meat. But we had a great fever amongst us, and all the children died, almost whole families not one left alive. This is a true account of the siege of Londonderry. . . .

QUEEN ANNE: two points of view

(a) *Source: Memoirs of Sir John Clerk*, quoted in *Select Documents for Queen Anne's Reign*, ed. Trevelyan, Cambridge, 1929, pp. 217–18.

Sir John Clerk was one of the Scots Commissioners engaged in drawing up the Act of Union of 1707.

In the great room above mentioned [in the Palace of Westminster] was a long table, sufficient to hold all the Commissioners for both Kingdoms, being about 50 feet in length. At the head of the table, under a canopy, was placed a large chair, ornamented with gold lace and crimson velvet, for the Queen, when she desired to come amongst us. . . . The Queen came amongst us three several times, once at our first or second meeting, to acquaint us of her intentions and ardent good wishes for our success and unanimity in this great transaction. At about a month thereafter she came again to enquire of our success . . . , and for the last time to approve of what we had done. . . .

All this time I neglected not to cultivate that friendship with the Duke of Queensberry, my patron, which he had always shown me. I was frequently at Kensington with him, where the Queen kept her Court. . . . One day I had occasion to observe the calamities which attend human nature even in the greatest dignities of life. Her majesty was labouring under a fit of the gout, and in extreme pain and agony, and on this occasion everything about her was much in the same disorder as about the meanest of her subjects. Her face, which was red and spotted, was rendered something frightful by her negligent dress, and the foot affected was tied up with a poultice and some nasty bandages. I was much affected at this sight. . . .

(b) Source: *Private Correspondence of Sarah, Duchess of Marlborough:* London, 1838, vol. ii, pp. 119–25.

As maid of honour to Princess Anne, Sarah Jennings became famous at the court of Charles II for her beauty, vivacity and deter-mination. After a long and stormy courtship, she consented to marry John Churchill—Turenne's 'handsome Englishman'. Princess Anne helped the young couple with friendship and money. As Lady of the Bedchamber she acquired a dominating influence over her mistress, whom she persuaded to accept William III as king. In the next reign she lost her hold over the Queen by her violent temper and arrogance; and to her fury was dismissed. After the death of the Duke, whose devotion she never lost, she gave herself up to family quarrels, to lawsuits and money. The reputation of Pope's Atossa is emphasised by the mock epitaph:

> ' Here Duke and Duchess ashes blend
> O Death! For once thy laws suspend.
> Keep her in thy cold bed-of-state.
> 'Tis *à-la-mode* to separate.
> Let fighting John return to life.
> We want the Hero, not the wife.'

The spitefulness of the rejected favourite comes out in this descrip-tion of Queen Anne.

Queen Anne had a person and appearance not at all ungraceful, till she grew exceeding gross and corpulent. There was some-thing of majesty in her look, but mixed with a sullen and constant frown, that plainly betrayed a gloominess of soul and a cloudiness of disposition within. . . .

Her memory was exceeding great, almost to a wonder, and had these two peculiarities very remarkable in it, that she could, whenever she pleased, forget what others would have thought themselves obliged by truth and honour to remember, and remember all such things as others would think it an happiness to forget. Indeed she chose to retain in it very little besides cere-monies and customs of courts and such like insignificant trifles, so that her conversation, which otherwise might have been enlivened by so great a memory, was only made the more empty and trifling by its chiefly turning upon fashions and rules of precedence, or observations upon the weather or some such poor topics, without any variety or entertainment. Upon which account it was a sort of unhappiness to her that she naturally loved to have a great crowd come to her, for when they were come to Court she never cared to have them come in to her, nor to go out herself to them, having little to say to them but that it was either hot or cold, and little to inquire of them but how long they had been in town, or the like weighty matters. . . . Her love to the prince seemed in the eye of the world to be prodigiously great; and great as was the passion of her grief her stomach was greater, for that very day he died she ate three very large and hearty meals, so that one would think that as other persons' grief takes away their appetites, her appetite took away her grief. Nor was it less remarkable, where there was so great an appearance of love, the peculiar pleasure she took before his funeral in settling the order of it, and naming the persons that were to attend, and placing them according to their rank and to the rules of precedence, which was the entertainment she gave herself every day till that solemnity was over. I know that in some libels she has been reproached as one who indulged herself in drinking strong liquors; but I believe this was utterly groundless, and that she never went beyond such a quantity of strong wines as her physicians judged to be necessary for her. . . .

She loved fawning and adoration, and hated plain dealing, even in the most important cases. She had a soul that nothing could so effectually move as flattery or fear. A sudden surprise, in an unguarded moment, would make the truth sometimes discover itself in her look or in some unlucky word, but if she had time and warning enough to learn her lesson, all the arguments and reason in the world could extort nothing from her that she had not a mind to acknowledge. In such cases she seemed to have the insensibility of a rock, and would resolutely dissemble or disown anything in the world, and by repeating one single answer in the same words could tire out the patience and elude all such inquiries as were disagreeable to herself.

She had no native generosity of temper, nor was often known of herself to do a handsome action either as a reward or as a piece of friendship. The diligence and faithfulness of a servant signified but little with her, where she had no passion for the person. Nor did she hardly ever think either of rewarding any because they were deserving, or of raising any because they were miserable, till such things were urged upon her by those whom she loved. And even to such as she professed to love her presents were very few and generally very insignificant, as fruit, or venison, or the like, unless in cases where she was directed by precedents in the former reigns. In a word, she had little zeal for the happiness of others, but a selfishness that was great enough to make every other consideration yield to it. She was headstrong and positive in matters of the utmost importance, and at last preferred her own humour and passion before the safety and happiness of her own people and of all Europe, which she had either not sense enough to see, or not enough goodness to regard. Whether her memory will be celebrated by posterity with blessings or curses, time will show.

BATH UNDER THE RULE OF BEAU NASH

Richard Nash (1674–1761)

' By birth a gentleman, an ancient Briton,' begins Dr. Oliver's famous epitaph. 'A man placed in the middle rank of life . . . whose vices and virtues were open to the eye of the most undiscerning spectator; who was placed in public view without power to repress censure or command adulation; who had too much merit not to become remarkable, yet too much folly to arrive at greatness,' is Oliver Goldsmith's balanced summary.

Richard Nash was born in Swansea. His father, a Pembrokeshire man, had settled in Swansea as partner in a glass-works; his mother was a niece of John Poyer, Mayor of Pembroke and a prominent man among the Welsh Roundheads in the first Civil War. In the second Civil War, Poyer changed sides and, after the capitulation of Pembroke, he was shot by a firing-squad in London, in April, 1649. His widow was pensioned by Charles II.

Educated at Caermarthen Grammar School and at Jesus College, Oxford, Nash went down without a degree under circumstances which are amusingly described by Goldsmith. He tried the Army and then the Law with equal lack of success, but attracted the attention of William III by the skill and taste with which he organised the pageant, presented by the Inns of Court, in honour of the King's accession. He became an arbiter of fashion in London, supporting himself on the proceeds of gambling. Grasping the possibilities of a summer centre of fashionable life, he went to Bath in 1705, and set on foot a revolution which changed the face of English life to a greater or less degree in every part of the kingdom. He established the Assembly Rooms, forbade duelling, and promulgated a code of behaviour and dress which he rigidly and successfully enforced. From Bath Beau Nash's code of polite manners spread quickly among the upper classes and largely contributed to make the society of eighteenth-century England remarkable for good sense and civilisation. England is heavily indebted to two Pembrokeshire Welshmen; Henry Tudor enforced good government, and Beau Nash good manners. Unlike the former, the latter died in poverty. Goldsmith's *Life of Richard Nash, Esquire*, with its famous description of Bath, provides an indispensable key to the history of England in the eighteenth century.

Upon a stranger's arrival at Bath he is welcomed by a peal of the Abbey Bells, and, in the next place, by the voice and music of the city waits. For these civilities, the ringers have generally a present made them of half-a-guinea, and the waits of half-a-crown, or more, in proportion to the person's fortune, generosity, or ostentation. These customs, though disagreeable, are however, liked or they would not continue. The greatest incommodity attending them is the disturbance the bells must give the sick. But the pleasure of knowing the name of every family that comes to town recompenses the inconvenience. Invalids are fond of news, and upon the first sound of the bells everybody sends out to inquire for whom they ring.

After the family is thus welcomed to Bath, it is the custom for the master of it to go to the public places, and subscribe two guineas at the assembly-houses towards the balls and music in pump-house, for which he is entitled to three tickets every ball night. His next subscription is a crown, half-a-guinea, or a guinea, according to his rank and quality, for the liberty of walking in the private walks belonging to Simpson's assembly-house; a crown or half-a-guinea is also given to the booksellers, for which the gentleman is to have what books he pleases to read at his lodgings, and at the coffee-house another subscription is taken for pen, ink, and paper, for such letters as the subscriber shall write at it during his stay. The ladies, too, may subscribe to the booksellers, and to a house by the pump-room, for the advantage of reading the news, and for enjoying each other's conversation.

Things being thus adjusted, the amusements of the day are generally begun by bathing, which is no unpleasing method of passing away an hour or so.

The baths are five in number. On the south-west side of the Abbey Church is the King's Bath, which is an oblong square; the walls are full of niches, and at every corner are steps to descend into it: this bath is said to contain 427 tons and 50 gallons of water; and on its rising out of the ground over the springs, it is sometimes too hot to be endured by those who bathe therein. Adjoining to the King's Bath, there is another, called the Queen's Bath; this is of a more temperate warmth, as borrowing its water from the other.

In the south-west part of the city are three other baths, viz: the Hot Baths, which is not much inferior in heat to the King's Bath, and contains 53 tons, 2 hogsheads, and 11 gallons of water; the Cross Bath, which contains 52 tons, 3 hogsheads, and 11 gallons; and the Leper's Bath, which is not so much frequented as the rest.

The King's Bath (according to the best observations) will fill in about nine hours and a half; the Hot Bath in about eleven hours and a half; and the Cross Bath in about the same time.

The hours for bathing are commonly between six and nine in the morning, and the baths are every morning supplied with fresh water; for when the people have done bathing, the sluices in each bath are pulled up, and the water is carried off by drains into the River Avon.

In the morning the lady is brought in a close chair, dressed in her bathing clothes, to the bath; and, being in the water, the woman who attends presents her with a little floating dish like a basin; into which the lady puts a handkerchief, a snuff-box, and a nosegay. She then traverses the bath; if a novice, with a guide; if otherwise, by herself; and having amused herself thus while she thinks proper, calls for her chair, and returns to her lodgings.

C

The amusement of bathing is immediately succeeded by a general assembly of people at the pump-room; some for pleasure, and some to drink the hot waters. Three glasses at three different times is the usual portion for every drinker; and the intervals between every glass are enlivened by the harmony of a small band of music, as well as by the conversation of the gay, the witty, or the forward.

From the pump-room the ladies, from time to time, withdraw to a female coffee-house, and from thence return to their lodgings to breakfast. The gentlemen withdraw to their coffee-houses, to read the papers, or converse on the news of the day, with a freedom and ease not to be found in the metropolis.

People of fashion make public breakfasts at the assembly-houses, to which they invite their acquaintances, and they sometimes order private concerts; or, when so disposed, attend lectures on the arts and sciences, which are frequently taught there in a pretty superficial manner, so as not to tease the understanding, while they afford the imagination some amusement. The private concerts are performed in the ball-rooms; the tickets a crown each.

Concert breakfasts at the assembly-houses sometimes make also a part of the morning's amusement here, the expenses of which are defrayed by a subscription among the men. Persons of rank and fortune who can perform are admitted into the orchestra, and find a pleasure in joining with the performers.

Thus we have the tedious morning fairly over. When noon approaches, and church (if any please to go there) is done, some of the company appear upon the parade, and other public walks, where they continue to chat and amuse each other, till they have formed parties for the play, cards, or dancing for the evening. Another part of the company divert themselves with reading in the booksellers' shops, or are generally seen taking the air and exercise, some on horseback, some in coaches. Some walk in the meadows round the town, winding along the side of the River Avon and the neighbouring canal; while others are seen scaling some of those romantic precipices that overhang the city.

When the hour of dinner draws nigh, and the company are returned from their different recreations, the provisions are generally served with the utmost elegance and plenty. Their mutton, butter, fish, and fowl, are all allowed to be excellent, and their cookery still exceeds their meat.

After dinner is over, and evening prayers ended, the company meet a second time at the pump-house. From this they retire to the walks, and from thence go to drink tea at the assembly-houses, and the rest of the evenings are concluded either with balls, plays, or visits. A theatre was erected in the year 1705, by subscription, by people of the highest rank, who permitted their arms to be engraven on the inside of the house, as a public testimony of their liberality towards it. Every Tuesday and Friday evening is concluded with a public ball, the contributions to which are so numerous, that the price of each ticket is trifling. Thus Bath yields a continued rotation of diversions, and people of all ways of thinking, even from the libertine to the methodist, have it in their power to complete the day with employments suited to their inclinations.

DOCTOR SACHEVERELL, as seen by the
Duchess of Marlborough.

Henry Sacheverell (1674–1724) became famous when he attacked the Whig ministers as enemies of the Church in two violent sermons delivered in 1709: one at Derby, the other in St. Paul's before the Lord Mayor of London. The Government, already much weakened, mistakenly decided to impeach Sacheverell. The mob rioted in his favour and set fire to the meeting houses of Dissenters. The House of Lords found Sacheverell guilty: the voting was 52 for acquittal, 69 for conviction. The sentence was a three-years' suspension from preaching and the burning of the two offending sermons at the Royal Exchange. The impeachment was one of the reasons for the downfall of the Ministry.

Source: Private Correspondence of Sarah, Duchess of Marlborough, London, 1838. vol. ii, pp. 142–4.

Further Reading: G. Every: *The High Church Party,* 1688–1718. S.P.C.K. 1956.

. . . Of the man himself no more need be said, than that he had not one good quality that any man of sense ever valued him for. He once professed himself a great Whig. But King William dying, he thought it best to change with the torrent. It must be owned that a person more fitted for a tool, could not have been picked out of the whole nation, for he had not learning enough to write or speak true English (as all his own compositions witness), but an heap of bombast, ill-connected words at command, which do excellently well with such as he was to move. He had so little sense, as even to design and effect that popularity, which now became his portion, and which a wise and good man knows not how to bear with. He had a haughty insolent air, which his friends found occasion often to complain of; but it made his presence more graceful in public.

His person was framed well for the purpose, and he dressed well. A good assurance, clean gloves, white handkerchief well-managed, with other suitable accomplishments, moved the hearts of many at his appearance, and the solemnity of a trial added much to a pity and concern which had nothing in reason or justice to support them. The weaker part of the ladies were more like mad or bewitched, than like persons in their senses.

At length, by the help of proper officers and tools, great mobs and tumults were raised, to whose outrages and violence nothing more conduced than a prevailing opinion, artfully spread amongst them, that one above was herself on the side of these disorders. . . .

Several eminent clergymen, who despised the man in their hearts, were engaged to stand publicly by him in the face of the world, as if the poor Church of England was now tried in him. A speech exquisitely contrived to move pity, was put into his mouth, full of an impious piety, denying the greatest part of the charge (which the man had been known to boast of before) with solemn appeals to God, and such applications of Scripture as would make any serious person tremble. . . . This speech was ready printed, contrary to all rule and decency, dispersed over the nation by himself, and had a great part in heightening our disorders. The sentence passed upon him could have been no punishment to any man, but one who was full of his own excellencies, and never thought himself so great as in a pulpit.

Everybody knows that he was afterwards sent about several counties; where, with his usual grace, he received as his due, the homage and adoration of multitudes; never thinking that respect enough was paid to his great merit, using some of his friends insolently, and raising mobs against his enemies, and giving ample proof of how great meanness the bulk of mankind is capable. . . .

THE DUKE OF MARLBOROUGH

Eldest surviving son of Sir Winston Churchill and educated at St. Paul's, he gained the confidence of James, Duke of York, and served in the army at Tangiers and on the Continent. He was principally responsible for crushing Monmouth's rebellion, but joined William III and was made Earl of Marlborough in 1689. William III distrusted Marlborough but on the accession of Anne he came into power. Given command of the English army against France, he gained by his famous campaigns and the victories of Blenheim, Ramillies, Oudenarde and Malplaquet the reputation of the greatest general in the history of his country. Created a Duke in 1702, given Blenheim Palace by a grateful Queen and parliament, he was finally dismissed in 1711. He actively supported the succession of George I in 1714, but in 1716 he had a paralytic stroke which was followed by senile decay. The story is famous of the broken man, hobbling to gaze at Kneller's portrait which showed him in the full splendour of manhood, and then murmuring ' that was once a man '.

Source: Sicco van Goslinga—*Memoires,* quoted by Sir Winston Churchill in *Marlborough,* Harrap, 1934 ed., vol. i, p. 479.

Van Goslinga was one of the three Dutch deputies of the Army. He was appointed in 1706. Sir Winston Churchill calls him ' a military-minded civilian.'

Further Reading: Sir J. Fortescue: *Marlborough,* Peter Davies, 1932.

Here is his portrait, drawn to the best of my insight. He is a man of birth: about the middle height, and the best figure in the world: his features without fault, fine, sparkling eyes, good teeth, and his complexion such a mixture of white and red as the fairer sex might envy: in brief, except for his legs, which are too thin, one of the handsomest men ever seen. His mind is keen and subtle, his judgment very clear and sound, his insight both quick and deep, with a consummate knowledge of men which no false show of merit can deceive. He expresses himself well, and even his very bad French is agreeable: his voice is harmonious, and as a speaker in his own language he is reckoned among the best. His address is most courteous, and while his handsome and well-graced countenance engages everyone in his favour at first sight, his perfect manners and his gentleness win over even those who start with a prejudice or grudge against him. He has courage, as he has shown in more than one conjuncture: he is an experienced soldier, and plans a campaign to admiration. So far his good qualities. Now for the weak points which if I am not mistaken I have found in him. The Duke is a profound dissembler, all the more dangerous that his manner and his words give the impression of frankness itself. His ambition knows no bounds, and an avarice which I can only call sordid, guides his entire conduct. If he has courage—and of this there is no question, whatever may be said by those who envy or hate him—he certainly wants that firmness of soul which makes the true hero. Sometimes, on the eve of an action, he is irresolute, or worse; he will not face difficulties, and occasionally lets reverses cast him down: of this I could adduce more than one instance as an eyewitness. Yet I saw nothing of the kind, either at Ramillies or Malplaquet, so it may be that some constitutional weakness, unfitting him to support fatigue, has something to do with it. He does not know much of discipline, and gives too much rein to his men who have now and then indulged in frightful excesses. Moreover he lacks the precise knowledge of military detail which a Commander-in-Chief should possess. But these defects are light in the scale against the rare gifts of this truly great man.

THE ACTION OF THE SCHELLENBERG,
Wednesday, July 2, 1704

Marlborough, marching from the Netherlands into Germany to frustrate the Franco-Bavarian designs on Vienna, wished to secure the crossing of the Danube at Donauwörth. Franco-Bavarian troops of Marshal Marsin's army therefore occupied the Schellenberg, a bell-shaped hill dominating Donauwörth. In a short but most severe action in which British casualties were very heavy, Marlborough drove the enemy from the hill. Donauwörth surrendered immediately and the bridgehead on the Danube was thus secured.

Source: Colonel Jean de la Colonie: *Chronicles of an old Campaigner,* 1692–1717 trans. Horsley. London, 1904, pp. 182–92.

de la Colonie commanded the French grenadiers behind the breastworks at the edge of the wood on the top of the Schellenberg.

Further Reading: Fortescue, *History of the British Army i:* Churchill, *Marlborough book i,* Harrap, two volume ed., 1947.

. . . . the enemy's battery opened fire upon us and raked us through and through. They concentrated their fire on us, and with their first discharge carried off Count de la Bastide, the Lieutenant of my own company with whom at the moment I was speaking, and twelve grenadiers, who fell side by side in the ranks, so that my coat was covered with brains and blood. So accurate was the fire that each discharge of the cannon stretched some of my men on the ground. . . . Hardly had our men lined the little parapet when the enemy broke into the charge, and rushed at full speed, shouting at the tops of their voices, to throw themselves into our entrenchments. . . .

The English infantry led this attack with the greatest intrepidity, right up to our parapet, but there they were opposed with a courage at least equal to their own. Rage, fury and desperation were manifested by both sides, with the more obstinacy as the assailants and assailed were perhaps the bravest soldiers in the world. The little parapet which separated the two forces became the scene of the bloodiest struggle that could be conceived. . . . It would be impossible to describe in words strong enough the details of the carnage that took place during this first attack, which lasted a good hour or more. We were all fighting hand to hand, hurling them back as they clutched at the parapet; men were slaying, or tearing at the muzzles of guns and the bayonets which pierced their entrails; crushing under their feet their own wounded comrades, and even gouging out their opponents' eyes with their nails, when the grip was so close that neither could make use of their weapons. . . .

At last the enemy, after losing more than eight thousand men in this first onslaught, were obliged to relax their hold, and they fell back for shelter to the dip of the slope, where we could not harm them. . . . The ground around our parapet was covered with dead and dying, in heaps almost as high as our fascines, but our whole attention was fixed on the enemy and his movements; we noticed that the tops of his standards still showed at about the same place as that from which they had made their charge in the first instance, leaving little doubt but that they were reforming before returning to the assault. As soon as possible we set vigorously to work to render their approach more difficult for them than before, and by means of an increasing fire swept their line of advance with a torrent of bullets, accompanied by numberless grenades, of which we had several waggon loads in rear of our position. These, owing to the slope of the ground, fell right amongst the enemy's ranks, causing them great annoyance and doubtless added not a little to their hesitation in advancing the second time to the attack. They were so disheartened by the first attempt that their generals had the greatest difficulty in bringing them forward again, and indeed would never have succeeded in this . . . had they not dismounted and set an example by placing themselves at the head of the column, and leading them on foot.

Their devotion cost them dear, for General Stirum and many other generals and officers were killed. They once more, then, advanced to the assault, but with nothing like the success of their first effort, for not only did they lack energy in their attack, but after being vigorously repulsed, were pursued by us at the point of the bayonet for more than eighty yards beyond our entrenchments. . . . [but other regiments retreated and M. de la Colonie's troops were taken in flank].

They arrived within gunshot of our flank, about 7.30 in the evening, without our being at all aware of the possibility of such a thing, so occupied were we in defence of our own particular post. . . .

But I noticed all at once an extraordinary movement on the part of our infantry, who were rising up and ceasing fire withal. I glanced around on all sides to see what had caused this behaviour, and then became aware of several lines of infantry in greyish white uniforms on our left flank. . . . I verily believed that reinforcements had arrived for us, and anybody else would have believed the same. No information whatever had reached us of the enemy's success, or even that such a thing was the least likely, so . . . I shouted to my men that they were Frenchmen, and friends, and they at once resumed their former position behind the parapet.

Having, however, made a closer inspection, I discovered bunches of straw and leaves attached to their standards, badges the enemy are in the custom of wearing on the occasion of battle, and at that very moment was struck by a ball in the right lower jam, which wounded and stupefied me to such an extent that I thought it was smashed. I probed my wound as quickly as possible with the tip of my finger, and finding the jaw itself entire, did not make much fuss about it; but the front of my jacket was so deluged with the blood which poured from it that several of our officers believed that I was dangerously hurt. I reassured them, however, and exhorted them to stand firmly with their men. . . . I at once, therefore, shouted as loudly as I could that no one was to quit the ranks, and then formed my men in column along the entrenchments facing the wood, fronting towards the opposite flank, which was the direction in which we should have to retire. Thus, whenever I wished to make a stand, I had but to turn my men about, and at any moment could resume the retirement instantaneously, which we thus carried out in good order.

THE BATTLE OF BLENHEIM,
Wednesday, August 13th, 1704

At Blenheim Marlborough and Prince Eugene defeated the Franco-Bavarian army under Tallard. Vienna was saved, and French prestige suffered severely. Blenheim was the first big defeat French arms had suffered in the reign of Louis XIV.

Source: Marlborough's own account of the battle from *The Complete History of Spain*, London, 1707.

Further Reading: G. M. Trevelyan: *England under Queen Anne: Blenheim*, Longmans, 1930. S. H. F. Johnston: *British Soldiers*, Collins, 1944.

Sir: I gave you an account on Sunday last of the situation we were then in, and that we expected to hear the enemy would pass the Danube at Lawringen, in order to attack Prince Eugene at eleven of the clock that night. We had an express from him, that the enemy were come, and desiring he might be reinforced as soon as possible. Whereupon I ordered my Brother Churchill to advance at one of the clock in the morning with his two battalions, and by three the whole Army was in motion; for the greater expedition, I ordered part of the troops to pass over the Danube, and follow the march of the twenty battalions; and with most of the Horse and the Foot of the First Line, I passed the Lech at Rain, and came over the Danube at Donawert. So that we all joined the prince that night, intending to advance and take this Camp at Hochstet: in order whereto we went out early on Tuesday with forty squadrons to view the ground, but found the enemy had already possessed themselves of it.

Whereupon we resolved to attack them, and accordingly we marched between three and four yesterday morning from the Camp at Munster, leaving all our tents standing. About six we came in view of the enemy, who, we found, did not expect so early an onset. The cannon began to play about half an hour after eight. They formed themselves in two bodies, the Elector with Monsieur Marsin and their troops on our right, and Monsieur de Tallard with all his on our left; which last fell to my share; they had two rivulets, besides a morass before them which we were obliged to pass over in their view, and Prince Eugene was forced to take a great compass to come to the enemy, so that it was one of the clock before the battle began. It lasted with great vigour till sunset, when the enemy were obliged to retire, and by the blessing of God we obtained a complete victory.

We have cut off great numbers of them, as well in the action as in the retreat, besides upwards of twenty squadrons of the French, which I pushed into the Danube, where we saw the greater part of them perish. Monsieur Tallard, with several of his general officers being taken prisoners at the same time, and in the village of Blenheim, which the enemy had entrenched and fortified, and where they made the greatest opposition, I obliged twenty-six entire battalions, and twelve squadrons of dragoons, to surrender themselves prisoners at discretion. We took likewise all their tents standing, with their cannon and ammunition, as also a great number of standards, kettle-drums, and colours in the action, so that I reckon the greatest part of Monsieur Tallard's army is taken or destroyed.

The bravery of all our troops on this occasion cannot be expressed, the Generals, as well as the officers and soldiers, behaving themselves with the greatest courage and resolution. The horse and dragoons were obliged to charge four or five several times. The Elector and Monsieur de Marsin were so advantageously posted, that Prince Eugene could make no impression on them, till the third attack, near seven at night, when he made a great slaughter of them. But being near a wood-side, a great body of Bavarians retired into it, and the rest of that army retreated towards Lawringen, it being too late, and the troops too much tired to pursue them far.

I cannot say too much in praise of that Prince's good conduct, and the bravery of his troops on this occasion. You will please to lay this before her Majesty and his Royal Highness, to whom I send my Lord Tunbridge with the good news. I pray you likewise inform yourself, and let me know her Majesty's pleasure, as well relating to Monsieur Tallard and the other general officers, as for the disposal of near one thousand two hundred other officers, and between eight and nine thousand common soldiers, who being all made prisoners by her Majesty's troops, are entirely at her disposal: but as the charge of subsisting these officers and men must be very great, I presume her Majesty will be inclined that they be exchanged for any other prisoners that offer.

I should likewise be glad to receive her Majesty's directions for the disposal of the standards and colours, whereof I have not yet the number, but guess there cannot be less than one hundred, which is more than has been taken in any battle these many years.

You will easily believe that, in so long and vigorous an action, the English, who had so great a share in it, must have suffered as well in officers as men; but I have not the particulars.

I am, Sir,

Your most obedient,

humble servant,

Marlborough.

From the camp at Hochstet
August the 4th (old style) 1704.

THE DUKE OF MARLBOROUGH AT RAMILLIES,
Sunday, May 23rd, 1706

(*b*) *Source:* Colonel Cranstoun: from the *Portland Papers*, quoted by Sir Winston Churchill in *Marlborough*, vol. ii, two volume ed., Harrap, 1947, p. 149.

Major-General Murray, who was posted on the left of the
second line, was so happy visibly to save the Duke of Marlborough, who fulfilled that day all the parts of a great captain,
except in that he exposed his person as the meanest soldier. The
attack being to be made by the Dutch on our left against the
enemy's right where all the King's household and their best
troops were, the Duke put himself at the head of the Dutch
horse; and the guards du corps, Mousquetaires, and gensdarmes,
happening to encounter them, ten of the Dutch squadrons were
repulsed, renversed and put in great disorder. The Duke, seeing
this, and seeing that things went pretty well elsewhere, stuck by
the weak part to make it up by his presence, and led up still new
squadrons there to the charge, till at last the victory was obtained.
It was here where those squadrons being renversed and in absolute
deroute and the French mixed with them in the pursuit, the Duke,
flying with the crowd, in leaping a ditch fell off his horse and some
rode over him. Major-General Murray, who had his eye there
and was so near he could distinguish the Duke in the flight, seeing
him fall, marched up in all haste with two Swiss battalions to
save him and stop the enemy who were hewing all down in their
way. The Duke when he got to his feet again saw Major-General
Murray coming up and ran directly to get in to his battalions.
In the meantime Mr. Molesworth quited his horse and got the
Duke mounted again, and the French were so hot in the pursuit
that some of them before they could stop their horses ran in
upon the Swiss bayonets and were killed, but the body of them,
seeing the two battalions, shore off to the right and retired.

COFFEE-HOUSES

Coffee-houses, where the new beverages, tea and coffee, could be
drunk, were opened in London from the middle of the seventeenth
century. They soon became centres of political discussion and their
influence was thus feared by governments. In the reign of Charles II
an attempt had been made to close them. It was unsuccessful, and the
number of coffee-houses rapidly increased so that by 1710 it is estimated
that there were 2,000 in London. Only men were admitted to them.
The first coffee-house to admit women as well as men—the Golden
Lion—did so in 1717.

(*a*) *Source:* de Saussure—*A Foreign View of England in the Reigns of George I and George II*, trans. by Mme. van Muyden, Murray, 1902. London 1902.

de Saussure was a Swiss citizen, of French Huguenot origin.

In London there are a great number of coffee-houses, most of which, to tell the truth, are not over clean or well furnished, owing to the quantity of people who resort to these places and because of the smoke, which would quickly destroy good furniture. Englishmen are great drinkers. In these coffee-houses you can partake of chocolate, tea, or coffee, and of all sorts of liquors, served hot; also in many places you can have wine, punch, or ale. . . . What attracts enormously in these coffee-houses are the gazettes and other public papers. All Englishmen are great newsmongers. Workmen habitually begin the day by going to coffee-rooms in order to read the latest news. I have often seen shoeblacks and other persons of that class club together to purchase a farthing paper. . . . Some coffee-houses are a resort for learned scholars and for wits; others are the resort of dandies or of politicians, or again of professional newsmongers.

(*b*) *Source:* Abbé Prévost: ' Les Aventures d'un Homme de Qualité ' quoted in *Strange Island* by F. M. Wilson and trans. F. M. Wilson, Longmans, 1955, p. 86. The Abbé Prévost, author of *Manon Lescaut*, lived in London for some time in the 1730s.

Further Reading: Trevelyan, *English Social History.*

I have had pointed out to me in several coffee-houses, a couple of lords, a baronet, a shoemaker, a tailor, a wine-merchant and some others of the same sort, all sitting round the same table and discussing familiarly the news of the court and town. The government's affairs are as much the concern of the people as of the great. Every man has the right to discuss them freely. Men condemn, approve, revile, rail with bitter invectives, both in speech and writing without the authorities daring to intervene. The King himself is not secure from censure. The coffee-houses and other public places are the seats of English liberty. For two pence you have the right to read all the papers for and against the government and to take a cup of tea or coffee as well.

(*c*) *Source: Travels of Carl Philipp Moritz in England in* 1782. Reprint of English translation of 1795. London, Humphrey Milford, 1924, pp. 86–87. See page 133.

From the church we went to a coffee-house, opposite to it, and there we dined. We had not been long there before the same clergyman, whom we had just heard preaching, also came in. He called for pen and ink, and hastily wrote down a few pages on a long sheet of paper which he put into his pocket; I suppose it was some rough sketch, or memorandum, that occurred to him at that moment, and which he thus reserved for some future sermon. He too ordered some dinner; which he had no sooner eat than he returned immediately to the same church. We followed him, and he again mounted the pulpit, where he drew from his pocket a written paper, or book of notes, and delivered, in all probability, those very words which he had just before composed in our presence, at the coffee-house.

In these coffee-houses, however, there generally prevails a very decorous stillness and silence. Every one speaks softly to those only who sit next him. The greater part read the news-papers, and no one ever disturbed another. The room is commonly on the ground floor, and you enter it immediately from the street, the seats are divided by wooden wainscot partitions. Many letters and projects are here written and planned, and many of those that you find in the papers are dated from some of these coffee-houses. There is, therefore, nothing incredible, nor very extraordinary, in a persons composing a sermon there. . . .

COCK-FIGHTING

Source: von Uffenbach: *Merkwuerdige Reisen* quoted and trans-lated by F. M. Wilson in *Strange Island:* Longmans, 1955, pp. 58–9.

von Uffenbach was a German, interested in old books and manu-scripts, who came to England in 1710 to add to his collection.

18 June, 1710.

In the afternoon we went to see the cock-fighting. This is a sport peculiar to the English, which, however great the pleasure this nation takes in it, seems very foolish to foreigners. A special building has been erected for it near ' Grays Inn '. When there is to be a fight, printed bills are carried round and sometimes invitations to fanciers appear in the news-sheets as well as the amount of the wagers and the number and species of cocks that are to fight. The building is round like a tower and inside it is just like a 'theatrum anatomicum' as all round it there are benches in tiers, on which the spectators sit. In the middle is a round table covered with mats, on which the cocks have to fight. When it is time to begin the persons appointed to do so bring in the cocks hidden in two sacks and then, before they have seen the birds, everyone starts to shout their wagers. The people, gentlefolk as well as commoners (they all sit together), act like madmen and go on raising the odds to twenty guineas and more. As soon as one of the bidders calls ' done ' . . . , the other is held to his bargain. Then the cocks are taken out of the sacks and fitted with silver spurs, . . . As soon as the cocks appear, the shouts grow even louder and the betting is continued. When they are put on to the table, some attack at once while others run away from the rest and, as we ourselves saw, try in their fright to jump down from the table among the crowd; they are then however thrown back with loud cries (especially from those who have put their money on the lively cocks which chase the others) and are thrust at each other until they get angry. Then one should just see how they peck at each other, and especially how they hack with their spurs. Their combs bleed quite horribly and they often slit each other's crop and abdomen with the spurs. There is nothing so amusing as when one cock seems quite exhausted and there are great shouts of joy and terrific bets and then, though he seemed quite done for, he suddenly recovers and masters the other. When one of the two is dead, the victor never fails to start crowing and jumping on the other and it often happens that they sing their song of triumph before victory is assured and the other wins after all. Sometimes when both are exhausted and neither will attack the other again, they are removed and others take their place; in this case the wagers are cancelled. But if one of them wins those who put their money on the loser have to pay immediately, so that an ostler in his apron often wins several guineas from a lord. If a man has made a bet and is unable to pay he is made, as a punishment, to sit in a basket tied to the ceiling and is drawn up in it amidst mighty laughter. The people become as heated about their wagers as the cocks themselves. . . .

BULL-BAITING

Source: von Uffenbach: *London in* 1710, translated and edited by W. H. Quarrell and M. Mare, London, 1934.

June 23, 1710: Towards evening we drove to see the bull-baiting, which is held here nearly every Monday in two places. On the morning of the day the bull, or any other creature that is to be baited, is led round. It takes place in a large open space or courtyard, on two sides of which high benches have been made for the spectators. First a young ox or bull was led in and fastened by a long rope to an iron ring in the middle of the yard; then about thirty dogs, two or three at a time, were let loose on him, but he made short work of them, goring them and tossing them high in the air above the height of the first storey. Then amid shouts and yells the butchers to whom the dogs belonged sprang forward and caught their beasts right side up to break their fall. They had to keep fast hold of the dogs to hinder them from returning to the attack without barking. Several had such a grip of the bull's throat or ear that their mouths had to be forced open with poles. When the bull had stood it tolerably long, they brought out a small bear and tied him up in the same fashion. As soon as the dogs had at him, he stood up on his hind legs and gave some terrific buffets; but if one of them got at his skin, he rolledabout in such a fashion that the dogs thought themselves lucky if they came out safe from beneath him. But the most diverting and worst of all was a common little ass, who was brought out saddled with an ape on his back. As soon as a couple of dogs had been let loose on him, he broke into a prodigious gallop—for he was free, not having been tied up like the other beasts—and he stamped and bit all round himself. The ape began to scream most terribly for fear of falling off. If the dogs came too near him, he seized them with his mouth and twirled them round, shaking them so much that they howled prodigiously. Finally another bull appeared, on whom several crackers had been hung: when these were lit and several dogs let loose on him on a sudden, there was a monstrous hurly-burly. And thus was concluded this truly English sport, which vastly delights this nation but to me seemed nothing very special.

PUBLIC EXECUTIONS AT TYBURN

Source: de Saussure: *A Foreign View of England in the Reigns of George I and George II*, Murray, 1902.

Some time after my arrival in London I witnessed a spectacle which certainly was not as magnificent or as brilliant as the Lord Mayor's Show; it is true it was quite a different kind of entertainment. I saw thirteen criminals all hanged at the same time. It will interest you, no doubt, to know something about justice in England, how it is practised, how criminals are punished, in what manner they are executed, as here it is done in quite a different way to what it is in other countries.

The day before the execution those who desire it may receive the sacrament, provided the chaplain thinks that they have sincerely repented and are worthy of it. On the day of execution the condemned prisoners, wearing a sort of white linen shirt over their clothes and a cap on their heads, are tied two together and placed on carts with their backs to the horses' tails. These carts are guarded and surrounded by constables and other police officers on horseback, each armed with a sort of pike. In this way part of the town is crossed, and Tyburn, which is a good half-mile from the last suburb, is reached, and here stands the gibbet. One often sees criminals going to their death perfectly unconcerned, others so impenitent that they fill themselves full of liquor and mock at those who are repentant. When all the prisoners arrive at their destination they are made to mount on a very wide cart made expressly for the purpose, a cord is passed round their necks and the end fastened to the gibbet, which is not very high. The chaplain who accompanies the condemned men is also on the cart; he makes them pray and sing a few verses of the Psalms. The relatives are permitted to mount the cart and take fare-well. When the time is up—that is to say about a quarter of an hour—the chaplain and the relations get off the cart, which slips from under the condemned men's feet, and in this way they remain all hanging together. You often see friends and relations tugging at the hanging men's feet so that they should die quicker and not suffer. The bodies and clothes of the dead belong to the executioner; relatives must, if they wish for them, buy them from

D

him, and unclaimed bodies are sold to surgeons to be dissected. You see most amusing scenes between the people who do not like the bodies to be cut up and the messengers the surgeons have sent for the bodies; blows are given and returned before they can be got away, and sometimes in the turmoil the bodies are quickly removed and buried. Again, the populace often come to blows as to who will carry the bought corpses to the parents who are waiting in coaches and cabs to receive them, for the carriers are well paid for their trouble. All these scenes are most diverting, the noise and confusion is unbelievable, and can be witnessed from a sort of amphitheatre erected for spectators near the gibbet.

THE OLD PRETENDER

The Old Pretender, whom the Jacobites called James III, landed in Scotland at the end of December 1715 to lead the rebellion. When reinforcements sent to the government troops in Scotland made further Jacobite military activity impossible, James left for France on February 4, 1716.

He was titular King of England, Scotland, France and Ireland for sixty-four years, a year longer than Queen Victoria's reign. The only son of James II and Mary of Modena was said and possibly believed by the Whigs to be a supposititious child, smuggled into the palace in a warming-pan. He was secretly conveyed by his mother to France on the outbreak of the Revolution. In 1719 he married a Polish princess, Maria Clementina Sobieska. On the outbreak of the 'Fifteen' he crossed from Dunkirk in a small privateer, but he was unable to put life into the Jacobite cause, and he returned to Lorraine. He sent his son to head the 'Forty-five'. The ill luck which pursued him from the cradle to the grave overthrew neither his dignity nor his fortitude. Without the cynicism of his uncle, the stupidity of his father, or the dash of his son, the Chevalier de St. George became Old Mr. Misfortunate. Dying in Rome, he was buried in St. Peter's where George IV helped with a subscription to employ Canova to erect a monument over his tomb. The monument was commissioned by Pius VII in 1819. His birthday, 10th June, was long celebrated by the Jacobites as White Rose Day.

'When our white roses all appear
For sake of Jamie the Rover.'

(a) Source: True Account of the Proceedings at Perth, by a Rebel, p. 19. Quoted Mahon, History of England, John Murray, 1858, pp. 184–5.

His person was tall and thin, seeming to incline to be lean rather than to fill as he grows in years. His countenance was pale, yet he seems to be sanguine in his constitution, and has something of a vivacity in his eye that perhaps would have been more visible, if he had not been under dejected circumstances and surrounded with discouragements, which it must be acknowledged, were sufficient to alter the complexion even of his soul as well as of his body. His speech was grave, and not very clearly expressing his thoughts, nor overmuch to the purpose, but his words were few, and his behaviour and temper seemed always composed. What he was in his diversions we knew not; here was no room for such things. It was no time for mirth. Neither can I say I ever saw him smile. . . . I must not conceal, that when we saw the man whom they called our King we found ourselves not at all animated by his presence, and if he was disappointed in us, we were tenfold more so in him. We saw nothing in him that looked like spirit. He never appeared with cheerfulness and vigour to animate us. Our men began to despise him; some asked if he could speak. His countenance looked extremely heavy. He cared not to come abroad amongst us soldiers, or to see us handle our arms or do our exercise. Some said the circumstances he found us in dejected him; I am sure the figure he made dejected us; and, had he sent us but 5,000 men of good troops, and never himself come amongst us, we had done other things than we have now done.

(b) *Source: A letter from Mr. Lesly to a Member of Parliament in London* quoted in *English Historical Documents* viii, pp. 910–11.

And first for the person of the Chevalier, which you desire to know. He is tall, straight and clean-limbed, slender, yet his bones pretty large. He has a very graceful mien, walks fast; and his gait has great resemblance to his uncle, King Charles II, and the lines of his face grow daily more and more like him. He uses exercise more for health than diversion; he walks abroad, shoots or hunts every day, but is not what they call a keen sportsman. Being asked what he most delighted in, he said it would be to hear wise men discourse upon useful subjects.

He is always cheerful but seldom merry, thoughtful but not dejected, and bears his misfortunes with a visible magnanimity of spirit. He frequents the public devotions, but there is no sort of bigotry about him. He has a great application to business, spends much time in his closet, and writes much, which no man does better and more succinctly. I have often admired his criticalness in the choice of words. He apprehends readily, and gives the direct answer. He is very affable, and has something strangely engaging in his voice and deportment, that none who ever conversed with him but are charmed with his good sense and sweetness of temper. Nor can any take it ill even when he grants not their request, for he always gives such a reason as must satisfy. Yet he can show displeasure, but without anger. . . .

He has informed himself of past miscarriages and knows well the difference betwixt the office of a King and a missionary. He will concern himself with no man's religion, but is resolved to defend that which is legally established and whose principles are true to monarchy and safe for government, for whose satisfaction and for his own restoration he thinks himself obliged to do everything that is consistent with conscience and honour. . . . I would not have said so much were it not to do him justice, and expose the vile clamours of his enemies that he has no regard to Protestants, which is known to be notoriously false to all who have the honour to attend him. He has given all the demonstrations possible to the contrary except parting with his conscience and honour, which some would have him do that they might object it against him, and represent him as unworthy to reign for so doing. . . .

THE CORONATION BANQUET OF GEORGE II

He came to England from Hanover with his father in 1714, and was created Prince of Wales. He quarrelled with his father, George I, and was excluded from the Court. He became king in 1727. At the battle of Dettingen he personally led the allied army into battle against the French. His horse, unbroken to musketry, bolted with him to the rear. Disentangling himself from his mount, the king led his men forward. In spite of his bravery his unpopularity was at times considerable. Lady Mary Wortley Montagu once remarked that ' he looked upon all men and women as creatures he might kick or kiss for his diversion ', and Lord Chesterfield amused the wits by suggesting that Hanover should be presented to the Old Pretender, which would destroy all hopes of a Stuart restoration; ' for the English will never endure another king from that country '. In affairs of state he was largely guided by his Queen, Caroline. When he died in 1760 the

French had been driven from Canada and checked in Europe. ' What an enviable death! ' wrote Walpole to Mann: ' In the greatest period of the glory of this country and of his reign, in perfect tranquillity at home, at seventy-seven, growing blind and deaf, to die without a pang before any reversal of fortune; nay but two days before a ship-load of bad news! '

Source: de Saussure: *A Foreign View of England in the Reigns of George I and George II*, trans. by Mme. van Muyden, Murray, 1902.

I was seated behind several ladies and gentlemen who were acquainted with some of the peers and peeresses seated at the table beneath us. When we saw that they had finished eating we let down a small rope, which, to tell the truth, we had made up by knotting our garters together. The peers beneath were kind enough to attach a napkin filled with food to our rope, which we then hauled up, and in this way got plenty of good things to eat and drink. This napkin took several journeys up and down, and we were not the only people who had this idea, for from all the galleries round the same sight could be seen.

Shortly after the Champion had challenged and retired, the King, Queen, and Princesses rose from table, and passing into another apartment, retired to St. James's Palace very fatigued and weary. Their example was followed by the peers and peeresses, after which the big doors were thrown open and the crowd allowed to enter and take possession of the remains of the feast, of the table linen, of the plates and dishes, and of everything that was on the table. The pillage was most diverting; the people threw themselves with extraordinary avidity on everything the hall contained; blows were given and returned, and I cannot give you any idea of the noise and confusion that reigned. In less than half an hour everything had disappeared, even the boards of which the tables and seats had been made.

VERNON AT CARTAGENA

Captain Edward Vernon was one of the most persistent critics of Walpole's peace policy in the House of Commons. When war came in 1739 he got the chance to prove his contention that the Spanish Empire was weak. In November 1739 he captured Porto Bello and lost only seven men in doing it. The government then wanted Vernon to attack Spanish strongholds in the West Indies, and after twelve months' delay the necessary troops and supplies reached him. It was not Vernon's fault that everything went wrong. Tropical fevers were partly responsible, but the incompetence of General Wentworth, who commanded the troops, was the chief factor. There were failures at Cartagena—in spite of the optimistic tone of the letter printed here —at Santiago de Cuba and at the Panama Isthmus. The novelist Tobias Smollett sailed on board the *Cumberland*, one of the largest ships in the force which went to reinforce Vernon in 1740, as surgeon's mate. Smollett was present at the attack on Cartagena. He used his experiences during the voyage as material for his novel *Roderick Random*, and in 1756 published a straightforward factual account in *A Compendium of Authentic and Interesting Voyages*. In this he blames both leaders: Wentworth ' wholly defective in point of experience, confidence and resolution '; Vernon ' of weak understanding, strong prejudices, boundless arrogance, and overboiling passions '. Nor did Smollett approve of the ' grog ' invented by Vernon (a quart of water mixed with the half-pint of spirits which men on the West India station were allowed, and called ' grog ' after Vernon's grogram cloak). Smollett says: ' the water was corrupted and stunk so abominably, that a man was fain to stop his nose with one hand, while with the other he conveyed the can to his head. . . . With respect to the allowance of brandy, granted to each individual, the Admiral, in his great sagacity, ordered it to be mixed in a proportion of the water, without sweetening or souring, so as to compose a most unpalatable drench, which no man could swallow without reluctance '.

Source: A letter from Admiral Vernon to his wife printed in H. Moorhouse: *Letters of the English Seamen*, Chapman and Hall, 1910.

Further Reading: D. Ford: *Admiral Vernon and the Navy*, T. Fisher Unwin, 1907.

Princess Caroline, in the harbour of
Cartagena, 31st March, 1741.

My dear,—After the glorious success it has pleased Almighty God so wonderfully to favour us with, Whose manifold mercies I hope I shall never be unmindful of, I cannot omit laying hold of the opportunity of an express I am sending home to acquaint you of the joyful news, though in my present hurries I have no leisure to enter into many particulars. . . .

The first attack was by three of my 80-gun ships on the forts of St. Jago and St. Philip, lying without Boca Chica Castle, to secure a descent; and we drove the enemy out of them in less than an hour, and secured a descent to the army, and without their having so much as a single musket-shot fired at them. And my gallant sailors twice stormed and took two batteries on the opposite side of the harbour; the one of fifteen, the other of five 24-pounders, which the general complained of to me galled his army; they having remounted guns and repaired it after our first destroying it, as it lay well to play on our land battery.

On the propitious 25th March, the day I took charge, the General sent me word he intended to storm Boca Chica Castle; upon which, before the time he proposed, I sent all my boats manned and armed to land at those destroyed batteries a third time, for making a diversion on that side, to favour their storming it. But the enemy was under such consternation, that our troops marched into the castle over the breach without having a single shot fired at them, and about ten at night my gallant sailors stormed St. Joseph's fort without the ceremony of a breach, from whence, all the first of the night, the enemy had been firing partridge-shot at our men through the bushes, but with little injury to them; but they would not stand the assault, but deserted the fort, leaving only three drunken Spaniards behind them. Flushed with this success, my officers finding the Spaniards burning and sinking their ships, part of the boats were detached, to try what could be saved; and they boarded and took the Spanish admiral's ship, the *Gallicia*, with the flag flying, and in her the captain of the ship, the captain of the marines, an ensign, and 60 men, who, not having boats to escape, gave us the opportunity of saving this ship, which they had orders to sink likewise. Besides the admiral's ship taken, of 70 guns, they burnt the *St. Philip*, of 80 guns, and sunk the *St. Carlos* and *Africa*, of 60 guns each, across the channel; and they have this day sunk the *Conquistador* and *Dragon*, of 60 guns each, the only remaining men-of-war here, as they have done all the galleons and other vessels lying above Castillo Grande near five leagues higher up the harbour.

I have only time to add, it has pleased Almighty God to preserve me in good health, to go through all these glorious fatigues, and in a full disposition to push this beginning with all possible vigour, to humble the proud Spaniards, and bring them to repentance for all the injuries and long-practised depredations on us.

I have only time to send you my sincerest love and affection
for you and blessing to our dear boys; and with services to all
our good neighbours, and honest Will Fisher,

I am, my dearest,

Your most affectionate husband,

E. Vernon.

ANSON'S VOYAGE ROUND THE WORLD

In 1739 Walpole was forced by public opinion into war with Spain
—the War of Jenkins' Ear. A squadron of 6 ships under Commodore
George Anson was sent in 1740 to attack the South American posses-
sions of Spain. The squadron sailed through the Straits of Magellan,
and after attacking Spanish ports and shipping crossed the Pacific,
refitted at Macao, and captured the Manilla Galleon returning laden
with silver from its trading voyage to South America. Anson returned
to England round the Cape in June 1744: he had been away for 3 years
and 9 months.

Source: Lord Anson's Voyage Round the World, by Richard Walter,
ed, S. W. C. Pack. Penguin, pp. 120–9.

Richard Walter was chaplain to the expedition.

From prisoners it was learnt that the customs-house of the port
of Paita contained a large sum of money. Paita was therefore attacked
by a force under Lieutenant Brett.

Further Reading: Sir G. Callender: *Sea Kings of Britain* vol. ii.
Longmans, 1911. Somerville: *Commodore Anson's World Voyage,* Heine-
mann, 1934.

But about ten o'clock at night, the ships being then within
five leagues of the place, Lieutenant Brett, with the boats under
his command, put off, and arrived at the mouth of the bay without
being discovered, though no sooner had he entered it than some
of the people on board a vessel riding at anchor there perceived
him, who instantly getting into their boat, rowed towards the
fort, shouting and crying, ' The English, the English dogs,' etc.,
by which the whole town was suddenly alarmed, and our people
soon observed several lights hurrying backwards and forwards
in the fort, and other marks of the inhabitants being in great
motion. Lieutenant Brett, on this, encouraged his men to pull
briskly up, that they might give the enemy as little time as
possible to prepare for their defence. However, before our
boats could reach the shore, the people in the fort had got ready

some of their cannon, and pointed them towards the landing-place; and though in the darkness of the night it might well be supposed that chance had a greater share than skill in their direction, yet the first shot passed extremely near one of the boats, whistling just over the heads of the crew. This made our people redouble their efforts, so that they had reached the shore and were in part disembarked by the time the second gun fired. As soon as our men landed, they were conducted by one of the Spanish pilots[1] to the entrance of a narrow street, not above fifty yards distant from the beach, where they were covered from the fire of the fort; and being formed in the best manner the shortness of the time would allow, they immediately marched for the parade, which was a large square at the end of this street, the fort being one side of the square, and the governor's house another. In this march (though performed with tolerable regularity) the shouts and clamours of threescore sailors, who had been confined so long on shipboard, and were now for the first time on shore in an enemy's country, joyous as they always are when they land, and animated besides in the present case with the hopes of an immense pillage—the huzzas, I say, of this spirited detachment, joined with the noise of their drums, and favoured by the night, had augmented their numbers, in the opinion of the enemy, to at least three hundred, by which persuasion the inhabitants were so greatly intimidated that they were much more solicitous about the means of flight than of resistance: so that though on entering the parade our people received a volley from the merchants who owned the treasure then in the town, and who, with a few others, had ranged themselves in a gallery that ran round the governor's house, yet that post was immediately abandoned upon the first fire made by our people, who were thereby left in quiet possession of the parade.

On this success Lieutenant Brett divided his men into two parties, ordering one of them to surround the governor's house, and, if possible, to secure the governor, whilst he himself at the head of the other marched to the fort, with an intent to force it. But, contrary to his expectation, he entered it without opposition; for the enemy, on his approach, abandoned it, and made their

[1] Prisoners captured in previous actions.

escape over the walls. By this means the whole place was
mastered in less than a quarter of an hour's time from the first
landing, and with no other loss than that of one man killed on the
spot, and two wounded, one of which was the Spanish pilot of
the *Teresa*, who received a slight bruise by a ball which grazed
on his wrist. Indeed, another of the company, the Honourable
Mr. Kepple, son to the Earl of Albemarle, had a very narrow
escape; for having on a jockey cap, one side of the peak was
shaved off close to his temple by a ball, which, however, did him
no injury.

Lieutenant Brett, when he had thus far happily succeeded,
placed a guard at the fort, and another at the governor's house,
and appointed sentinels at all the avenues of the town, both to
prevent any surprise from the enemy, and to secure the effects
in the place from being embezzled. This being done, his next
care was to seize on the custom-house, where the treasure lay,
and to examine if any of the inhabitants remained in the town,
that he might know what further precautions it was necessary
to take; but he soon found that the numbers left behind were no
ways formidable, for the greatest part of them (being in bed when
the place was surprised) had run away with so much precipitation
that they had not given themselves time to put on their clothes.
In this general rout the governor was not the last to secure
himself, for he fled betimes half naked, leaving his wife, a young
lady of about seventeen years of age, to whom he had been
married but three or four days, behind him, though she too was
afterwards carried off in her shift by a couple of sentinels, just
as the detachment ordered to invest the house arrived before it.
This escape of the governor was an unpleasing circumstance, as
Mr. Anson had particularly recommended it to Lieutenant
Brett to secure his person if possible, in hopes that by that means
we might be able to treat for the ransom of the place; but it seems
his alertness rendered the execution of these orders impracticable.
The few inhabitants who remained were confined in one of the
churches under a guard, except some stout negroes which were
found in the town; these, instead of being shut up, were employed
the remaining part of the night to assist in carrying the treasure
from the custom-house and other places to the fort; however,

there was care taken that they should be always attended by a file of musqueteers.

The transporting the treasure from the custom-house to the fort was the principal occupation of Mr. Brett's people after he had got possession of the place. But the sailors, while they were thus busied, could not be prevented from entering the houses which lay near them in search of private pillage: where the first things which occurred to them being the clothes that the Spaniards in their flight had left behind them, and which, according to the custom of the country, were most of them either embroidered or laced, our people eagerly seized these glittering habits, and put them on over their own dirty trousers and jackets, not forgetting at the same time, the tie or bag-wig and laced hat which were generally found with the clothes; and when this practice was once begun, there was no preventing the whole detachment from imitating it: but those who came latest into the fashion not finding men's clothes sufficient to equip themselves, were obliged to take up with women's gowns and petticoats, which . . . they made no scruple of putting on and blending with their own greasy dress. So that when a party of them thus ridiculously metamorphosed first appeared before Mr. Brett, he was extremely surprised at the grotesque sight, and could not immediately be satisfied they were his own people. . . .

We had finished sending the treasure on board the *Centurion* the evening before, so that the third morning . . . the boats were employed in carrying off the most valuable part of the effects that remained in the town. And the commodore intending to sail in the afternoon, he, about ten o'clock, pursuant to his promise, sent all his prisoners, amounting to eighty-eight, on shore, giving orders to Lieutenant Brett to secure them in one of the churches under a strict guard till the men were ready to be embarked. Mr. Brett was at the same time ordered to burn the whole town, except the two churches . . . and then he was to abandon the place and to return on board. These orders were punctually complied with . . . setting fire to those houses which were most to the windward, he collected his men and marched towards the beach, where the boats waited to carry them off. . . .
The Spaniards on the hill perceiving he was retreating, resolved

to try if they could not precipitate his departure, and thereby lay some foundation for their future boasting. To this end a small squadron of their horse . . . marched down the hill with much seeming resolution, so that had we not entertained an adequate opinion of their prowess, we might have imagined that now we were on the open beach with no advantage of situation, they would certainly have charged us, but we presumed (and we were not mistaken) that this was mere ostentation. For, notwithstanding the pomp and parade they at first came on with, Mr. Brett had no sooner ordered his men to halt and face about, than the enemy stopped their career, and never dared to advance a step further. . . .

. . . The acquisition we made, though inconsiderable in comparison of what we destroyed, was yet far from despicable, for the wrought plate, dollars and other coin which fell into our hands, amounted to upwards of £30,000 sterling, besides several rings, bracelets, and jewels, whose intrinsic value we could not then determine; and over and above all this, the plunder which became the property of the immediate captors was very great, so that upon the whole it was by much the most important booty we met with upon that coast.

GEORGE II AND QUEEN CAROLINE

Lord Hervey (1696–1743) whose *Memoirs* are so important for the study of his age, was Vice-Chamberlain of the Royal Household to George II and Queen Caroline, and a member of the Privy Council. His influence with the Queen made him useful to Walpole. Hervey became Lord Privy Seal in 1740, but was dismissed in 1742.

Lord Hervey suffered from epilepsy and his physicians prescribed a strict diet: asses' milk and a biscuit a day, and once a week an apple. He sometimes had to paint his face to hide its ghastly pallor.

(*a*) *Source:* John, Lord Hervey, *Memoirs of the Reign of George II*, ed. Croker, 2 vols., Murray 1848.

Further Reading: J. H. Plumb: *The First Four Georges*, Batsford, 1956.

[The Queen's] predominant passion was pride, and the darling pleasure of her soul was power; . . . She was at least seven or eight hours tête-à-tête with the King every day, during which time she was generally saying what she did not think, assenting to what she did not believe, and praising what she did not approve. . . . For all the tedious hours she spent then in watching him whilst he slept, or the heavier task of entertaining him whilst he was awake, her single consolation was in reflecting she had power, and that people in coffee-houses and *ruelles* were saying she governed the country, without knowing how dear the government of it cost her.

The Queen . . . loved reading and the conversation of men of wit and learning. But she did not dare to indulge herself as much as she wished to do in this pleasure for fear of the King, who often rebuked her for dabbling in all that lettered nonsense (as he termed it). . . .

(*b*) George II and Hanover.

After this last journey [1735] Hanover had so completed the conquest of his affections that there was nothing English ever commended in his presence that he did not always show, or pretend to show, was surpassed by something of the same kind in Germany. No English or even French cook could dress a dinner; no English confectioner set out a dessert; no English player could act; no English coachman could drive; or English jockey ride, nor were any English horses fit to be drove or fit to be ridden; no Englishman knew how to come in to a room, nor any Englishwoman how to dress herself; nor were there any diversions in England, public or private; nor any man or woman in England whose conversation was to be borne—the one, as he said, talking of nothing but their dull politics, and the others of nothing but their ugly clothes. Whereas at Hanover all these things were in the utmost perfection: the men were patterns of politeness, bravery, and gallantry; the women of beauty, wit, and entertainment; his troops there were the bravest in the world, his counsellors the wisest, his manufacturers the most ingenious, his subjects the happiest. . . .

(*c*)

In the absence of the King, the Queen had taken several very bad pictures out of the great drawing room at Kensington, and put very good ones in their places: the King, affecting, for the sake of contradiction, to dislike this change, or, from his extreme ignorance in painting, really disapproving it, told Lord Hervey, as Vice-Chamberlain, that he would have every new picture taken away, and every old one replaced. Lord Hervey, who had a mind to make his court to the Queen by opposing this order, asked if His Majesty would not give leave for the two Vandykes, at least, on each side of the chimney to remain, instead of those two sign-posts, done by nobody knew who, that had been removed to make way for them. To which the King answered, ' My Lord, I have a great respect for your taste in what you understand, but in pictures I beg leave to follow my own. I suppose you assisted the Queen with your fine advice when she was pulling my house to pieces and spoiling all my furniture: thank God, at least she has left the walls standing! As for the Vandykes, I do not care whether they are changed or no; but for the picture with the dirty frame over the door, and the three nasty little children, I will have them taken away, and the old ones restored; I will have it done too to-morrow morning before I go to London, or else I know it will not be done at all. . . .

Lord Hervey told the Queen, next morning at breakfast, what had passed the night before, who affected to laugh, but was a good deal displeased, and more ashamed. She said the King, to be sure, was master of his own furniture; and asked Lord Hervey if the pictures were changed; who told her ' No ', and why it was impossible. [The displaced pictures had been sent to other palaces and the frames had been altered to fit the new pictures]. She charged him not to tell the King why, but to find out some other reason. Whilst they were speaking the King came in, but, by good luck, said not one word of the pictures: his Majesty stayed about five minutes in the gallery, snubbed the Queen, who was drinking chocolate, for being always stuffing, the Princess Emily for not hearing him, the Princess Caroline for being grown fat, the Duke [of Cumberland] for standing awkwardly, Lord Hervey for not knowing what relation the Prince of Sultzbach was to the Elector Palatine: and then carried the Queen to walk, and be resnubbed, in the garden. The pictures were altered according to the King's direction soon after; and the excuse Lord Hervey made for their not being done that morning was the man's being out of the way who was always employed on these occasions.

THE BATTLE OF DETTINGEN: Platoon-Fire
of the Royal Welch Fusileers
Thursday, June 27th, 1743

The Royal Welch Fusiliers were attacked by the French cavalry, to quote the late Sir John Fortescue, ' at full trot with pistols in both hands and swords dangling by the wrist. Arrived within range they fired their pistols, dashed the empty weapons in the faces of the British, and then fell to with the sword; but the Fusiliers, as it was said, fought like devils, their platoon-fire thundering out as regularly as on parade, and the French horse fell back repulsed.'

This letter from one of their officers illustrates exactly the method and effect of this platoon-fire in the last battle in which an English king personally commanded his troops on the battlefield. The colonel, contrary to the hopes of the writer of the letter, died of his wounds; and his place was taken by Huske.

Source: Gentleman's Magazine, xiii, p. 386.

We attack'd the Regiment of *Navarre*, one of their prime regiments. Our People imitated their Predecessors in the last war gloriously, marching in close Order, as firm as a Wall, and did not fire till we came within 60 Paces, and still kept advancing; so that we had soon closed with the Enemy, if they had not retreated: For when the Smoak blew off a little, instead of being among their Living, we found the Dead in Heaps by us; and the second Fire turn'd them to the Right about, and upon a long Trot. We engaged two other Regiments afterwards, one after the other, who stood but one fire each; and their Blue *French* Foot Guards made the best of their Way without firing a Shot. Our Colonel fell in the first Attack, shot in the Mouth, and out at the Neck; but there are Hopes of his Recovery. The Gens d'Armes are quite ruin'd, who are their chief Dependance, and intended to cut us all to Pieces without firing a Shot. Our Regiment sustain'd little Loss, tho' much engaged; And indeed our whole Army gives us great Honour. Brigadier Huske who behaved gloriously, and quite cool was shot thro' the Foot at the Time that our Colonel fell, yet continued his Post. We have no more than 50 kill'd and wounded, and one Officer besides the Colonel. What preserved us, was our keeping close Order, and advancing near the Enemy ere we fir'd. Several that popp'd at 100 Paces lost more of their Men, and did less Execution; for the *French* will stand Fire at a distance, tho' 'tis plain they cannot look Men in the Face.

JOHN WESLEY, 1703-1791

John Wesley was the son of Samuel Wesley, the rector of Epworth in Lincolnshire, and Susanna his wife. John Wesley was educated at Charterhouse and Lincoln College, Oxford. He took Holy Orders, and after his religious experience in the Moravian Meeting House in Aldersgate Street, London, in 1738, he began his great work of evangelisation. During the next 53 years he travelled 224,000 miles, mostly on horseback, and preached over 40,000 sermons. The hostility of the Anglican Church to his work compelled him more and more to organise his followers outside the Establishment, though he had no wish to found a new religious body. These extracts from Wesley's Journal show something of the hostility he had to meet; they also show his courage.

Source: Journal of John Wesley.

Further Reading: G. E. Harrison, *Son to Susanna*, Penguin Book. J. H. Overton, *John Wesley*, Methuen, 1891. M. Piette, *John Wesley in the Evolution of Protestantism*, Sheed and Ward, 1937. R. A. Knox, *Enthusiasm*, Oxford University Press, 1950.

Friday, March 19, 1742—I rode once more to Pensford, at the earnest request of several serious people. The place where they desired me to preach was a little green spot near the town. But I had no sooner begun, than a great company of rabble, hired (as we afterwards found) for that purpose, came furiously upon us, bringing a bull which they had been baiting and now drove in among the people. But the beast was wiser than his drivers, and continually ran either on one side of us or the other, while we quietly sang praise to God and prayer for about an hour. The poor wretches finding themselves disappointed, at length seized upon the bull, now weak and tired after being so long torn and beaten both by dogs and men, and by main strength partly dragged and partly thrust him in among the people. When they had forced their way to the little table on which I stood, they strove several times to throw it down by thrusting the helpless beast against it, who of himself stirred no more than a log of wood. I once or twice put aside his head with my hand, that the blood might not drop upon my clothes, intending to go on as soon as the hurry should be a little over. But the table falling down, some of our friends caught me in their arms and carried me right away on their shoulders, while the rabble wreaked their vengeance on the table which they tore bit from bit. We went a little way off, where I finished my discourse without any noise or interruption.

Wednesday, June 9, 1742—I rode over to a neighbouring town to wait upon a Justice of Peace, a man of candour and understanding, before whom their angry neighbours had carried a whole waggon-load of these new heretics. But when he asked what they had done there was a deep silence; for that was a point their conductors had forgot. At length one said, ' Why, they pretended to be better than other people. And besides, they prayed from morning to night.' Mr. S. asked, ' But have they done nothing besides? ' ' Yes, Sir,' said an old man, 'An't please your worship, they have *convarted* my wife. Till she went among them she had such a tongue! And now she is as quiet as a lamb.' ' Carry them back, carry them back ', replied the Justice, ' and let them convert all the scolds in the town '.

Thursday, April 17, 1743. As I was preaching at Pelton, one of the colliers, not much accustomed to things of this kind, in the middle of the sermon began shouting amain for mere satisfaction and joy of heart. But their usual token of approbation (which somewhat surprised me at first) was clapping me on the back.

Wednesday, October 18, 1749. I rode, at the desire of John Bennet, to Rochdale, in Lancashire. As soon as ever we entered the town, we found the streets lined on both sides with multitudes of people, shouting, cursing, blaspheming and gnashing upon us with their teeth. Perceiving it would not be practicable to preach abroad, I went into a large room, open to the street and called aloud ' Let the wicked forsake his way, and the unrighteous man his thoughts.' . . . None opposed or interrupted; and there was a very remarkable change in the behaviour of the people as we afterwards went through the town.

We came to Bolton about five in the evening. We had no sooner entered the main street than we perceived the lions at Rochdale were lambs in comparison of those at Bolton. Such rage and bitterness I scarce ever saw before in any creatures that bore the form of men. They followed us in full cry to the house where we went and, as soon as we were gone in, took possession

E

of all the avenues to it, and filled the street from one end to the other. . . . When the first stone came among us through the window, I expected a shower to follow, and the rather because they had now procured a bell to call their whole forces together; but they did not design to carry on the attack at a distance. Presently one ran up and told us the mob had bursted into the house; he added that they had got J[ohn] B[ennet] in the midst of them. They had; and he laid hold on the opportunity to tell them of ' the terrors of the Lord '.

Meantime D[avid] T[aylor] engaged another part of them with smoother and softer words. Believing the time was now come, I walked down into the thickest of them. They had now filled all the rooms below. I called for a chair. The winds were hushed and all was calm and still. My heart was filled with love, my eyes with tears, and my mouth with arguments. They were amazed, they were ashamed, they were melted down, they devoured every word.

Sunday, May 6, 1750 [Athlone]. . . . In the midst of the sermon, a man with a fine curveting horse drew off a large part of the audience. I paused a little, and then, raising my voice, said, ' If there are any more of you who think it is of more concern to see a dancing horse than to hear the Gospel of Christ, pray go after them.' They took the reproof; the greater part came back directly and gave double attention.

Tuesday, 19 September, 1769—Between twelve and one I preached at Freshford, and on White's Hill, near Bradford, in the evening. I had designed to preach there again the next evening, but a gentleman in the town desired me to preach at his door. The beasts of the people were tolerably quiet till I had nearly finished my sermon. Then they lifted up their voice, especially one, called a gentleman, who had filled his pocket with rotten eggs. But a young man coming unawares, clapped his hands on each side and mashed them all at once. In an instant he was perfume all over, though it was not so sweet as balsam!

GIBBON'S DECLINE AND FALL OF THE ROMAN EMPIRE

Edward Gibbon (1737–1794) was educated at Westminster and spent fourteen months at Magdalen College, Oxford (1752–3)—'the most idle and unprofitable of my whole life.' He read Bossuet's *Exposition* and his *History of Protestant Variations* and became a convert to the Church of Rome. His father was thus compelled to remove him from Oxford. He sent him to Lausanne where his tutor, Mr. Pavillard, was able to teach him the art of steady and consistent reading. Under his guidance, too, Gibbon's adherence to Catholicism was abbreviated to a period of eighteen months, though at the cost ultimately of reducing him to a savage if polished scepticism. Gibbon's *Autobiography* describes with delightful and inimitable self-satisfaction the main events of his life. His *Decline and Fall* is, as Sir Llewellyn Woodward has said, 'unique not merely in English historical writing, but in the historical writing of any country'. Newman remarked somewhere that it was the only considerable example of ecclesiastical history in English. Gibbon summarised it in the famous sentence: 'I have described the triumph of barbarism and religion'. In consequence, it has been suggested, Gibbon consciously dramatised the setting of the book's inception to fit the theme. As Mr. G. M. Young has pointed out, the usually accurate Gibbon misread the scene of his decision. It was the Temple of Juno in which the 'bare-footed friars' were singing Vespers. As for the Temple of Jupiter, its ruins were what he was sitting upon. But so great a book deserves so great an inception.

Source: Autobiography of Edward Gibbon, ed. by Lord Sheffield, 'World's Classics', Oxford University Press, 1907, pp. 160 and 205.

Further Reading: G. M. Young: *Gibbon*, 1932, Nelson.

It was at Rome, on the 15th of October, 1764, as I sat musing amidst the ruins of the Capitol, while the bare-footed friars were singing Vespers in the Temple of Jupiter, that the idea of writing the decline and fall of the City first started to my mind.

I have presumed to mark the moment of conception: I shall now commemorate the hour of my final deliverance. It was on the day, or rather night, of the 27th of June, 1787, between the hours of eleven and twelve, that I wrote the last lines of the last page, in a summer house in my garden. After laying down my pen, I took several turns in a *berceau*, or covered walk of acacias, which commands a prospect of the country, the lake, and the mountains. The air was temperate, the sky was serene, the silver orb of the moon was reflected from the waters, and all nature was silent. I will not dissemble the first emotions of joy on recovery of my freedom, and, perhaps, the establishment of my fame. But my pride was soon humbled, and a sober melancholy was spread over my mind, by the idea that I had taken an ever-lasting leave of an old and agreeable companion, and that what-soever might be the future fate of my *History*, the life of the historian must be short and precarious.

THE JACOBITE REBELLION OF 1745
The Battle of Prestonpans
Tuesday, September 21st, 1745

On Tuesday, September 21 the forces of Sir John Cope were dispersed by the army of Prince Charles Edward in 15 minutes. Only 30 Jacobites were killed.

Elder son of the Old Pretender, the Prince was born and bred in Rome. The Gaelic form of his name, *Teàrlach* as it sounded to English ears, is probably the reason why he has been universally known as Prince Charlie. So late as 1777 Dr. Johnson observed: ' If England were fairly polled, the present King would be sent away to-night and his adherents hanged to-morrow.' The Pretender in fact inherited a cause for which no Englishman would fight but to whose success many Englishmen would drink. He led the forlorn hope of the Forty-Five with such dash that at one point success seemed not impossible. He subsequently visited London in disguise, inspected the defences of the Tower, and made a formal abjuration of Catholicism, probably in St. Martin-in-the-Fields. Some years later he was reconciled to the Church of Rome. A mistress whom his followers believed to be a spy, bouts of drunkenness and an unhappy marriage all contributed to diminish his active adherents.

By 1783 he was a solitary old man, playing old tunes to himself on his violincello, in a room hung with crimson damask and lighted by two candles, with two loaded pistols on the table beside him. The music would come to an end with ' Lochaber No More ! ' for then the old man broke down and wept. He died at Rome on January 30th, 1788, the anniversary of Charles I's death on the scaffold in Whitehall.

Source: Narrative of O'Sullivan printed in *The* 1745 *and After*, by A. and H. Tayler. Nelson, 1938.

John William O'Sullivan was one of the ' Seven Men of Moidart '. After Culloden he shared the wanderings of the Prince for some days;

then they separated, and O'Sullivan got aboard a ship for the Nether-lands and went to France. At the French Court he asked that a ship be sent to Scotland to rescue Prince Charles Edward.

The date of O'Sullivan's death is not known.

Further Reading: Petrie, *The Jacobite Movement: The Last Phase,* 1716–1807. Eyre and Spottiswoode, 1950. K. Tomasson, *The Jacobite General.* Blackwood, 1958.

We began to march an hour before day, and happily for us, found no opposition, so that we had time to form before the enemy perceived us. The irregularity of the day before, or the difficulty of the passes, caused a general changement in the order of battle, for the Macdonalds who pretend it is due to them, took the right, though they were to have the left by lot, and the Camerons who were to have the right, had the left, but things did not go the worse for that changement, for every man did his duty, and no troops in the world could show more valour, than the Highlanders did that day. The Duke of Perth was at the right, and Lord George at the left; it was not yet day, so that we saw the enemy in good order of battle before they could see us; our dark clothes were advantageous to us.

As soon as they perceived us, their Cannon began to fire, but did little or no damage, and did not at all relent our march. Sullivan, who was at the right, seeing we had out-winged the enemy, cried out, ' Let the Macdonalds come to this hedge, we have out-winged them '; the Dragoons hearing this made a motion, as if they would extend themselves; upon which Sullivan cried out again, ' Let the first rank fire,' which they did; the Dragoons answered by a very irregular discharge, and went off, as fast as they could drive, and the Macdonalds after them, as fast as they; the foot finding themselves abandoned by the horse, flinched immediately after, so that there was a general deroute, and never such a one I believe in any action. The left, composed of the Camerons, Stewards of Appen and the Duke of Perth's Regiment which were almost all MacGregors, behaved most gloriously, for they rushed in with such fury upon the enemy, after their first discharge, that they had not time to charge their cannon, and then the broadswords played their part, for with one stroke, arms, and legs were cut off, and heads were split to the shoulders, never such wounds were seen. Cope escaped with the few that followed him by the breaches that he caused to be made in those stone walls near Gardener's House and it was there really where the great slaughter was, for the poor soldiers that could not pass in those breaches because of the Dragoons that filled them up, were cut to pieces, and the Dragoons themselves were pursued so closely . . . that they were obliged to abandon their horses and throw themselves into those parks where the most of them were taken. The Dragoons, in their flight, threw away their Standards, the foot their Colours; one found in one place, another in another, but the people of the country took away a great many of them, there were eighty-four officers made prisoners, of all ranks and about fourteen hundred private men. . . .

. . . But when people begun to be cool, they reflected on the danger the Prince exposed himself to, notwithstanding what he promised. . . . The Prince answered that he was obliged to them all, for the care and tenderness they had of him, that he only did what he ought to do, and that he would never forget their behaviour that day. They then proposed him to refresh and repose himself, that he had great need of it; ' No,' says he, with a tender heart and in a most feeling way, ' I can't rest until I see my own poor men taken care of, and the other wounded too, for they are the King's subjects as well as we, and it's none of their fault if they are led on blindly ', upon which he immediately sent orders, to the neighbouring villages, upon pain of military execution that houses and everything necessary should be provided for the wounded, and that the inhabitants should come with spades and other instruments to bury the dead. He spoke to the surgeons, first to dress the Highlanders, and afterwards to neglect nothing for the others; he neither would eat or drink until he saw people set about this.

MANCHESTER DURING THE REBELLION

Source: Private Journal and Literary Remains of John Byrom, ed. R. Parkinson for the Cheetham Society, 1854–7. From a letter written by Byrom and dated March 1st, 1745.

Byrom was typical of many Englishmen with Jacobite sympathies who did not commit themselves to the cause of the Pretender.

As they [the Highlanders] came forward, the apprehension of our people increased, a great many of them left the town and sent away their effects, and some of their provisions, their bread and their cheese and their liquor, . . . We were told one morning that they were gone to Liverpool, but it was false intelligence, for that day about noon there came a sergeant and a drummer in a Highland dress, with a woman on horseback carrying a drum, which they beat up, soon after their arrival, for volunteers. My curiosity led me to my sister's window at the Cross, where I beheld this extraordinary event of two men and a half taking our famous town of Manchester without any resistance or opposition. . . . That night there came in a party of horse, and the next day the whole army. The Prince (for so he has been called in all places when present, or near it, but, at a proper distance, Pretender), came in about noon, walking in a Highland habit, in the middle of a large party, and went to Mr. Dickenson's house. . . . The officers and the men were sent up and down to the several houses . . . we had only a single Highlander, who came into the house of himself, and, behaving civilly, we entertained him civilly, and he was content to lie in the stable during their stay. The town was exceeding still and quiet. The day that the Prince came in the proclamation of his father was read at the Cross, and the two constables were forced to be there, and one of them to repeat the words. I came by as they were at it, but there was no great crowd or hurry about it nor any soldiers, only an officer or two, who I suppose performed this ceremony wherever they came. It was easy enough for friend or foe that was curious enough to see the Prince, to have an opportunity; he rode through the streets the day after his coming, and to do justice to his person, whatever his pretensions may be, he makes a very graceful and amiable appearance; he is fair complexioned, well shaped, has a sensible and comely aspect. . . .

There were about thirty of our neighbours that listed under him, among whom three sons of poor Dr. Deacon, who engaged without their father's consent as I am told, and two of them without his knowledge . . . there was no mobbing till the return of the Highlanders from Derby, where to my surprise they ventured and came back again. The first returning party was about thirty horse, which passed by our house, coming into the town that way, and the foolish mob clodded them with dirt or stones, and then I thought there would have been mischief done, but there was not. They came in all that night, and the next day laid a mulct of £5,000 upon the town for the mobbing, which was moderated to half the sum, and raised with much ado. . . . A Highlander was shot upon the road by a fellow that, for no reason but his being one, killed him as he was passing with some others; a butcher was killed in the same manner by a fellow that took him for a Highlander; nobody else killed about us on this occasion, which we thought would have slain half of us. . . .

THE DECISION TO RETREAT AT DERBY

Source: O'Sullivan's Narrative in A. and H. Tayler's *The 1745 and After*, Nelson, 1938.

. . . The accounts we had from all sides were that Cumberland marched with the greatest diligence to get before us, and that each trooper carried a foot soldier behind him; that Wade was in march on the other side, and 6000 men that marched from London, or at least all the forces they could spare; that the three armies could join together and that we could not possibly make our way, nor pretend to conquer them, for they would be four against one. Lord George comes very early the next morning to H.R.H.'s, represents him the situation he was in, and that it was everybody's opinion that the only party that was to be taken was to retire. The Prince was astonished at this proposition. . . .

The Chiefs and others were sent for, who were the most part of them for the retreat, and really according to all the rules of war, and prudence it was the only party to be taken (Sullivan proposed it at Manchester finding that not a man of any consequence appeared;) but a young Prince, that sees himself within three days, or at utmost four days, march of the capital, where if he was once arrived, would in all appearance restore the King, could not relish the word of retreat, and really he would not hear that word from the beginning, he had an aversion to the word itself, but finding everybody almost of that opinion was obliged to consent. I never saw anybody so concerned as he was for this disappointment, nor never saw him take anything after so much to heart as he did it.

THE REBELLION SEEN FROM LONDON

Source: Horace Walpole: *Letters,* ed. Toynbee, Oxford 1903, vol. ii, pp. 159–60.

From a letter to Sir Horace Mann dated from Arlington Street, December 9, 1745.

In the winter of 1739, Horace Walpole, the youngest son of Sir Robert, visited Florence. He was doing the Grand Tour in company with Thomas Gray. The British chargé d'affaires in Florence, Horace Mann, was a distant relation of the Walpole family, and one of their protégés. He and Horace Walpole found each other's society most congenial, and Walpole stayed in Florence for 13 months. The bulk of Horace Walpole's correspondence consists of letters to Mann written between 1741 and 1786.

. . . The Duke, from some strange want of intelligence, lay last week for four-and-twenty hours under arms at Stone, in Staffordshire, expecting the rebels every moment, while they were marching in all haste to Derby. The news of this threw the town into great consternation; but his Royal Highness repaired his mistake, and got to Northampton, between the Highlanders and London. They got nine thousand pounds at Derby. . . . Then they retreated a few miles, but returned again to Derby, got ten thousand pounds more, plundered the town, and burnt a house of the Countess of Exeter. They are gone again, and go back to Leake, in Staffordshire, but miserably harassed. . . . The Duke has sent General Hawley with the dragoons to harass them in their retreat. . . . They must either go to North Wales, where they will probably all perish, or to Scotland, with great loss. We dread them no longer. We are threatened with great preparations for a French invasion, but the coast is exceedingly guarded; and for the people, the spirit against the rebels increases every day. Though they have marched thus into the heart of the Kingdom, there has not been the least symptom of a rising, not even in the great towns of which they possessed themselves . . . here in London the aversion to them is amazing: on some thoughts of the King's going to an encampment at Finchley, the weavers not only offered him a thousand men, but the whole body of the Law formed themselves into a little army, under the command of Lord Chief Justice Willes, and were to have done duty at St. James's, to guard the royal family in the King's absence.

THE YOUNG PRETENDER IN 1770

Source: Letters from Italy by an Englishwoman (Mrs. Miller), London, 1776, vol. ii, p. 198, quoted Mahon: *History of England*, John Murray, 1858 vol. iii, pp. 352-3.

The Pretender is naturally above the middle size, but stoops excessively; he appears bloated and red in the face; his countenance heavy and sleepy, which is attributed to his having given into excess of drinking: but when a young man he must have been esteemed handsome. His complexion is of the fair tint, his eyes blue, his hair light brown, and the contour of his face a long oval; he is by no means thin, has a noble person, and a graceful manner. His dress was scarlet laced with broad gold lace; he wears the blue riband outside of his coat, from which depends a cameo, antique, as large as the palm of my hand; and he wears the same Garter and motto as those of the noble order of St. George in England. Upon the whole, he has a melancholy, mortified appearance. Two gentlemen constantly attend him; they are of Irish extraction, and Roman Catholics you may be sure. . . .

THE BLACK HOLE OF CALCUTTA,
Monday, June 21st, 1756

Suraj-ud-Daulah, the ruler of Bengal, had captured the British fort at Calcutta. Many British subjects, including the Governor, Roger Drake, fled in panic down the river Hooghly; those who remained and fell into Suraj-ud-Daulah's power were treated in the manner described here. Clive and Admiral Watson restored British power and influence at Calcutta several months later, but the battle of Plassey, when Suraj-ud-Daulah was defeated, really ends the story.

Source: Letter of J. Z. Holwell printed in the *Annual Register* for 1758, pp. 278-85.

Since the flight of the Governor, Holwell had been the senior official.

Further Reading: Philip Woodruff: *The Men who ruled India: I. The Founders.* Macaulay: Essay on Clive.

. . . Figure to yourself, my friend, if possible, the situation of a hundred and forty-six wretches, exhausted by continual fatigue and action, crammed together in a cube of eighteen feet, in a close sultry night, in Bengal, shut up to the eastward and southward (the only quarters from whence air could reach us) by dead walls, and by a wall and door to the north, open only to the westward by two windows, strongly barred with iron, from which we could receive scarce any the least circulation of fresh air.

What must ensue, appeared to me in lively and dreadful colours, the instant I cast my eyes round and saw the size and situation of the room. Many unsuccessful attempts were made to force the door; for having nothing but our hands to work with, and the door opening inwards, all endeavours were vain and fruitless. . . .

We had been but few minutes confined before every one fell into a perspiration so profuse, you can form no idea of it. This brought on a raging thirst, which increased in proportion as the body was drained of its moisture.

. . . Before nine o'clock every man's thirst grew intolerable, and respiration difficult. Efforts were made again to force the door but in vain. Many insults were used to the guard to provoke them to fire in upon us. For my own part, I hitherto felt little pain or uneasiness, but what resulted from my anxiety for the sufferings of those within. By keeping my face between two of the bars, I obtained enough air to give my lungs easy play, though my perspiration was excessive and my thirst commencing.

Now everybody, excepting those situated in and near the windows, began to grow outrageous, and many delirious: ' Water, Water,' became the general cry. And the old Jemmaut-daar[1] . . . , taking pity on us, ordered the people to bring some skins of water. This was what I dreaded. I foresaw it would prove the ruin of the small chance left us, and essayed many times to speak to him privately to forbid its being brought; but the clamour was so loud, it became impossible. The water appeared. Words cannot paint to you the universal agitation and raving the sight of it threw us into. . . .

We had no means of conveying it into the prison, but by hats forced through the bars; and thus myself and Messieurs Coles and Scott . . . supplied them as fast as possible. But those who have experienced intense thirst . . . will be sufficiently sensible it could receive no more than a momentary alleviation; the cause

[1] One of the guards outside the windows.

still subsisted. Though we brought full hats within the bars, there ensued such violent struggles, and frequent contests to get at it, that before it reached the lips of any one, there would be scarcely a small tea cup left in them. These supplies like sprinkling water on fire, only served to feed and rouse the flame. . . . The confusion now became general and horrid. Several quitted the other window (the only chance they had for life) to force their way to the water, and the throng and press upon the window was beyond bearing; many forcing their passage from the further part of the room, pressed down those in their way, who had less strength, and trampled them to death.

From about nine to near eleven, I sustained this cruel scene and painful situation, still supplying them with water, though my legs were almost broke with the weight against them. By this time I myself was near pressed to death, and my two companions, with Mr. William Parker (who had forced himself into the window) were really so. . . .

For a great while they preserved a respect and regard to me, more than indeed I could well expect, . . . but now all distinction was lost. My friend Baillie . . . and several others . . . had for some time been dead at my feet: and were now trampled upon by every corporal or common soldier, who, by the help of more robust constitutions, had forced their way to the window, and held fast by the bars over me, till at last I became so pressed and wedged up, I was deprived of all motion.

Determined now to give everything up, I called to them, and begged, as the last instance of their regard, they would remove the pressure upon me, and permit me to retire out of the window to die in quiet. They gave way; and with much difficulty I forced a passage into the centre of the prison, where the throng was less by the many dead (then I believe amounting to one third) and the numbers who flocked to the windows. . . .

In the black-hole there is a platform. . . . I travelled over the dead and repaired to the further end of it, just opposite to the other window. Here my poor friend Mr. Edward Eyre came staggering over the dead to me, and with his usual coolness and good nature, asked me how I did? but fell and expired before I had time to make him a reply. I laid myself down on some of the dead behind me, on the platform; and, recommending myself to heaven, had the comfort of thinking my sufferings could have no long duration.

My thirst grew now insupportable, and the difficulty of breathing much increased; and I had not remained in this situation I believe, ten minutes, when I was seized with a pain in my breast, and palpitation of heart. . . . These roused and obliged me to get up again. . . . I instantly determined to push for the window opposite to me, and . . . gained the third rank at it, with one hand seized a bar, and by that means gained the second. . . .

In a few moments the pain, palpitation, and difficulty of breathing ceased; but my thirst continued intolerable. I called aloud for 'Water for God's sake.' But from the water I had no relief; my thirst was rather increased by it; so I determined to drink no more but patiently wait the event; and kept my mouth moist from time to time by sucking the perspiration out of my shirt-sleeves, and catching the drops as they fell, like heavy rain, from my head and face; you can hardly imagine how unhappy I was if any of them escaped my mouth. . . .

By half an hour past eleven, the much greater number of those living were in an outrageous delirium, and the others quite ungovernable; few retaining any calmness, but the ranks next the window. . . . They whose strength was exhausted, laid themselves down and expired quietly upon their fellows: others who had yet some strength and vigour left, made a last effort for the windows, and several succeeded by leaping and scrambling over the backs and heads of those in the first ranks: and got hold of the bars, from which there was no removing them. Many to the right and left sunk with the violent pressure, and were soon suffocated; for now a steam arose from the living and the dead. . . .

I need not, my dear friend, ask your commiseration, when I tell you, that in this plight, from half an hour after eleven till near two in the morning, I sustained the weight of a heavy man, with his knees on my back, and the pressure of his whole body on my head; a Dutch sergeant, who had taken his seat upon my left shoulder, and a Topaz[1] bearing on my right: all which,

[1] A black Christian soldier: subject of Portugal.

nothing could have enabled me long to support, but the props
and pressure equally sustaining me all around. The two latter I
frequently dislodged, by shifting my hold on the bars, and driving
my knuckles into their ribs; but my friend above stuck fast, and,
as he held by two bars, was immoveable.

The repeated trials and efforts I made to dislodge this insuffer-
able incumbrance upon me, at last quite exhausted me, and towards two o'clock, finding I must quit the window, or sink where
I was, I resolved on the former.

I was at this time sensible of no pain, and little uneasiness. I
found a stupor coming on apace, and laid myself down by that
gallant old man, the reverend Mr. Jervas Bellamy, who lay dead
with his son the Lieutenant, hand in hand, near the southernmost
wall of the prison.

When I had lain there some little time, I still had reflexion
enough to suffer some uneasiness in the thought that I should be
trampled upon when dead. . . . With some difficulty I raised
myself and gained the platform a second time, where I presently
lost all sensation. Of what passed in this interval to the time of
my resurrection from this hole of horrors, I can give you no
account.

When the day broke, and the gentlemen found that no entreat-
ies could prevail to get the door opened, it occurred to one of them
(I think to Mr. Secretary Cooke) to make a search for me, in
hopes I might have influence enough to gain a release from this
scene of misery. Accordingly Messrs. Lushington and Walcot
undertook the search, and by my shirt discovered me under the
dead upon the platform. They took me from thence and imagin-
ing I had some signs of life, brought me towards the window I
had first possession of.

But as life was equally dear to every man (and the stench
arising from the dead bodies was grown so intolerable), no one
would give up his station in or near the window: so they were
obliged to carry me back again. But soon after Captain Mills . . .
who was in possession of a seat in the window, had the humanity
to offer to resign it. I was again brought by the same gentlemen
and placed in the window. At this juncture the *suba*, who had
received an account of the havoc death had made amongst us,

sent one of his Jemmautdaars to enquire if the chief survived. They showed me to him; told I had appearance of life remaining; and believed I might recover if the door was opened very soon. This answer being returned to the *suba*, an order came immediately for our release, it being then near six in the morning.

As the door opened inwards, and as the dead were piled up against it, and covered all the rest of the floor, it was impossible to open it by any efforts from without; it was therefore necessary that the dead should be removed by the few that were within, who were become so feeble, that the task, though it was the condition of life, was not performed without the utmost difficulty, and it was 20 minutes after the order came before the door could be opened.

About a quarter after six in the morning, the poor remains of 146 souls, being no more than three and twenty, came out of the Black-hole alive, but in a condition which made it very doubtful whether they would see the morning of the next day. . . . The bodies were dragged out of the hole by the soldiers, and thrown promiscuously into the ditch of an unfinished ravelin, which was afterwards filled with earth. . . . Mr. Holwell, when he came out of the prison was in a high fever, and not able to stand; he was, however, sent for to be examined by the viceroy, and was in this condition carried to his presence. It was some time before he could speak, but as soon as he was able, he began to relate the sufferings and death of his unhappy companions.

The viceroy, without taking any notice of this tale of distress, stopped him short, by telling him, that he had been informed there was treasure to a very considerable value secreted in the fort, and that if he did not discover it, he must expect no mercy. Mr. Holwell replied, that he knew of no such treasure; and then began to remind him of his assurance the day before, that no hurt should come either to himself or his friends. To this remonstrance he paid no more regard than he had done to the complaint, but proceeded in his enquiry concerning the treasure; and when he found no intelligence could be got, he ordered the general of his household troops, whose name was Mir Muddon, to take charge of Mr. Holwell as his prisoner. . . . Mr. Holwell and his associates in captivity, were conveyed in a kind of coach, drawn by oxen, called a hackery, to the camp, where they were loaded with fetters, and lodged in the tent of a Moorish soldier, which being no more than four feet by three feet, they were obliged to lie, sick as they were, half in and half out the whole night, which happened to be very rainy; yet the next day their fever happily came to a crisis, and boils broke out on every part of their bodies, which, though they were extremely painful, were the certain presages of their recovery. The next day they were removed to the coast, and, by order of General Mir Muddon, were soon after sent by sea to Maxadavad, the Metropolis of Bengal, to wait the viceroy's return, and be disposed of as he should farther determine.

At Maxadavad they arrived, after a voyage of thirteen days, in a large boat, in which they had no better provision than rice and water, and no softer beds than some bamboos laid on the bottom timber of the vessel; they were, besides, exposed alternately to excessive heat and violent rains, without any covering, but a bit of old mat and some scraps of sacking. The boils that covered them were become running sores, and the irons on their legs had consumed the flesh almost to the bone.

When they arrived at Maxadavad, Mr. Holwell sent a letter to Mr. Law, the chief of the French factory, with an account of their distress, and Mr. Law, with great politeness and humanity, sent them not only clothes, linen, provision and liquors, in great plenty, but money.

[The prisoners were then set free, and Mr. Holwell was able to take ship for England.]

THE BATTLE OF PLASSEY,
Thursday, June 23rd, 1757

Robert Clive was the eldest son of a Shropshire squire. At school, at Market Drayton, his turbulent temper made his father decide to ship him off to India as a clerk in the East India Company's service. Friendless and in debt, the boy tried to shoot himself after his arrival in India. He obtained an ensign's commission. His defence of Arcot in 1751 laid the foundation of British rule in India, and he rose to the governorship of Fort St. David. In 1756 he was given the task of avenging the Black Hole of Calcutta. In 1757 he won the Battle of Plassey. On his return to England in 1760 he was given an Irish peerage. In 1765 he returned to India as Governor of Bengal. In 1766 he came back to England with his health broken. His enemies tried to secure his impeachment for corruption. He defended himself with vigour, concluding his speech with this sentence: ' Before I sit down, I have but one request to make to the House, that when they come to decide upon my honour, they will not forget their own.' The House of Commons passed a resolution that ' Robert Lord Clive had rendered great and meritorious services to his country.' In November, 1774, his mind gave way under calumny, ill health and opium, and he committed suicide.

Source: Letter of Robert Clive to the Secret Committee of the Court of Directors of the East India Company: dated July 26, 1757, in Malcolm, *Memoirs of Lord Clive*, vol. i, pp. 263 et sqq.

I gave you an account of the taking of Chandernagore; the subject of this address is an event of much higher importance, no less than the entire overthrow of Nabob Suraj-ud-Daulah, and the placing of Meer Jaffier on the throne. I intimated in my last how dilatory Suraj-ud-Daulah appeared in fulfilling the articles of the treaty. This disposition not only continued but increased, and we discovered that he was designing our ruin by a conjunction with the French. To this end Monsieur Bussy was pressingly invited to come into this province, and Monsieur Law of Cossimbazar was ordered to return from Patna.

About this time some of his principal officers made overtures to us for dethroning him. At the head of these was Meer Jaffier, then Bukhshee to the army, a man as generally esteemed as the other was detested. As we had reason to believe this disaffection pretty general, we soon entered into engagements with Meer Jaffier to put the crown on his head. All necessary preparations being completed with the utmost secrecy, the army, consisting of about one thousand Europeans and two thousand sepoys, with eight pieces of cannon, marched from Chandernagore on the 13th and arrived on the 18th at Cutwa Fort. The 22nd, in the evening, we crossed the river, and landing on the island, marched straight for Plassey Grove, where we arrived by one in the morning.

At daybreak we discovered the Nabob's army moving towards us, consisting, as we since found, of about fifteen thousand horse and thirty-five thousand foot, with upwards of forty pieces

F

of cannon. They approached apace, and by six began to attack with a number of heavy cannon, supported by the whole army, and continued to play on us very briskly for several hours, during which our situation was of the utmost service to us, being lodged in a large grove with good mud banks. To succeed in an attempt on their cannon was next to impossible, as they were planted in a manner round us, and at considerable distances from each other. We therefore remained quiet in our post, in expectation of a successful attack upon their camp at night.

About noon the enemy drew off their artillary, and retired to their camp. . . . We immediately sent a detachment accompanied with two field-pieces, to take possession of a tank with high banks, which was advanced about three hundred yards above our grove, and from which the enemy had considerably annoyed us with some cannon managed by Frenchmen. This motion brought them out a second time; but on finding them make no great effort to dislodge us, we proceeded to take possession of one or two more eminences lying very near an angle of their camp. . . . They made several attempts to bring out their cannon, but our advance field-pieces played so warmly and so well upon them that they were always drove back. Their horse exposing themselves a good deal on this occasion, many of them were killed, and among the rest four or five officers of the first distinction, by which the whole army being visibly dispirited and thrown into some confusion, we were encouraged to storm both the eminence and the angle of their camp, which were carried at the same instant, with little or no loss. . . . On this a general rout ensued; and we pursued the enemy six miles, passing upwards of forty pieces of cannon they had abandoned, with an infinite number of carriages filled with baggage of all kinds. Suraj-ud-Daulah escaped on a camel, and reaching Moorshedabad early next morning, despatched away what jewels and treasure he conveniently could, and he himself followed at midnight with only two or three attendants.

It is computed there are killed of the enemy about five hundred. Our loss amounted to only twenty-two killed and fifty wounded, and those chiefly blacks. During the warmest part of the action we observed a large body of troops hovering on our right, which proved to be our friends; but as they never discovered themselves by any signal whatsoever, we frequently fired on them to make them keep their distance. When the battle was over they sent a congratulatory message, and encamped in our neighbourhood that night. The next day Meer Jaffier paid me a visit, and expressed much gratitude at the service done him, assuring me in the most solemn manner that he would faithfully perform his engagement to the English. . . .

THE IMPEACHMENT OF WARREN HASTINGS

Born of ancient but impoverished stock, Hastings determined as a child to make a fortune and recover the family estate of Daylesford in Worcestershire. As first King's Scholar at Westminster he formed a close friendship with Cowper, the future poet. In 1750 he went to Bengal in the service of the East India Company. He quickly gave evidence of ability. In 1772 he became Governor of Bengal, and in consequence of the Regulating Act, in 1773 Governor-General. He triumphed over his opponents in the Council, expelled Haidar Ali from the Carnatic, deposed Chait Singh and secured his treasure. He was accused of imprisoning the Begums of Oudh, seizing their money, and conniving at the torture of two of their servants. During the crisis of the War of American Independence the preservation of English predominance in India was largely his achievement. In 1785 he left India. In 1788 he was impeached for corruption and cruelty: he was acquitted in 1795. As Hastings said, he had been arraigned before one generation and acquitted by another. The last twenty-four years of his life were passed mainly at Daylesford, where he was occupied with his farm and his gardens. Macaulay's description of Hastings, as he stood in Westminster Hall, may perhaps be applied to his career: ' he looked like a great man, and not like a bad man.'

Source: Diary and Letters of Madame d'Arblay, edited by her niece, Colburn, 1843, vol. iv, pp. 56–62.

Madame d'Arblay (1752–1842) was the daughter of Dr. Burney, the celebrated musician. She wrote *Evelina,* a novel which had great success. Dr. Johnson was one of those who thought highly of it. Miss Burney, as she then was, accepted the position of Second Keeper of the Robes to Queen Charlotte in 1786. She resigned in 1791 and married General d'Arblay, a French refugee. Her diary contains news and gossip of the Court, and of the literary and political figures of her time. It was reviewed at length by Macaulay in the *Edinburgh Review.*

Further Reading: Penderel Moon: *Warren Hastings and British*

India, Hodder and Stoughton, 1947.   Macaulay: *Essays*, 'Warren Hastings'.

February 13th, 1788. . . . The Trial, so long impending, of Mr. Hastings, opened to-day. . . . The Grand Chamberlain's box is in the centre of the upper end of the Hall; there we sat. . . . To the left, on the same level, were the green benches for the House of Commons, which occupied a third of the up per end of the Hall, and the whole of the Left side: to the right of us, on the same level, was the Grand Chamberlain's gallery.

The left side of the Hall, opposite to the green benches for the Commons, was appropriated to the Peeresses and Peers' daughters. The bottom of the Hall contained the Royal Family's Box and the Lord High Stewards. . . .

A gallery also was run along the left side of the Hall, above the green benches, which is called the Duke of Newcastle's Box, the centre of which was railed off into a separate apartment for the reception of the Queen and four eldest Princesses, who were then *incog.*, not choosing to appear in state, and in their own box.

Along the right side of the Hall ran another gallery . . . and this was divided into boxes for various people. . . . Now for the disposition of the Hall itself, or ground.

In the middle was placed a large table, and at the head of it the seat for the Chancellor, and round it seats for the Judges . . . and all who belonged to the Law; the upper end, and the right side of the room, was allotted to the Peers in their robes; the left side to the Bishops and Archbishops.

Immediately below the Great Chamberlain's Box was the place allotted for the Prisoner. On his right side was a box for his own Counsel, on his left the Box for the Managers, or Committee, for the Prosecution. . . .

Almost the moment I entered I was spoken to by a lady I did not recollect, but found afterwards to be Lady Claremont, . . . she named to me all the order of the buildings, and all the company, pointing out every distinguished person, and most obligingly desiring me to ask her any questions I wanted to have solved, as she knew, she said, ' all those creatures that filled the green benches, looking so little like gentlemen, and so much like hairdressers.' These were the Commons. . . .

The business did not begin till near twelve o'clock. The opening to the whole then took place, by the entrance of the Managers of the Prosecution. . . .

I shuddered and drew involuntarily back, when, as the doors were flung open, I saw Mr. Burke, as Head of the Committee, make his solemn entry. He held a scroll in his hand, and walked alone, his brow knit with corroding care and deep labouring thought. . . .

Then began the procession, the clerks entering first, then the Lawyers according to their rank, and the Peers, Bishops and Officers, all in their coronation robes . . . and the whole ending by the Chancellor, with his train borne. Then they all took their seats.

A Serjeant-at-Arms, arose, and commanded silence in the Court, on pain of imprisonment.

Then some other officer, in a loud voice, called out, as well as I can recollect, words to this purpose—' Warren Hastings, Esquire, come forth! Answer to the charges brought against you; save your bail, or forfeit your recognizance!' . . .

The moment he came in sight, which was not for full ten minutes after his awful summons, he made a low bow to the Chancellor and Court facing him. I saw not his face, as he was directly under me. He moved on slowly . . . to the opening of his own Box; there, lower still, he bowed again; and then, advancing to the bar, he leant his hands upon it, and dropped on his knees; but a voice in the same moment proclaiming he had leave to rise, he stood up almost instantaneously, and a third time profoundly bowed to the Court.

What an awful moment this for such a man! . . . The Crier, I think it was, made, in a loud and hollow voice, a public proclamation, ' That Warren Hastings, Esquire, late Governor-General of Bengal, was now on his trial for high crimes and misdemeanours, with which he was charged by the Commons of Great Britain; and that all persons whatsoever who had aught to allege against him were now to stand forth.

A general silence followed, and the Chancellor, Lord Thurlow, now made his speech.

THE EXECUTION OF ADMIRAL BYNG

Admiral Byng was court-martialled for having retired before a slightly superior French naval force on May 20, 1756, thus making inevitable the capitulation of the British forces on Minorca. He was sentenced to be shot for negligence. It is to this execution that Voltaire refers in *Candide*: ' in this country it is thought well to kill an admiral from time to time to encourage the others '.

Source: Naval History of Great Britain 1758, vol. iv, p. 342, quoted in Montagu Burrows: *Life of Lord Hawke*, Allen, 1883.

On Monday, March 14th, 1757, all the men-of-war at Spithead were ordered to send their boats with the captains and all the officers of each ship, accompanied with a party of marines under arms, to attend the execution of Mr. Byng. Accordingly they rowed from Spithead, and made the harbour a little after 11 o'clock, with the utmost difficulty and danger, it blowing prodigiously hard at N.W. by N., and the tide of ebb against them. It was still more difficult to get up so high as the *Monarque* lay, on board which ship the admiral suffered. Notwithstanding it blew so hard and the sea ran very high, there was a prodigious number of other boats round the ship, on the outside of the ship's boats, which last kept all others off. Not a soul was suffered to be aboard the *Monarque*, except those belonging to the ship. Mr. Byng, accompanied by a clergyman who attended him during his confinement, and two gentlemen of his relations, about 12 came on the quarterdeck, when he threw his hat on the deck, kneeled on a cushion, tied a handkerchief over his eyes, and dropping another which he held in his hand as a signal, a volley from six marines was fired, five of whose bullets went through him, and he was no more. He died with great resolution and composure, not showing the least sign of timidity in the awful moment.

THE CAPTURE OF QUEBEC,
Thursday, September 13th, 1759

Source: *Journal of Captain John Knox*, vol. ii, Champlain Society, Toronto.

Further Reading: W. T. Waugh: *James Wolfe*, Manchester University Press, 1933.

Canada

ORDERS[1]

On board the *Sutherland*.

The enemy's force is now divided, great scarcity of provisions now in their camp, and universal discontent among the Canadians: . . . . a vigorous blow struck by the army at this juncture may determine the fate of Canada. Our troops below are in readiness to join us; all the light artillery and tools are embarked at the point of Levi, and the troops will land where the French seem least to expect it. The first body that gets on shore is to march directly to the enemy, and drive them from any little post they may occupy; the Officers must be careful that the succeeding bodies do not, by any mistake, fire upon those who go on before them. The battalions must form on the upper ground with expedition, and be ready to charge whatever presents itself. When the artillery and troops are landed, a corps will be left to secure the landing-place, while the rest march on and endeavour to bring the French and Canadians to a battle. The officers and men will remember what their country expects from them, and what a determined body of soldiers, inured to war, is capable of doing, against five weak French battalions, mingled with a disorderly peasantry. The soldiers must be attentive and obedient to their Officers, and resolute in the execution of their duty. . . .

. . . This evening all the boats of the fleet below the town were filled with marines, etc., covered by frigates and sloops of war, worked up, and lay half-channel over, opposite to Beauport, as if intending to land in the morning, and thereby fix the enemy's whole attention to that quarter; the ships attending them are to edge over, at break of day, as near as possible without grounding, and cannonade the French entrenchments. At nine o'clock this night, our army in high spirits, the first division of them put into the flat-bottomed boats, and, in a short time after, the whole squadron moved up the river with the tide of flood, and, about an hour before daylight next morning we fell down with the ebb. Weather favourable, a star-light night.

[1] Issued by Wolfe.

BATTLE OF QUEBEC

Thursday, September 13, 1759.

Before day-break this morning we made a descent upon the
north shore, about half a quarter of a mile to the eastward of
Sillery;... we had, in this debarkation, thirty flat-bottomed boats,
containing about sixteen hundred men. This was a great surprise
on the enemy, who, from the natural strength of the place, did not
suspect, and consequently were not prepared against, so bold
an attempt. . . . As fast as we landed, the boats put off for reinforcements . . . the General, with Brigadiers Monckton and
Murray, were a-shore with the first division. We lost no time
here, but clambered up one of the steepest precipices that can be
conceived, being almost a perpendicular, and of an incredible
height. As soon as we gained the summit, all was quiet, and not
a shot was heard, owing to the excellent conduct of the light
infantry under Colonel Howe; it was by this time clear day-light.
Here we formed again . . . we then faced to the right, and marched
towards the town by files, till we came to the plains of Abraham;
an even piece of ground which Mr. Wolfe had made choice of,
while we stood forming upon the hill. Weather showery: about
six o'clock the enemy first made their appearance upon the
heights, between us and the town; whereupon we halted, and
wheeled to the right, thereby forming the line of battle. . . . The
enemy had now likewise formed the line of battle, and got some
cannon to play on us, with round and canister shot; but what
galled us most was a body of Indians and other marksmen they
had concealed in the corn opposite to the front of our right wing
. . . but Colonel Hale . . . advanced some platoons . . . which,
after a few rounds, obliged these skulkers to retire. We were
now ordered to lie down, and remained some time in this position.
About eight o'clock we had two pieces of short brass six-pounders
playing on the enemy, which threw them into some confusion.
. . . About ten o'clock the enemy began to advance briskly in
three columns, with loud shouts and recovered arms, two of them
inclining to the left of our army, and the third towards our right,
firing obliquely at the two extremities of our line, from the distance of one hundred and thirty, until they came within forty

yards; which our troops withstood with the greatest intrepidity
and firmness, still reserving their fire, and paying the strictest
obedience to their Officers: this uncommon steadiness, together
with the havoc which the grape-shot from our field-pieces[1] made
among them, threw them into some disorder, and was most
critically maintained by a well-timed, regular and heavy discharge
of our small arms, such as they could no longer oppose; hereupon
they gave way, and fled with precipitation, so that, by the time
the cloud of smoke was vanished, our men were again loaded,
and profiting by the advantage we had over them, pursued them
almost to the gates of the town, and the bridge over the little
river, redoubling our fire with great eagerness, making many
Officers and men prisoners. The weather cleared up, with a
comfortably warm sunshine. . . . Our joy at this success is
inexpressibly damped by the loss we sustained of one of the
greatest heroes which this or any other age can boast of—General
James Wolfe, who received his mortal wound as he was exerting
himself at the head of the grenadiers of Louisbourg. . . . The
officers who are prisoners say that Quebec will surrender in a
few days: some deserters, who came out to us in the evening,
agree in that opinion, and inform us, that the Sieur de Montcalm
is dying, in great agony, of a wound he received today in their
retreat. . . .

After our late worthy general, of renowned memory, was
carried off wounded, to the rear of the front line, he desired those
who were about him to lay him down; being asked if he would
have a Surgeon, he replied, ' It is needless; it is all over with me '.
One of them then cried out, ' They run, see how they run '.
' Who runs? ' demanded our hero, with great earnestness, like a
person roused from sleep. The Officer answered, ' The enemy,
Sir, Egad they give way everywhere '. Thereupon the General
rejoined, ' Go one of you, my lads, to Colonel Burton; tell him
to march Webb's regiment with all speed down to Charles's
river, to cut off the retreat of the fugitives from the bridge '.
Then, turning on his side, he added, ' Now, God be praised, I
will die in peace: ' and thus expired.

[1] There were two field-pieces in action.

THE BATTLE OF MINDEN: The King's Own Yorkshire Light Infantry,
Wednesday, August 1st, 1759

The battle of Minden, one of the great British victories of the
Seven Years War, was fought on Wednesday, August 1, 1759. Prince
Ferdinand of Brunswick, the allied commander, had 42,000 men
against the 53,000 of the French Marshal Contades. The battle was
notable for three things: the perfect steadiness of the British infantry
as they marched (the result of a mistaken order) through an appalling
cross fire; their defeat first of the French cavalry and then of infantry
attacks; the inexplicable refusal of Lord George Sackville to obey a
four-times-repeated order to charge with his cavalry. The famous
' Men who fought at Minden were: the King's Own Yorkshire Light
Infantry, the Royal Welch Fusileers, the Lancashire Fusileers, the
Suffolk Regiment, the Hampshire Regiment and the King's Own
Scottish Borderers.

Source: A letter written by Lieut. Hugh Montgomery of the 12th
Foot, quoted in *History of the King's Own Yorkshire Light Infantry*, by
Col. H. C. Wylly, Lund Humphries, n.d., vol. i, pp. 48 et sqq.

Dear Madam,—The pursuit of the enemy, who have retired
with the greatest precipitation, prevents me from giving you so
exact an account of the late most glorious victory over the French
army as I would, had I almost any leisure, however here goes as
much as I can.

We marched from camp between 4 and 5 o'clock in the
morning, about seven drew up in a valley, from thence marched
about three hundred yards, when an eighteen pound ball came
gently rolling up to us. Now began the most disagreeable
march that I ever had in my life, for we advanced more than a
quarter of a mile through a most furious fire from a most infernal
battery of eighteen-pounders, which was at first upon our
front, but as we proceeded, bore upon our flank, and at last
upon our rear. It might be imagined, that this cannonade would
render the regiments incapable of bearing the shock of unhurt
troops drawn up long before on ground of their own choosing,
but firmness and resolution will surmount almost any difficulty.
When we got within about 100 yards of the enemy, a large body
of French cavalry galloped boldly down upon us; these our men
by reserving their fire until they came within thirty yards,
immediately ruined, but not without receiving some injury from

them, for they rode down two companies on the right of our regiment, wounded three officers, took one of them prisoner with our artillery Lieutenant, and whipped off the Tumbrells. This cost them dear for it forced many of them into our rear, on whom the men faced about and five of them did not return. These visitants being thus dismissed, without giving us a moment's time to recover the unavoidable disorder, down came upon us like lightning the glory of France in the persons of the Gens d'Armes. These we almost immediately dispersed without receiving hardly any mischief from the harmless creatures. We now discovered a large body of infantry consisting of seventeen regiments moving down directly on our flank in column, a very ugly situation; but Stewart's Regiment and ours wheeled, and showed them a front, which is a thing not to be expected from troops already twice attacked, but this must be placed to the credit of General Waldgravie and his aide-de-camp. We engaged this corps for about ten mtnutes, killed them a good many, and as the song says, ' the rest hen ran away '.

The next who made their appearance were some Regiments of the Grenadiers of France, as fine and terrible looking fellows as I ever saw. They stood us a tug, notwithstanding we beat them off to a distance, where they galded us much, they having rifled barrels, and our muskets would not reach them. To remedy this we advanced, they took the hint, and ran away. Now we were in hopes that we had done enough for one day's work, and that they would not disturb us more, but soon after a very large body of fresh infantry, the last resource of Contades, made the final attempt on us. With them we had a long but not very brisk engagement, at last made them retire almost out of reach, when the three English regiments of the rear line came up, and gave them one fire, which sent them off for good and all. But what is wonderful to tell, we ourselves after all this success at the very same time also retired, but indeed we did not then know that victory was ours. However we rallied, but all that could now be mustered was about 13 files private with our Colonel and four other officers one of which I was so fortunate to be. With this remnant we returned again to the charge, but to our unspeakable joy no opponents could be found. It is astonishing, that this victory was gained by six English regiments of foot, without their grenadiers, unsupported by cavalry or cannon, not even their own battalion guns, in the face of a dreadful battery so near as to tear them with grape-shot, against forty battalions and thirty-six squadrons, which is directly the quantity of the enemy which fell to their share.

It is true that two Hanoverian regiments were engaged on the left of the English, but so inconsiderably as to lose only 50 men between them. On the left of the army the grenadiers, who now form a separate body, withstood a furious cannonade. Of the English there was only killed one captain and one sergeant; some Prussian dragoons were engaged and did good service. Our artillery which was stationed in different places, also behaved well, but the grand attack on which depended the fate of the day, fell to the lot of the six English regiments of foot. From this account the Prince might be accused of misconduct for trusting the issue of so great an event to so small a body, but this affair you will have soon enough explained to the disadvantage of a great man whose easy part, had it been properly acted, must have occasioned to France one of the greatest overthrows it ever met with. The sufferings of our regiment will give you the best notion of the smartness of the action. We actually fought that day not more than 480 private and 27 officers, of the first 302 were killed and wounded, and of the latter 18. Three lieutenants were killed on the spot, the rest are only wounded, and all of them are in a good way except two. Of the officers who escaped there are only four who cannot show some marks of the enemy's good intentions, and as perhaps you may be desirous to know any little risks that I might have run, I will mention those of which I was sensible. At the beginning of the action I was almost knocked off my legs by my three right hand men, who were killed and drove against me by a cannon ball, the same ball also killed two men close to Ward, whose post was in the rear of my platoon, and in this place I will assure you that he behaved with the greatest bravery, which I suppose you will make known to his father and friends. Some time after I received from a spent ball just such a rap on my collar-bone as I have frequently from that once most dreadful weapon, your crooked-headed stick; it just swelled and grew red enough to convince the neighbours that I was not fibbing when I mentioned it. I got another of these also on one of my legs, which gave me about as much pain, as would a tap of Miss Mathews's fan. The last and greatest misfortune of all fell to the share of my poor old coat for a musket ball entered into the right skirt of it and made three holes. I had almost forgot to tell you that my spontoon[1] was shot through a little below my hand; this disabled it, but a French one now does duty in its room. The consequences of this affair are very great, we found by the papers, that the world began to give us up, and the French had swallowed us up in their imaginations. We have now pursued them above 100 miles with the advanced armies of the hereditary prince, Wanganheim, and Urff in our front, of whose success in taking prisoners and baggage, and receiving deserters, Francis Joy will give you a better account than I can at present. They are now entrenching themselves at Cassel, and you may depend on it they will not show us their faces again during this campaign.

I have the pleasure of being able to tell you that Captain Rainey is well; he is at present in advance with the Grenadiers plundering French baggage and taking prisoners. I would venture to give him forty ducats for his share of prize money.

I have now contrary to my expectations and in spite of many interruptions wrote you a long letter, this paper I have carried this week past in my pocket for the purpose, but could not attempt it before. We marched into this camp yesterday evening, and shall quit it early in the morning. I wrote you a note just informing you that I was well the day after the battle; I hope you will receive it in due time. Be pleased to give my most affectionate duty to my uncles and aunts . . . and believe me to be

With the greatest affection,

Your very dutiful son,

Camp at Paderton   H[h] Montgomery.
9th August, 1759.

. . . The noise of the battle frightened our sutler's wife into labour the next morning. She was brought to bed of a son, and we have had him christened by the name of Ferdinand.

[1] A kind of halberd used by infantry officers.

THE BATTLE OF QUIBERON BAY,
November 20th, 1759

The greatest task of the British Navy in the Seven Years War until 1759 was to prevent the junction of the two French fleets: the Mediterranean force based on Toulon; the Atlantic force at Brest. The junction of these two forces might have been followed by a French attempt to invade England. While Admiral Boscawen was blockading Toulon, Hawke was watching Brest. The French fleet escaped from Brest while Hawke was refitting in Torbay after a westerly gale. He pursued the French ships to Quiberon Bay.

(a) Source: A letter from ' a Chaplain in one of His Majesty's ships '. It is dated Quiberon Bay, November 25, 1759, and is quoted in Montagu Burrows: Life of Lord Hawke, Allen, 1883, p. 394.

Further Reading: G. Callender: Sea Kings of Britain, Longmans, 1909, vol. ii. D. Mathew: British Sailors, Collins, 1947.

. . . The firing now became very alert on both sides, and there was no distinguishing any longer English colours from French. M. du Verger, the French rear admiral, in the Formidable bore a very fierce cannonade from the Resolution; but upon the Royal George's coming up, they hauled down their flag, and struck to Sir Edward Hawke, . . . The Royal George continued advancing, and Sir Edward gave orders to his Master to carry him close alongside of M. Conflans in the Soleil Royal. The French admiral seemed to have the same ambition on his part, and it was a glorious sight to behold the blue and white flags, both at the maintop mast-head, bearing down to each other. The Royal George passed the Torbay, which was closely engaged with the Thésée of 74 guns, and soon after sent that unfortunate ship to the bottom. On the other side was the Magnanime, who kept an incessant fire on one of the largest of the French ships and in the end obliged her to strike. She afterwards ran ashore and was burnt.

The two commanders-in-chief were now very near, and M. Conflans gave the English admiral his broadside; the Royal George returned the uncivil salutation; but after two or three exchanges of this kind, the Marshal of France declined the combat and steered off. The French Vice-Admiral likewise gave Sir Edward his broadside, and soon followed the example of his superior. Another and another acted the same part; the fifth ship escaped not so well. Sir Edward poured his whole fire into her at once, and repeating the same, down she went along side of him. The *Royal George's* people gave a cheer, but it was a faint one; the honest sailors were touched at the miserable state of so many hundreds of poor creatures. The blue flag was now encountered with seven ships at the same time, and appeared to be in the very centre of the French rear. Every observer pitied the *Royal George*, to see her singly engaged against so many of the enemy . . . her situation would have been lamentable if the enemy had preserved any degree of composure, or fired with any sort of direction; but their confusion was so great, that of many hundreds of shot, I do not believe that more than 30 or 40 struck the ship.

Sir Charles Hardy, in the *Union*, with the *Mars*, *Hero*, and several other ships, were crowding to the Admiral's assistance, when the retreat of the French, covered by the obscurity of the evening, put an end to the engagement. Happy circumstance for the enemy, as an hour's daylight more would have brought on their total ruin!

The battle was fought so near the coast of Brittany, that ten thousand persons on the shore were sad witnesses of the white flag's disgrace. . . .

. . . The glory of the British flag has been nobly supported, while that of the enemy is vanished into empty air.

(*b*) *Source:* Letter from Admiral Sir Edward Hawke in Moorhouse: *Letters of the Eng ish Seamen*, 1910, pp. 119–122.

Royal George, of Penris Point,
November 24th, 1759.

Sir,

In my letter of the 17th by express, I desired you would acquaint their Lordships with my having received intelligence of eighteen sail of the line, and three frigates of the Brest squadron being discovered about twenty-four leagues to the north-west of Belleisle, steering to the eastward. All the prisoners, however, agree that on the day we chased them, their squadron consisted, according to the accompanying list, of four ships of eighty, six of seventy-four, three of seventy, eight of sixty-four, one frigate of thirty-six, one of thirty-four, and one of sixteen guns, with a small vessel to look out. They sailed from Brest the 14th instant, the same day I sailed from Torbay. Concluding that their first rendezvous would be Quiberon, the instant I received the intelligence I directed my course thither with a pressed sail. At first the wind blowing hard at S. b. E. and S. drove us considerably to the westward. But on the 18th and 19th, though variable, it proved more favourable. In the meantime having been joined by the *Maidstone* and *Coventry* frigates, I directed their commanders to keep ahead of the squadron, one on the starboard, and the other on the larboard bow.

At half-past eight o'clock on the morning of the 20th, Belleisle, by our reckoning, bearing E. b. N. $\frac{1}{4}$ N. about thirteen leagues, the *Maidstone* made the signal for seeing a fleet. I immediately spread abroad the signal for the line abreast, in order to draw all the ships of the squadron up with me. I had before sent the *Magnanime* ahead to make the land. At three-quarters past nine she made the signal for seeing an enemy. Observing, on my discovering them, that they made off, I threw out the signal for the seven ships nearest them to chase, and draw into a line of battle ahead of me, and endeavour to stop them till the rest of the squadron should come up, who were also to form as they chased, that no time might be lost in the pursuit. . . . Monsieur Conflans kept going off under such sail as all his squadron could carry, and at the same time keep together; while we crowded after him with every sail our ships could bear. At half-past two p.m. the fire beginning ahead, I made the signal for engaging. We were then to the south-ward of Belleisle, and the French Admiral headmost, soon after led round the Cardinals, while his rear was in action. About four o'clock the *Formidable* struck, and a little after, the *Thésée* and *Superbe* were sunk. About five, the *Heros* struck, and came to an anchor, but it blowing hard, no boat could be sent to board her. Night was now come, and being on a part of the coast, among islands and shoals, of which we were totally ignorant, without a pilot, as was the greatest part of the squadron, and blowing hard on a lee shore, I made the signal to anchor, and come-to in fifteen-fathom water. . . . In the night we heard many guns of distress fired, but, blowing hard, want of knowledge of the coast, and whether they were fired by a friend or an enemy, prevented all means of relief. . . .

As soon as it was broad daylight, in the morning of the 21st, I discovered seven or eight of the enemy's line-of-battle ships at anchor between Point Penris and the river Vilaine, on which I made the signal to weigh in order to work up and attack them. But it blowed so hard from the N.W. that instead of daring to cast the squadron loose, I was obliged to strike topgallant masts. Most of the ships appeared to be aground at low water. . . .

In attacking a flying enemy, it was impossible in the space of a short winter's day that all our ships should be able to get into action, or all those of the enemy brought to it. The commanders and companies of such as did come up with the rear of the French on the 20th behaved with the greatest intrepidity, and gave the strongest proofs of a true British spirit. In the same manner I am satisfied would those have acquitted themselves whose bad-going ships, or the distance they were at in the morning, prevented from getting up.

Our loss by the enemy is not considerable. For in the ships which are now with me, I find only one lieutenant and fifty seamen and marines killed, and about two hundred and twenty wounded.

When I consider the season of the year, the hard gales on the day of action, a flying enemy, the shortness of the day, and the coast they were on, I can boldly affirm that all that could possibly be done has been done. As to the loss we have sustained, let it be placed to the account of the necessity I was under of running all risks to break this strong force of the enemy. Had we had but two hours more daylight, the whole had been totally destroyed or taken; for we were almost up with their van when night overtook us. . . .

I am, etc.,
Edward Hawke.

G

THE YEAR OF VICTORIES, 1759

Source: Horace Walpole: *Letters.* From a letter to George Montagu,
Esq., dated from Strawberry Hill, October 21, 1759.

. . . Can we easily leave the remains of such a year as this?
It is still all gold. I have not dined or gone to bed by a fire till
the day before yesterday. Instead of the glorious and ever-memor-
able year 1759, as the newspapers call it, I call it this ever-warm
and victorious year. We have not had more conquest than fine
weather: one would think we had plundered East and West
Indies of sunshine. Our bells are worn threadbare with ringing
for victories. . . . One thing is very fatiguing—all the world is
made knights or generals. Adieu! I don't know a word of news
less than the conquest of America. . . .

P.S. You shall hear from me again if we take Mexico or China
before Christmas.

GEORGE III AT THE FUNERAL OF GEORGE II

Source: Horace Walpole: *Letters.* From a letter to George Montagu,
Esq., dated November 13, 1760.

. . . For the King [George III] himself, he seems all good-
nature, and wishing to satisfy everybody; all his speeches are
obliging. I saw him again yesterday, and was surprised to find
the levee-room had lost so entirely the air of the lion's den. This
Sovereign don't stand in one spot, with his eyes fixed royally
on the ground, and dropping bits of German news; he walks
about, and speaks to everybody. I saw him afterwards on the
throne, where he is graceful and genteel, sits with dignity, and
reads his answers to addresses well. . . .

Do you know, I had the curiosity to go to the burying t'other
night; I had never seen a royal funeral. . . . It is absolutely a
noble sight. The Prince's chamber, hung with purple, and a
quantity of silver lamps, the coffin under a canopy of purple
velvet, and six vast chandeliers of silver on high stands, had a
very good effect. . . . The procession, through a line of foot
guards, every seventh man bearing a torch, the horse guards
lining the outside, their officers with drawn sabres and crape

sashes on horseback, the drums muffled, the fifes, bells tolling, and minute guns,—all this was very solemn. But the charm was the entrance of the Abbey, where we were received by the Dean and Chapter in rich robes, the choir and alms-men bearing torches; the whole Abbey so illuminated, that one saw it to greater advantage than by day. . . . When we came to the chapel of Henry the Seventh, all solemnity and decorum ceased; no order was observed, people sat or stood where they could or would; the yeomen of the guard were crying out for help, oppressed by the immense weight of the coffin; the Bishop read sadly, and blundered in the prayers; . . . and the anthem, besides being immeasurably tedious, would have served as well for a nuptial. The real serious part was the figure of the Duke of Cumberland, heightened by a thousand melancholy circumstances. He had a dark brown adonis, and a cloak of black cloth, with a train of five yards. Attending the funeral of a father could not be pleasant; his leg extremely bad, yet forced to stand upon it near two hours; his face bloated and distorted with his late paralytic stroke, which has affected, too, one of his eyes, and placed over the mouth of the vault, into which, in all probability, he must himself so soon descend; think how unpleasant a situation! He bore it all with a firm and unaffected countenance. This grave scene was fully contrasted by the burlesque Duke of Newcastle. He fell into a fit of crying the moment he came into the chapel, and flung himself back in a stall, the Archbishop hovering over him with a smelling-bottle; but in two minutes his curiosity got the better of his hypocrisy, and he ran about the chapel with his glass to spy who was or was not there, spying with one hand, and mopping his eyes with the other. Then returned the fear of catching cold; and the Duke of Cumberland, who was sinking with heat, felt himself weighed down, and turning round, found it was the Duke of Newcastle standing upon his train, to avoid the chill of the marble. It was very theatric to look down into the vault, where the coffin lay, attended by mourners with lights. . . .

PITT DENOUNCES THE PEACE OF PARIS,
December 1762

Pitt, whose policy had won the Seven Years War, regarded the peace treaty, made by the government of Lord Bute, as a betrayal of the nation. He accused the government of having failed to destroy France as a commercial and maritime power, and of having betrayed England's ally Prussia.

Source: Horace Walpole: *Memoirs of the Reign of George III*, ed. Sir Denis le Marchant, 1845.

Further Reading: J. H. Plumb, *Chatham*, Collins, 1953.

The doors opened, and at the head of a large acclaiming concourse was seen Mr. Pitt, borne in the arms of his servants, who, setting him down within the bar, he crawled by the help of a crutch, and with the assistance of some few friends, to his seat; not without the sneers of some of Fox's party. In truth, there was a mixture of the very solemn and the theatric in this apparition. The moment was so well timed, the importance of the man and his services, the languor of his emaciated countenance, and the study bestowed on his dress, were circumstances that struck solemnity into a patriot mind, and did a little furnish ridicule to the hardened and insensible. He was dressed in black velvet, his legs and thighs wrapped in flannel, his feet covered with buskins of black cloth, and his hands with thick gloves. . . .

His speech it would be difficult to detail; it lasted three hours and twenty-five minutes, and was uttered in so low and faint a voice that it was almost impossible to hear him. At intervals he obtained the permission of the House to speak sitting, a permission he did not abuse; supporting himself with cordials, and having the appearance of a man determined to die in that cause and in that hour. This faintness and the prolixity with which he dwelt on the article of the fisheries, gave a handle to the courtiers to represent his speeches as unmeasurably dull, tedious, and uninteresting. But it contained considerable matter, much reason, and some parts of great beauty:—but thunder was wanting to blast such a treaty, and this was not a day on which his genius thundered! His health or his choice had led him to present himself as a subject of affliction to his country, and his ungrateful country was not afflicted.

PUBLIC OPINION IN AMERICA

Source: Journal of Nicholas Cresswell, 1774–1777, ed. Thornely. London, 1925, pp. 43–4, 46, 58, 203.

Nicholas Cresswell was born, the son of a landowner, at Crowden-le-Booth, Edale, in December, 1750. He was educated probably at Wakefield Grammar School. In 1774 he emigrated to North America but returned in 1777.

Alexandria, Virginia—Wednesday, October 19th, 1774.

. . . Everything here is in the utmost confusion, Committees are appointed to inspect into the characters and conduct of every tradesman, to prevent them selling Tea or buying British Manufactures. Some of them have been tarred and feathered, others had their property burnt and destroyed by the populace. Independent Companies are raising in every County on the Continent, appointed Adjutants and train their Men as if they were on the Eve of a War. A General Congress of the different Colonies met at Philadelphia on the 5th of last month are still sitting, but their business is a profound secret. Subscription is raising in every colony on the Continent for the relief of the people of Boston. The King is openly cursed, and his authority set at defiance. In short, everything is ripe for rebellion. The New Englanders by their canting, whining, insinuating tricks have persuaded the rest of the Colonies that the Government is going to make absolute slaves of them. . . . By everything that I can understand, in the different company I have been in, Independence is what the Massachusetts people aim at, but am not in the least doubt but the Government will take such salutary and speedy measure, as will entirely frustrate their abominable intentions. . . . All trade is almost at a stand, everyone seems to be at a loss in what manner to proceed. . . .

Thursday, November 3rd, 1774. . . . The Effigy of Lord North was shot at, then carried in great parade into the town and burnt. . . .

Tuesday, February 28th, 1775. This is the last day Tea is allowed to be drunk on the Continent, by an act of Congress. The ladies seem very sad about it. . . .

Monday, April 21st, 1777 (Alexandria, Virginia).

. . . Saw a Highlander (a soldier in the 71st Regiment, now a prisoner of War here) whipped by his comrades for enlisting into the Rebel service. He is the only one out of two hundred and odd who have been prisoners in this Colony, that has enlisted into their service. His fellow prisoners held a Court Martial over him, a Sergeant being the highest officer present, and condemned the poor wretch to receive 1500 lashes with a switch upon his bare back, 100 every day till the number was complete. The man enlisted when drunk and returned the money as soon as he was sober and absolutely refused to serve, but this would not satisfy his enraged companions.

THE BOSTON MASSACRE, March 1770

In June 1768, the Government had sent troops to Boston to help revenue officers to enforce the Acts of Trade. It was a small force which had been sent; too weak to overawe the Boston mob, which continually insulted the soldiers.

Source: *English Historical Documents ix.* American Colonial Documents to 1776, Eyre and Spottiswoode, 1955, pp. 751–2.

This is from the account of Captain Thomas Preston, who was arrested with some of his men after the incident and put on trial. He and six other soldiers were acquitted, and two found guilty of manslaughter.

On Monday night about 8 o'clock two soldiers were attacked and beat. But the party of the townspeople in order to carry matters to the utmost length, broke into two meeting houses and rang the alarm bells, which I supposed was for fire as usual, but was soon undeceived. About 9 some of the guard came to and informed me the town inhabitants were assembling to attack the troops, and that the bells were ringing as the signal for that purpose and not for fire, and the beacon intended to be fired to bring in the distant people of the country. This, as I was captain of the day, occasioned my repairing immediately to the main guard. In my way there I saw the people in great commotion, and heard them use the most cruel and horrid threats against the troops. In a few minutes after I reached the guard, about 100 people passed it, and went towards the custom house where the

King's money is lodged. They immediately surrounded the sentry posted there, and with clubs and other weapons threatened to execute their vengeance on him. I was soon informed by a townsman their intention was to carry off the soldier from his post and probably murder him: on which I desired him to return for further intelligence, and he soon came back and assured me he heard the mob declare they would murder him. This I feared might be a prelude to their plundering the King's chest. I immediately sent a non-commissioned officer and 12 men to protect both the sentry and the King's money, and very soon followed myself to prevent, if possible, all disorder, fearing lest the officer and soldiers, by the insults and provocations of the rioters, should be thrown off their guard and commit some rash act. They soon rushed through the people, and by charging their bayonets in half-circles, kept them at a little distance. Nay, so far was I from intending the death of any person that I suffered the troops to go to the spot where the unhappy affair took place without any loading in their pieces; nor did I ever give orders for loading them. This remiss conduct in me perhaps merits censure; yet it is evidence, resulting from the nature of things, which is the best and surest that can be offered, that my intention was not to act offensively, but the contrary part, and that not without compulsion. The mob still increased and were more outrageous, striking their clubs or bludgeons one against another, and calling out, "Come on you rascals, you bloody backs, you lobster scoundrels, fire if you dare, G—d damn you, fire and be damned, we know you dare not," and much more such language was used. At this time I was between the soldiers and the mob, parleying with, and endeavouring all in my power to persuade them to retire peaceably, but to no purpose. They advanced to the points of the bayonets, struck some of them and even the muzzles of the pieces, and seemed to be endeavouring to close with the soldiers. On which some well behaved persons asked me if the guns were charged. I replied yes. They then asked me if I intended to order the men to fire. I answered no, by no means, observing to them that I was advanced before the muzzles of the men's pieces, and must fall a sacrifice if they fired; that the soldiers were upon the half cock and charged bayonets, and

my giving the word fire under those circumstances would prove
me to be no officer. While I was thus speaking, one of the soldiers
having received a severe blow with a stick, stepped a little on
one side and instantly fired, on which turning to and asking him
why he fired without orders, I was struck with a club on my arm,
which for some time deprived me of the use of it, which blow
had it been placed on my head most probably would have destroyed me. On this a general attack was made on the men by
a great number of heavy clubs and snowballs being thrown at
them, by which all our lives were in imminent danger, some
persons at the same time from behind calling out, " damn your
bloods—why don't you fire." Instantly three or four of the
soldiers fired, one after another, and directly after three more in the
same confusion and hurry. The mob then ran away, except three
unhappy men who instantly expired, . . . one more is since dead,
three others are dangerously, and four slightly wounded. The
whole of this melancholy affair was transacted in almost 20
minutes. On my asking the soldiers why they fired without
orders, they said they heard the word fire and supposed it came
from me. This might be the case as many of the mob called out
fire, fire, but I assured the men that I gave no such order; that
my words were, don't fire, stop your firing. In short, it was
scarcely possible for the soldiers to know who said fire, or don't
fire, or stop your firing. On the people's assembling again to
take away the dead bodies, the soldiers supposing them coming
to attack them, were making ready to fire again, which I prevented by striking up their firelocks with my hand. Immediately after a townsman came and told me that 4 or 5000 people
were assembled in the next street, and had sworn to take my life
with every man's with me. On which I judged it unsafe to remain
there any longer, and therefore sent the party and sentry to the
main guard, where the street is narrow and short, there telling
them off into street firings, divided and planted them at each
end of the street to secure their rear, momently expecting an
attack, as there was a constant cry of the inhabitants " to arms, to
arms, turn out with your guns; " and the town drums beating
to arms, I ordered my drums to beat to arms, and being soon after
joined by the different companies of the 29th regiment, I formed

them as the guard into street firings. The 14th regiment also got under arms but remained at their barracks. I immediately sent a sergeant with a party to Colonel Dalrymple, the commanding officer, to acquaint him with every particular. Several officers going to join their regiment were knocked down by the mob, one very much wounded and his sword taken from him. The Lieutenant-Governor and Colonel Carr soon after met at the head of the 29th regiment and agreed that the regiment should retire to their barracks, and the people to their houses, but I kept the picket to strengthen the guard. It was with great difficulty that the Lieutenant-Governor prevailed on the people to be quiet and retire. At last they all went off, excepting about a hundred. . . .

THE BOSTON TEA PARTY

Source: Letters of John Andrews, Esq., of Boston, 1772–1776, ed. Winthrop Sargeant. (Reprinted from the Proceedings of the Massachusetts Historical Society, 1866).

December 18th (1773).

However precarious our situation may be, yet such is the present calm composure of the people that a stranger would hardly think that ten thousand pounds sterling of the East India Company's tea was destroyed the night, or rather evening, before last, yet it's a serious truth; and if yours, together with the other Southern provinces, should rest satisfied with their quota being stored, poor Boston will feel the whole weight of ministerial vengeance. However, it's the opinion of most people that we stand an equal chance now, whether troops are sent in consequence of it or not; whereas, had it been stored, we should inevitably have had them, to enforce the sale of it.

The affair was transacted with the greatest regularity and despatch. . . . A general muster was assembled, from this and all the neighbouring towns, to the number of five or six thousand, at 10 o'clock Thursday morning in the Old South Meeting House, where they passed a unanimous vote that the Tea should go out of the harbour that afternoon, and sent a committee with Mr. Rotch[1] to the Customhouse to demand a clearance, which the

[1] Owner of one of the tea ships.

Collector told them it was not in his power to give, without the duties being first paid. They then sent Mr. Rotch to Milton, to ask a pass from the Governor, who sent for answer, that ' consistent with the rules of government and his duty to the King he could not grant one without they produced a previous clearance from the office '. By the time he returned with this message the candles were light in the house, and upon reading it, such prodigious shouts were made, that induced me, while drinking tea at home, to go out and know the cause of it. The house was so crowded I could get no farther than the porch, when I found the moderator was just declaring the meeting to be dissolved, which caused another general shout, outdoors and in, and three cheers. What with that, and the consequent noise of breaking up the meeting, you'd thought that the inhabitants of the infernal regions had broke loose.

For my part, I went contentedly home and finished my tea, but was soon informed what was going forward; but still not crediting it without ocular demonstration, I went and was satisfied. They mustered, I'm told, upon Fort Hill to the number of about two hundred, and proceeded, two by two, to Griffin's wharf, where *Hall*, *Bruce*, and *Coffin* lay, each with 114 chests of the ill-fated article on board; the two former with only that article, but the latter, arrived at the wharf only the day before, was freighted with a large quantity of other goods, which they took the greatest care not to injure in the least, and before nine o'clock in the evening every chest from on board the three vessels was knocked to pieces and flung over the sides.

They say the actors were Indians from Narragansett. Whether they were or not, to a transient observer they appeared as such, being clothed in blankets with the heads muffled, and copper-coloured countenances, being each armed with a hatchet or axe, and pair pistols, nor was their dialect different from what I conceive these geniuses to speak, as their jargon was unintelligible to all but themselves. Not the least insult was offered to any person, save one Captain Connor, a letter of horses in this place, not many years since removed from dear Ireland, who had ripped up the lining of his coat and waistcoat under the arms, and watching his opportunity had nearly filled them with tea, but being detected, was handled pretty roughly. They not only stripped him of his clothes, but gave him a coat of mud, with a severe bruising into the bargain; and nothing but their utter aversion to make any disturbance prevented his being tarred and feathered.

Should not have troubled you with this, by this post, hadn't I thought you would be glad of a more particular account of so important a transaction than you could have obtained by common report; and if it affords my brother but a temporary amusement, I shall be more than repaid for the trouble of writing it.

SKIRMISH AT LEXINGTON

On Monday, April 18, 1774, General Gage sent troops to Concord, twenty miles from Boston, to seize some military stores. The utmost secrecy was observed and the troops moved off from Boston by night, but the colonists discovered what was afoot, and Paul Revere set out on his famous ride through darkened villages and hamlets to give the alarm. When the advanced British detachment arrived at Lexington it was fired on. These were the first shots of the War of Independence.

Source: A letter in the State Paper Office quoted in Mahon: *History of England,* John Murray, 1858, vol. vi, pp. 25–27.

Lieut.-Col. Smith to Governor Gage

Boston, April 22, 1775.

Sir,

In obedience to your Excellency's commands, I marched on the evening of the 18th inst. with the corps of grenadiers and light infantry for Concord, to execute your Excellency's orders with respect to destroying all ammunition, artillery, tents, &c., collected there, which was effected, having knocked off the trunnions of three pieces of iron ordnance, some new gun carriages, a great number of carriage wheels burnt, a considerable quantity of flour, some gunpowder and musket balls, with other small articles thrown into the river. Notwithstanding we marched with the utmost expedition and secrecy, we found the country had intelligence or strong suspicion of our coming, and fired many signal guns, and rung the alarm bells repeatedly; and were informed, when at Concord, that some cannon had been taken out of the town that day, that others, with some stores, had been carried three days before. . . .

I think it proper to observe, that when I had got some miles on the march from Boston, I detached six light infantry companies to march with all expedition to seize the two bridges on different roads beyond Concord. On these companies' arrival at Lexington, I understand, from the report of Major Pitcairn, who was with them, and from many officers, that they found on a green close to the road a body of the country people drawn up in military order, with arms and accoutrements, and, as appeared after, loaded; and that they had posted some men in a dwelling and Meeting-house. Our troops advanced towards them, without any intention of injuring them, further than to inquire the reason of their being thus assembled, and, if not satisfactory, to have secured their arms; but they in confusion went off, principally to the left, only one of them fired before he went off, and three or four more jumped over a wall and fired from behind it among the soldiers; on which the troops returned it, and killed several of them. They likewise fired on the soldiers from the Meeting and dwelling-house. We had one man wounded, and Major Pitcairn's horse shot in two places. Rather earlier than this, on the road, a country man from behind a wall had snapped his piece at Lieutenants Adair and Sutherland, but it flashed and did not go off. After this we saw some in the woods, but marched on to Concord without anything further happening. While at Concord we saw vast numbers assembling in many parts; at one of the bridges they marched down, with a very considerable body, on the light infantry posted there. On their coming pretty near, one of our men fired on them, which they returned; on which an action ensued, and some few were killed and wounded. In this affair, it appears that after the bridge was quitted, they scalped and otherwise ill-treated one or two of the men who were either killed or severely wounded, being seen by a party that marched by soon after. At Concord we found very few inhabitants in the town; those we met with both Major Pitcairn and myself took all possible pains to convince that we meant them no injury, and that if they opened their doors when required to search for military stores, not the slightest mischief would be done. We had opportunities of convincing them of our good intentions, but they were sulky; and one of them even struck Major Pitcairn. On our leaving Concord to return to Boston, they began to fire on us from behind the walls, ditches, trees, etc., which, as we marched, increased to a very great degree, and continued without the intermission of five minutes altogether, for, I believe, upwards of eighteen miles; so that I can't think but it must have been a preconcerted scheme in them, to attack the King's troops the first favourable opportunity that offered, otherwise, I think they could not, in so short a time as from our marching out, have raised such a numerous body, and for so great a space of ground. Notwithstanding the enemy's numbers, they did not make one gallant effort during so long an action, though our men were so very much fatigued, but kept under cover.

I have the honour, etc.
F. Smith, Lt-Col. 10th Foot.

THE ATTACK ON GIBRALTAR,
Friday, September 13th, 1782

When Spain and France allied with the United States and fought against Great Britain in the War of American Independence, Gibraltar was a prime object of attack. For three years and seven months the fortress held out under its eccentric and indomitable commander, General Eliott.

The attack described here was the supreme effort of the Franco-Spanish forces, who put great faith in a new secret weapon: the floating batteries, supposedly indestructible and unsinkable, invented by d'Arcon, a French engineer.

Source: Letter from Captain Curtis, of H.M.S. *Brilliant* to Mr. Stephens, dated *Camp at Europa, Gibraltar,* September 15, 1782. *Annual Register* 1782.

Further Reading: Fortescue: *History of the British Army,* vol. iii. S. H. F. Johnston: *British Soldiers,* Collins, 1944.

Be pleased to acquaint my Lords Commissioners that the Combined Fleet of France and Spain, consisting of thirty-eight sail of the line, arrived in this bay on the 12th instant: six sail of the line were here before.

At eight o'clock in the morning of the 13th, the ten battering ships of the enemy lying at the head of the bay, under the command of Admiral Moreno, began to get under sail in order to come against the garrison; everything was in readiness for their reception. At ten the admiral's ship was placed about one thousand yards from the King's Bastion, and commenced his fire. The others were very shortly afterwards posted to the north and south of him, at small distances asunder, and began their cannonade. They were all fixed to the stations allotted them in a masterly manner. Our batteries opened as the enemy came before them: the fire was very heavy on both sides; the red-hot shot were sent with such precision from the garrison, that in the afternoon the smoke was seen to issue from the upper part of the Admiral, and one other, and men were perceived to be using fire engines and pouring water into the holds, endeavouring to extinguish the fire. Their efforts proved ineffectual; by one o'clock in the morning the two before mentioned were in flames, and several others actually on fire, though as yet not in so great a degree. Confusion was now plainly observed among them, and the numerous rockets thrown up from each of the ships, was a clear demonstration of their great distress: their signals were answered from the enemy's fleet, and they immediately began to take away the men, it being impossible to move the ships. I thought this a fit opportunity to employ my gun-boats, and I advanced with the whole (12 in number, each carrying a twenty-four or eighteen-pounder) and drew them up so as to flank the line of the enemy's battering-ships, while they were annoyed extremely by an eccessive heavy and well-directed fire from the garrison. The fire from the gun-boats was kept up with great vigour and effect. The boats of the enemy durst not approach; they abandoned their ships and the men left in them to our mercy; or to the flames. The day-light now appeared, and two felucas, which had not yet escaped, endeavoured to get away; but a shot from a gun-boat, killing five men on board one of them, they submitted. The scene at this time before me was dreadful to a high degree; numbers of men crying from amidst the flames, some upon pieces of wood in the water, others appearing in the ships where the fire had as yet made but little progress, all expressing by speech and gesture the deepest distress, and all imploring assistance, formed a spectacle of horror not easily to be described. Every exertion was made to relieve them; and I have inexpressible happiness in informing my lords, that the number saved amounts to 13 officers and 344 men. One officer and 29 wounded (some of them dreadfully) taken from among the slain in the holds, are in our hospital, and many of them in a fair way. The blowing up of the ships around us, as the fire got to the magazines, and the firing of the cannon of others, as the metal became heated by the flames, rendered this a very perilous employment; but we felt it as much a duty to make every effort to relieve our enemies from so shocking a situation, as an hour before we did to assist in conquering them. The loss of the enemy must have been very considerable. Great numbers were killed on board, and in boats. Several launches were sunk. In one of them were fourscore men, who were all drowned, except an officer and twelve of them, who were floated under our walls upon the wreck. It was impossible that greater exertions could have been made to prevent it, but there is every reason to believe that a great many wounded perished in the flames. All the battering ships were set on fire by our hot shot except one, which we afterwards burnt. The admiral left his flag flying, and it was consumed with the ship.

A large hole was beat in the bottom of my boat; my coxswain was killed, and two of the crew were wounded by pieces of timber falling on her when one of the battering ships blew up. The same cause sunk one of my gun-boats and damaged another.
. . .

A considerable detachment of seamen did duty as artillerists upon the batteries, and gave great satisfaction.

The officers and men of the brigade of seamen under my command, in whatever situations they were placed, behaved in a manner highly becoming them.

JOHN WILKES AND THE MOB

The son of Israel Wilkes, a rich distiller, he early distinguished himself by being as witty as he was vicious. 'Vote for you, Sir! I'd sooner vote for the Devil,' said one of the Middlesex electors. 'But in case your friend should not stand?' enquired Wilkes. In 1757 he was elected a member for Aylesbury. In 1762 he started the *North Briton* in which he denounced Bute, the Ministry, and the Scots. Next year, in the famous 'Number 45', he attacked the Royal Speech at the end of the last session. He was prosecuted for libel. His prosecution began by being mainly of legal interest but developed into a constitutional issue. Successive Houses of Commons insisted on persecuting and expelling Wilkes. In 1774 they gave up the struggle and in 1782 all the proceedings of the House against him were expunged from its journals. He was considered to have established the right of every constituency to return the member of its choice. Boswell's account of the encounter between Wilkes and Dr. Johnson at Mr. Dilly's house is famous.

Source: Horace Walpole: *Letters.* From a letter to Sir Horace Mann dated Thursday, March 31, 1768.

He [Wilkes] stood for the City of London, and was the last on the poll of seven candidates, none but the mob, and most of them without votes, favouring him. He then offered himself to the County of Middlesex. The election came on last Monday. By five in the morning a very large body of Weavers etc, took possession of Piccadilly, and the roads and turnpikes leading to Brentford, and would suffer nobody to pass without blue cockades, and papers inscribed, 'No. 45, Wilkes and Liberty'. They tore to pieces the coaches of Sir W. Beauchamp Proctor, and Mr. Cooke, the other candidates, though the latter was not there, but in bed with the gout, and it was with difficulty that Sir William and Mr. Cooke's cousin got to Brentford. There, however, lest it should be declared a void election, Wilkes had the sense to keep everything quiet. But, about five, Wilkes, being considerably ahead of the other two, his mob returned to town and behaved outrageously. They stopped every carriage, scratched and spoilt several with writing all over them ' No. 45 ', pelted, threw dirt and stones, and forced everybody to huzza for Wilkes. I did but cross Piccadilly at eight, in my coach, with a French monsieur d'Angeul, whom I was carrying to Lady

Hertford's; they stopped us, and bid us huzza. I desired him to let down the glass on his side, but, as he was not alert, they broke it to shatters. At night they insisted, in several streets, on houses being illuminated, and several Scotch refusing, had their windows broken. Another mob rose in the City, and Harley, the present Mayor, being another Sir William Walworth, and having acted formerly and now with great spirit against Wilkes, and the Mansion House not being illuminated, and he out of town, they broke every window, and tried to force their way into the House. The Trained Bands were sent for, but did not suffice. At last a party of guards, from the Tower, . . . dispersed the tumult. At one in the morning a riot began before Lord Bute's house, in Audley Street, though illuminated. They flung two large flints into Lady Bute's chamber, who was in bed, and broke every window in the house. Next morning, Wilkes and Cooke were returned members. The day was very quiet, but at night they rose again, and obliged almost every house in town to be lighted up, even the Duke of Cumberland's and Princess Amelia's.

GEORGE III GOES TO WEYMOUTH

Son of Frederick, Prince of Wales, and grandson of George II, he came to the throne in 1760. With considerable private virtues, his declaration that he ' gloried in the name of Britain ' helped to give him after 1783 a popularity with the middle classes which was never forfeited. It was during his reign that the grandsons of the Jacobites and Nonjurors transferred their allegiance from the White Rose to the White Horse. In 1761 he married Charlotte of Mecklenburg-Strelitz. The years between 1763 and 1782 were generally disastrous. The King's relations with his ministers have been decisively re-interpreted by Sir Lewis Namier. The King's excitability of mind and oddity of manner developed in 1811 into final insanity. He had always spoken and thought in English; he had liked and disliked most of what his subjects had liked and disliked; he had patently tried to do his duty as he saw it; and his love of Handel's music remained to solace him in his blindness and insanity. When he died in 1820 he had never set foot in Hanover.

(*a*) *Source: Diary and Letters of Madame d'Arblay*, Colburn, 1846, vol. v, pp. 28–36.

On June 25, 1789, the Court left Windsor for Weymouth, where the King, who had recently recovered from his first attack of mental illness, was to stay.

H

Thursday, June 25th.

. . . At Romsey, on the steps of the Town Hall, an orchestra was formed and a band of musicians, in common brown coarse cloth and red neckcloths, and even in carters' loose gowns, made a chorus of ' God save the King ', in which the countless multitude joined. . . .

[At Lyndhurst] During the King's dinner, which was in a parlour looking into the garden, he permitted the people to come to the window; and their delight and rapture in seeing their monarch at table, with the evident hungry feeling it occasioned, made a contrast of admiration and deprivation, truly comic. They crowded, however, so excessively, that this can be permitted them no more. They broke down all the paling, and much of the hedges, and some of the windows, and all by eagerness and multitude, for they were perfectly civil and well-behaved. . . .

Tuesday, June 30th [at Weymouth].

. . . The King, and Queen, and Princesses, and their suite, walked out in the evening; an immense crowd attended them—sailors, bargemen, mechanics, countrymen; and all united in so vociferous a volley of ' God save the King ', that the noise was stunning. . . .

The preparations of festive loyalty were universal. Not a child could we meet that had not a bandeau round its head, cap, or hat, of ' God save the King ', all the bargemen wore it in cockades; and even the bathing-women had it in large coarse girdles round their waists. It is printed in golden letters upon most of the bathing-machines, and in various scrolls and devices it adorns every shop and almost every house. . . .

Wednesday, July 8th.

. . . The King bathes, and with great success; a machine follows the royal one into the sea, filled with fiddlers, who play ' God save the King ', as his Majesty takes his plunge!

Miss Burney to Dr. Burney.

Gloucester House, Weymouth,
July 13th, 1789.

. . . When the Mayor and burgesses came with the address, they requested leave to kiss hands; this was graciously accorded; but the Mayor advancing, in a common way, *to take the Queen's hand*, as he might that of any lady mayoress, Colonel Gwynn, who stood by, whispered, ' You must kneel, sir! ' He found, however, that he took no notice of this hint, but kissed the Queen's hand erect. As he passed him, in his way back, the Colonel said, ' You should have knelt, sir! '

' Sir ', answered the poor Mayor, ' I cannot '.

' Everybody does, sir,'

' Sir,—I have a wooden leg! '

(*b*) In 1791 Thomas Byam Martin had just been promoted Lieutenant, at the age of seventeen. He was serving in the frigate *Juno* which was ordered to Weymouth to attend on George III.

Source: Letters and Papers of the Fleet Sir Thomas Byam Martin, vol. i, Navy Records Society.

The sailing about in a ship of war, attended by several others, was so new and agreeable to his Majesty, that a thousand questions came from him that quite startled the nerves of persons unaccustomed to his rapid and rambling volubility. It is beyond description the incoherence with which he would fly from one thing to another, to the great distress of we young folks, who were so awed in the presence of royalty as not to feel much at ease under any circumstances. The King, however, generally supplied our want of promptness in replying to his questions, by kindly answering them himself in a sort of way, to show an impatient desire to get on with his catechismal habit of addressing people. I own I often thought the royal mind had not, at that time, recovered the bewilderment under which it laboured three years before in 1788 or '9, and which at a subsequent period rendered him incapable of holding the reins of government.

The King, as he advanced towards anyone, had a peculiar

sort of stare, and half smile, which tended to discompose those who, like myself, would rather have been a hundred miles off than be found within his orbit, for although meant as good humour and condescension, it was more than an awkward, uncourtier-like boy could encounter with composure. One day, very soon after I began to move in the circle of royalty, his Majesty seeing me on the Esplanade at Weymouth, advanced towards me with the sort of look I have described, and for the life of me I had no means of escape. I knew not what to be at. I was truly in what is vulgarly called a funk, and as the royal personage slowly advanced I became more and more hurried and nervous; at last losing all self-command and without waiting his first word, I burst out, ' How do you do, Sir? ' upon which his Majesty seeing the thing in its true light laughed very heartily, and then went on with a thousand good-humoured questions.

I remember an unfortunate young midshipman being pent up, as it were, in the corner of the after part of the quarter-deck one day, just when some of the seabirds called gulls were hovering about. The King burst out in a moment, ' Young gentleman, what birds are those—pigeons? ' ' No, your Majesty, gulls.' ' Gulls, gulls ', continued the King; ' Where do they come from? What do they feed upon? Where do they roost? ' All this was uttered with the greatest rapidity and without waiting any reply to either question; indeed the poor mid. was so confounded that he was ready to sink into the deck, and it may also be said that his life was saved by his Majesty's attention being drawn to some other object.

Whenever the royal family came on board, and the ship under sail, the people were kept at their different stations, and the lower deck quite clear. One day the King and Queen came out of the cabin together and were inclined to pay a visit to the lower deck. When I discovered the intended frolic, I found his Majesty with infinite awkwardness trying how it was best to go down the ladder; first his foot was planted on the upper step, as if to descend in the usual way of going down stairs, presently he turned to try the other way to make a stern board of it; but not quite satisfied that he was right, I found on my approach that he and the Queen were holding a council of war, and being called in to assist in the deliberations, the latter mode of proceeding was adopted.

My accidental appearance was very fortunate; I do believe if left to themselves they would have encountered a very bumping, disagreeable passage from one deck to the other, for if the heel slips in going down, the hinder part of the human body is sure to strike each step in the descent. I endeavoured to explain this hazard in the most delicate terms I could employ, and with sufficient clearness to make her Majesty at once take the lead with her face towards the ladder. This is a caution which I always give to ladies, however contrary to court etiquette such mode of presentation.

Having reached the lower deck my duty was to think of the safety of another part of the royal person, and that a very tender one, too, considering the King's then recent malady—I mean the head. The height of a frigate of the *Juno* class, the old 32, is about 5 feet 4 inches between decks, so that there was a constant danger of his Majesty throwing his head suddenly up and receiving a severe blow; it kept me quite in a nervous fidget the whole time. We were the only three persons at the time on the lower deck, and I was desired to explain everything as they walked round. His Majesty, getting tired of stooping so long, was not sorry to sit himself down in the midshipmen's berth, and then commenced innumerable questions as to my professional service, etc., etc. Finding I had served with Prince William (Duke of Clarence) in every ship he had ever commanded, the conversation became very interesting, and occasioned them to tarry so long in this unfrequented part of the ship that a sort of hue and cry made us aware that some uneasiness prevailed on account of their Majesties' long absence from the quarter-deck. This was still more increased when one of the anxious attendants, Colonel Price, reconnoitred the cabin and found the royal couple missing. The alarm soon reached those above, and set one of the lords off, accompanied by one of the officers of the ship, in search of the absentees. We were found very snug in the midshipmen's berth; the Queen in the enjoyment of a half-broken chair, while his Majesty was politely content to take his seat on a poor mid.'s chest. For myself I can't say much for enjoyment; I stood before them almost exhausted answering the thousand questions put to me, and they ceased not even when the intruders discovered our retreat. The King long recollected his visit to the lower deck, and had always a question ready for me relating to the conversation on that occasion.

REMINISCENCES OF PITT AND FOX

Source: Memoirs of the Lady Hester Stanhope as related by herself in Conversations with her Physician, Dr. Meryon. 2nd edition, 1846.

Lady Hester Stanhope was born in 1776. Her mother (who died when Lady Hester was four years old) was the daughter of Chatham, and her father was that Earl Stanhope who had defended the French Revolution in the House of Lords and had erased the ' damned aristo-cratical nonsense ' of armorial bearings from his carriages and his plate. To his family Earl Stanhope was a tyrant and a bully, and to escape from him Lady Hester went to live with her grandmother, Lady Chatham. Three years later when Lady Chatham died, her uncle, William Pitt, offered her a home at Walmer. There she stayed, devoted to her uncle, until his death. In 1810 her travels began. Finally she settled in Djoun on Mount Lebanon. After some time, to quote Lytton Strachey—' Her habits grew more and more eccentric. She lay in bed all day, and sat up all night, talking unceasingly for hour upon hour to Dr. Meryon, who alone of her English attendants remained with her '. She died at Djoun in 1839.

Further Reading: Lytton Strachey: Essay on Lady Hester Stanhope in *Books and Characters.* Chatto and Windus, 1922.

Hobhouse: *Fox*, Constable, 1934.   Erich Eyck: *Pitt versus Fox*, Bell, 1950.

William Pitt
' *The pilot who weathered the storm.* '

Born in the Year of Victories, the son of the first Earl of Chatham and Lady Hester Grenville provides an example of a precocious genius which more than fulfilled its early promise. He was educated at Pem-broke College, Cambridge, where he read classics and mathematics. As the younger son of an impoverished father he had his way to make in the world. In 1780 he was called to the Bar and in the same year he entered the House of Commons as member for Appleby and immediately made his mark as a speaker. In December 1783 he became Prime Minister: 'A sight to make surrounding nations stare, Three kingdoms trusted to a schoolboy's care.' Between 1784 and 1788 his India Bill, the National Debt, parliamentary reform, the impeachment of Warren Hastings, the slave trade and the question of the Regency, were the chief subjects of political interest. Then unexpectedly came the French Revolution and war. He succeeded in bringing about the union with Ireland, but was prevented from combining it with Catholic Emancipation which alone, he believed, would make it effective. He therefore resigned in 1801, but returned to power in 1804. On October 11th, 1805, came Trafalgar; on December 2nd, Austerlitz; on January 23rd, Pitt died. At his funeral Lord Wellesley said ' What grave contains such a father and such a son? '

(*a*) *Source:* the same, vol. II, pp. 58–59.

People little knew what he [Pitt] had to do. Up at eight in the morning, with people enough to see for a week, obliged to talk all the time he was at breakfast, and receiving first one, then another, until four o'clock; then eating a mutton-chop, hurrying off to the House, and there badgered and compelled to speak and waste his lungs until two or three in the morning!—who could stand it? After this, heated as he was, and having eaten nothing, in a manner of speaking, all day, he would sup with Dundas, Huskisson, Rose, Mr. Long, and such persons, and then go to bed to get three or four hours sleep, and to renew the same thing the next day, and the next, and the next. . . .

. . . When Mr. Pitt was at Walmer, he recovered his health prodigiously. He used to go to a farm near Walmer, where hay and corn were kept for the horses. He had a room fitted up there with a table and two or three chairs, where he used to write sometimes, and a tidy woman to dress him something to eat. Oh! what slices of bread and butter I have seen him eat there, and hunches of bread and cheese big enough for a ploughman! He used to say that, whenever he could retire from public life, he would have a good English woman cook. Sometimes, after a grand dinner, he would say, ' I want something—I am hungry ': and when I remarked ' Well, but you are just got up from dinner ', he would add, ' Yes, but I looked round the table, and there was nothing I could eat—all the dishes were so made up, and so un-natural '. Ah, doctor! in town, during the sitting of parliament, what a life was his! Roused from his sleep (for he was a good sleeper) with a despatch from Lord Melville;—then down to Windsor, then, if he had half an hour to spare, trying to swallow something:—Mr. Adams with a paper, Mr. Long with another, then Mr. Rose, then, with a little bottle of cordial confection in his pocket, off to the House until three or four in the morning; then home to a hot supper for two or three hours more, to talk over what was to be done next day:—and wine, and wine!— Scarcely up next morning, when tat-tat-tat—twenty or thirty people, one after another, and the horses walking before the door from two till sunset, waiting for him. It was enough to kill a man—it was murder!

(*b*) *Source:* the same, vol. II, p. 62.

. . . In regarding him [Pitt] I should have said that he had a sort of slovenly or negligent look: and the same when he was in a passion. His passion did not show itself by knitting his brows or pouting his mouth, nor were his words very sharp: but his eyes lighted up in a manner quite surprising. It was something that seemed to dart from within his head, and you might see sparks coming from them. At another time, his eyes had no colour at all.

Charles James Fox was the third son of Henry Fox, first Baron Holland, and descended through his mother, Lady Catherine Lennox, daughter of the second Duke of Richmond, from Charles II. It has been remarked that his grandfather, Sir Stephen Fox, had attended Charles I on the scaffold and lived to hear of the execution of Lord Derwentwater, while his aunt, Lady Sarah Napier, survived until 1826. Educated at Eton and Hertford College, Oxford, he became member for Midhurst in 1768. A brilliant debater, he was rewarded with an appointment as Junior Lord of the Admiralty in 1770. In 1772 he resigned and opposed the Royal Marriage Act. Taken again into the Ministry, he broke with North and joined the opposition, of which he eventually became the leader. He was elected member for Westminster. In 1783 he was reconciled to North with whom he served under the Duke of Portland. Dismissed in 1783, he failed to overthrow Pitt. He hailed the news of the French Revolution and, far longer than most Englishmen, sympathised with events in France. He was a close friend of the Prince of Wales whom he supported against Pitt over the Regency Bill. His passion for liberty was genuine and his personality attractive.

(*c*) *Source:* the same, vol. III, pp. 146–7.

' Fox, I think, was thrown into a position with the Prince and his dissipated friends from which he never afterwards could extricate himself, otherwise he would have been a different man;

but, mixed up with them, the King could never bear him: for, when Mr. Pitt took office in 1803, the King wrote to him (for I saw the letter) ' Would you force on me Mr. Fox, who debauched my son? ' etc. The last time I saw Mr. Fox, he was at Vauxhall with Mrs. Fox. She was dressed as some respectable housekeeper might be, with a black bonnet and some sort of a gown. . . . Mr. Fox looked like the landlord of a public-house; yet, when he spoke, doctor, he was sometimes very eloquent. On Mr. Hastings' trial he made many people cry. There were all the peers with their pocket-handkerchiefs out—quite a tragedy! but he made such a business of it—' (here Lady Hester sat up in bed, and, to show what she meant, threw her arms first to the right and then to the left, and then thumped the bed violently, making me wonder where she had found such strength;)—' he was worse than Punch'.

(*d*) *Source: Table-talk of Samuel Rogers.*, ed. Dyce.

Samuel Rogers (1763–1855) the ' banker-poet ', was immensely influential in the literary world. He was offered the laureateship when Wordsworth died in 1850, but refused it. Alexander Dyce wrote down much of the conversation of Rogers, and published it in 1856 under the title of *Recollections of the Table-talk of Samuel Rogers*.

It is quite true, as stated in several accounts of him, that Fox, when a very young man, was a prodigious dandy—wearing a little odd French hat, shoes with red heels, etc. He and Lord Carlisle once travelled from Paris to Lyons for the express purpose of buying waistcoats; and during the whole journey they talked about nothing else.

Fox (in his earlier days, I mean), Sheridan, Fitzpatrick, etc., led *such* a life! Lord Tankerville assured me that he has played cards with Fitzpatrick at Brookes's from ten o'clock at night till near six o'clock the next afternoon, a waiter standing by to tell them ' whose deal it was ', they being too sleepy to know.

After losing large sums at hazard, Fox would go home—not to destroy himself, as his friends sometimes feared, but—to sit down quietly, and read Greek.

He once won about eight thousand pounds; and one of his bond-creditors, who soon heard of his good luck, presented himself and asked for payment. ' Impossible, sir ', replied Fox; ' I must first discharge my debts of honour '. The bond-creditor remonstrated. ' Well, sir, give me your bond.' It was delivered to Fox, who tore it in pieces and threw them into the fire. ' Now, sir,' said Fox, ' my debt to you is a debt of honour ', and immediately paid him.

When I became acquainted with Fox, he had given up that kind of life entirely, and resided in the most perfect sobriety and regularity at St. Anne's Hill. There he was very happy delighting in study, in rural occupations, and rural prospects. He would break from a criticism on Porson's *Euripides* to look for the little pigs. I remember his calling out to the Chertsey hills, when a thick mist, which had for some time concealed them, rolled away: ' Good morning to you! I am glad to see you again '. There was a walk in his grounds which led to a lane through which the farmers used to pass; and he would stop them, and talk to them, with great interest, about the price of turnips, etc. I was one day with him in the Louvre, when he suddenly turned from the pictures, and, looking out of the window, exclaimed, ' This hot sun will burn up my turnips at St. Anne's Hill '. . . .

Never in my life did I hear anything equal to Fox's *speeches in reply*—they were wonderful. Burke did not do himself justice as a speaker: his manner was hurried, and he always seemed to be in a passion. Pitt's voice sounded as if he had worsted in his mouth.

Porson said that ' Pitt carefully considered his sentences before he uttered them; but that Fox threw himself into the middle of his, and left it to God Almighty to get him out again '. . . .

Lady Holland announced the death of Fox in her own odd manner to those relatives and intimate friends of his who were sitting in a room near his bed-chamber, and waiting to hear that he had breathed his last;—she walked through the room with her apron thrown over her head.

How fondly the surviving friends of Fox cherished his memory! Many years after his death, I was at a fête given by the Duke of Devonshire at Chiswick House. Sir Robert Adair and I wandered about the apartments, up and down stairs. ' In which room did Fox expire? ' asked Adair. I replied, ' In this very room '. Immediately Adair burst into tears with a vehemence of grief such as I hardly ever saw exhibited by a man.

SLAVERY IN THE WEST INDIES

Source: Journal of Nicholas Cresswell, 1774–77, ed. Thornely, London, 1925, pp.35–40.

Cresswell was on a voyage from Virginia to Barbados.

Tuesday, September 13th, 1774. Went ashore and saw a Cargo of Slaves land. One of the most shocking sights I ever saw. About 400 Men, Women, and Children, brought from their native Country, deprived of their liberty, and themselves and posterity become the property of cruel strangers without a probability of ever enjoying the Blessings of Freedom again, or a right of complaining, be their sufferings never so great. The idea is horrid and the practice unjust. They were all naked, except a small piece of blue cloth about a foot broad to cover their nakedness, and appear much dejected. . . .

Friday, September 16th, 1774.

. . . The British nation famed for humanity suffers it to be tarnished by their Creolian subjects—the Cruelty exercised upon the Negroes is at once shocking to humanity and a disgrace to human nature. For the most trifling faults, sometimes for mere whims of their Masters, these poor wretches are tied up and whipped most unmercifully. I have seen them tied up and flogged with a twisted piece of Cowskin till there was very little signs of Life. . . . Some of them die under the severity of these barbarities, others whose spirits are too great to submit to the insults and abuses they receive put an end to their own lives. If a person kills a slave he only pays his value as a fine. It is not a hanging matter. Certainly these poor beings meet with some better place on the other side of the Grave, for they have a hell on earth. It appears they are sensible of this, if one may judge from their behaviour at their funerals. Instead of weeping and wailing, they dance and sing and appear to be the happiest mortals on earth.

JOHN WOOLMAN THE QUAKER

John Woolman (1720–1772) was an American Quaker, born in West Jersey. About 1743 he set out to preach and persuade against the slave trade, addressing himself particularly towards the American Quakers. In 1772 he came to England on the same errand. He was taken ill, died and was buried at York. His *Journal* was first published in 1775, the larger part being concerned with his struggle against slavery and ill-paid or unpaid labour. Lamb's advice, ' Get the writings of John Woolman by heart,' may be taken together with Sir G. M. Trevelyan's suggestion that by contrasting Woolman with Rousseau as reformers, the difference between the two main movements for social reform can best be appreciated. These two extracts from the *Journal* illustrate and explain Woolman's attitude towards social justice in general and slavery in particular.

Further Reading: ed. Eyre: *European Civilisation* vol. vii Oxford 1939, chapter on ' Negro Slavery ', by Carter G. Woodson. Trevelyan: *Clio: a Muse*, ' John Woolman the Quaker '. Nelson, 1913.

(*a*) *Source: The Journal of John Woolman.* Melrose, 1898, pp. 293-5, 289-91.

' Twenty-sixth of Eighth Month.—Being now at George Crosfield's, in the county of Westmorland, I feel a concern to commit to writing the following uncommon circumstance:—

In a time of sickness, a little more than two years and a half ago, I was brought so near the gates of death that I forgot my name. Being then desirous to know who I was, I saw a mass of matter of a dull gloomy colour between the south and the east, and was informed that this mass was human beings in as great misery as they could be and live, and that I was mixed up with them, and that henceforth I might not consider myself as a distinct or separate being. In this state I lived several hours. I then heard a soft melodious voice, more pure and harmonious than any I had heard with my ears before; and I believed it was the voice of an Angel who spake to the other Angels; and the words were ' John Woolman is dead '. . . . I was then carried in spirit to the mines where poor oppressed people were digging rich treasures for those called Christians, and heard them blaspheme the name of Christ, at which I was grieved, for His name to me was precious. I was then informed that these heathens were told that those who oppressed them were the followers of Christ, and they said among themselves, ' If Christ directed them to use us in this sort, then Christ is a cruel tyrant '. . . . My tongue was often so dry that I could not speak till I had moved it about and gathered some moisture, and as I lay still for a time I at length felt a divine power prepare my mouth that I could speak, and then I said, ' I am crucified with Christ, nevertheless

I live; yet not I, but Christ liveth in me. And the life which I now live in the flesh I live by the faith of the Son of God, who loved me and gave Himself for me '. Then the mystery was opened and I perceived there was joy in heaven over a sinner who had repented, and that the language ' John Woolman is dead ' meant no more than the death of my own will.

(b) The same, pp. 289-291.

' Sixteenth of Eighth Month and the first of the week, I was at Settle. . . . On inquiry at many places I find the price of rye about five shillings; wheat eight shillings per bushel; oatmeal, twelve shillings for a hundred and twenty pounds; mutton from threepence to fivepence per pound; bacon from sevenpence to ninepence; cheese, from fourpence to sixpence; butter, from eightpence to tenpence; house-rent for a poor man from twenty-five shillings to forty shillings per year, to be paid weekly; wood for fire very scarce and dear; coal in some places two shillings and sixpence per hundredweight; but near the pits not a quarter so much. Oh, may the wealthy consider the poor!

The wages of labouring men in several counties towards London at tenpence per day in common business, the employer finds small beer and the labourer finds his own food; but in harvest and hay time wages are about one shilling per day, and the labourer hath all his diet. In some parts of the north of England, poor labouring men have their food where they work, and appear in common to do rather better than nearer London. Industrious women who spin in the factories get some fourpence, some fivepence, and so on to six, seven, eight, nine or tenpence per day, and find their own house-room and diet. Great numbers of poor people live chiefly on bread and water in the southern parts of England, as well as in the northern parts; and there are many poor children not even taught to read. May those who have abundance lay these things to heart. . . .

So great is the hurry in the spirit of this world, that in aiming to do business quickly and to gain wealth, the creation at this day doth loudly groan.

THE ENGLISH LOVE OF FISTICUFFS

Source: Misson de Valbourg: *Mr. Misson's Memoirs and Observations in England;* trans. Ozell. London 1719.
Misson de Valbourg, a Huguenot refugee, came to England in 1685.

If two little boys quarrel in the street, the passengers stop, make a ring round them in a moment, and set them against one another, that they may come to fisticuffs. . . . During the fight the ring of bystanders encourages the combatants with great delight of heart, and never parts them while they fight according to the rules. And these bystanders are not only other boys, porters, and rabble, but all sorts of men of fashion, some thrusting by the mob that they may see plainly, others getting upon stalls, and all would hire places, if scaffolds could be built in a moment. The fathers and mothers of the boys let them fight on as well as the rest, and hearten him that gives the ground, or has the worst. These combats are less frequent among grown men than children, but they are not rare. If a coachman has a dispute about his fare with a gentleman that has hired him, and the gentleman offers to fight him to decide the quarrel, the coachman consents with all his heart. The gentleman pulls off his sword, lays it in some shop with his cane, gloves and cravat, and boxes in the same manner as I have described above. If the coachman gets soundly drubbed, which happens almost always, that goes for payment, but if he is the beater, the beatee must pay the money about which they quarrelled. I once saw the late Duke of Grafton at fisticuffs in the open street, with such a fellow, whom he lambed most horribly. In France we punish such rascals with our cane, and sometimes with the flat of the sword; but in England this is never practised. They use neither sword nor stick against a man that is unarmed, and if an unfortunate stranger (for an Englishman would never take it into his head) should draw his sword upon one that had none, he'd have a hundred people upon him in a moment, that would, perhaps, lay him so flat that he would hardly ever get up again until the Resurrection.

THE GORDON RIOTS, June 2-8, 1780

Parliament had passed the Catholic Relief Act, to remove some of the worst disabilities of Catholics. Lord George Gordon (1751–1793) the third son of the Duke of Gordon and Whig M.P. for the pocket borough of Ludgershall, formed the Protestant Association to secure the repeal of this Act. He called an enormous meeting at St. George's Fields from which thousands went to petition Parliament. Mob violence broke out almost at once and for four days the mob terrorised London. Order was restored only when George III ordered troops to disperse the rioters. Lord George Gordon was put on trial for high treason but was acquitted. He died in Newgate, however, while serving a sentence of five years' imprisonment for having insulted the Queen of France and the French ambassador. Before his death he had been converted to Judaism.

This extract describes the attack on Newgate Prison. The mob was trying to rescue some rioters arrested and imprisoned the previous day.

Source: Life of George Crabbe by his son, London, 1947. This life of George Crabbe (1754–1832), the poet, was written by his son George (1785–1857), who was, like his father, an Anglican clergyman.

Further Reading: Dickens: *Barnaby Rudge.* David Mathew: *Catholicism in England,* 1535–1935, Longmans, 1936, pp. 136–45.

June 8th, 1780:—I left Westminster when all the members, that were permitted, had entered the House, and came home. In my way I met a resolute band of vile-looking fellows, ragged, dirty, and insolent, armed with clubs, going to join their companions. I since learned that there were eight or ten of these bodies in different parts of the city.

About seven o'clock in the evening I went out again. . . . I crossed St. George's Fields, which were empty, and came home again by Blackfriars Bridge; and in going from thence to the Exchange, you pass the Old Bailey; and here it was that I saw the first scene of terror and riot ever presented to me. The new prison was a very large, strong, and beautiful building, having two wings, . . . besides these, were the Keeper's (Mr. Akerman's) house. . . . Akerman had in his custody four prisoners, taken in the riot; these the mob went to his house and demanded. He begged he might send to the sheriff, but this was not permitted. How he escaped, or where he is gone, I know not; but just at the time I speak of they set fire to his house, broke in, and threw every piece of furniture they could find into the street, firing them also in an instant. The engines came, but were only suffered to preserve the private houses near the prison.

As I was standing near the spot, there approached another

body of men, I suppose 500, and Lord George Gordon in a
coach, drawn by the mob towards Alderman Bull's, bowing as
he passed along. He is a lively-looking young man in appearance,
and nothing more, though just now the reigning hero.

By eight o'clock, Akerman's house was in flames. I went
close to it, and never saw anything so dreadful. The prison was,
as I have said, a remarkably strong building; but, determined
to force it, they broke the gates with crows and other instruments,
and climbed up the outside of the cell part, which joins the two
great wings of the building, where the felons were confined;
and I stood where I plainly saw their operations. They broke the
roof, tore away the rafters, and having got ladders they descended.
. . .

The prisoners escaped. I stood and saw about twelve women
and eight men ascend from their confinement to the open air,
and they were conducted through the street in their chains.
Three of these were to be hanged on Friday. You have no
conception of the frenzy of the multitude, . . . Tired of the scene
I went home, and returned again at eleven o'clock at night.
I met large bodies of horse and foot soldiers coming to guard the
Bank, and some houses of Roman Catholics near it. Newgate
was at this time open to all; any one might get in, and, what
was never the case before, any one might get out. I did both;
for the people were now chiefly lookers-on. The mischief was
done, and the doers of it gone to another part of the town. . . .

On comparing notes with my neighbours, I find I saw but
a small part of the mischief. They say Lord Mansfield's house
is now in flames. . . .

A SHROPSHIRE RECTOR ABROAD IN 1779

John Fletcher (1729–1785) came of an aristocratic Swiss family. His
father was an officer in the French army. He anglicised his name,
de la Flechere, on settling in England. He was ordained in 1757 at the
Chapel Royal of St. James's. In 1760 he was presented to the living of
Madeley in Shropshire, which he chose in preference to a more attractive living where, as the patron put it, ' the parish is small, the duty
light, the income good (£400 per annum) and it is situated in a fine
healthy sporting country '. Madeley was at this time ' notorious for
ignorance and impiety '. Here for a quarter of a century until his death

in 1785 this holy and humble man lived and worked, effecting a remarkable reformation in his parish. A close friend of John Wesley, Fletcher provides an admirable example of the achievement of the Evangelical Movement in the Church of England in the eighteenth century.

This extract illustrates how war between two governments did not necessarily prevent travel, the Englishman's opinion of French inns and French food, and how the acerbity of doctrinal principle was in practice tempered by charity, good manners and good sense. Fletcher's encounters with the Capuchins and with Pius VI are more typical of the contemporary English attitude to Giant Pope than the Gordon Riots might suggest.

Source: John Wesley's A Short Account of the Life and Death of the Reverend John Fletcher. W. Milner, Halifax, 1851. pp. 76–84.

Dear Sir,

As you desire me to send you some account of my journey, now I am a little settled, I will do it in the best manner I am able.

I set out from London, on Tuesday, November the seventeenth; we arrived at Dover about three on Wednesday morning; embarked on Thursday, and arrived at Calais in about three hours.

Though it was in war time, yet we did not meet with the least incivility, either here or in any part of France: but the badness of the inns makes the travelling through this country disagreeable. The rooms in general are so dirty, as to be fitter for swine than for men: each room both above and below stairs, is provided with two, three or four beds, and they are so high as to require steps to go up to them; for there is on each bed, first, a monstrous canvass bag, stuffed with a huge quantity of straw; over this a feather bed, and on this as many mattresses as the hosts can furnish. But the worst is, the sheets are not damp, but rather down-right wet; yet the good woman would constantly scold us, if we attempted to dry them even at our own fire: insisting upon it that it was impossible they should be damp at all.

At table every one is furnished with a spoon and a fork, but with no knives; and in general they are not needful, for both flesh and vegetables are so stewed down, as to be properly termed spoon-meat. However, at the meanest inn, every one is provided with a clean napkin; and both after dinner and after supper, there is a fine dessert of fruit. . . .

I

... On Good Friday, there being no service here, Mr. Fletcher and I crossed the lake into Savoy, in order to hear a celebrated Capuchin, who was to preach that day. He made a very good discourse; and afterwards, he and his brethren invited us to dine with them. This we declined, but after dinner, paid our respects to them; and we spent two or three agreable hours in serious and friendly conversation. [The tour was continued and the party reached Rome.] While he was here, as Mr. Ireland and he were one day going through one of the streets in a coach, they were informed the Pope was coming forward, and it would be required of them to come out of the coach, and kneel while he went by, as all the people did; and if they did not, in all probability, the zealous mob would fall upon them, and knock them on the head. But this, whatever might be the consequence, they flatly refused to do—judging the paying such honour to a man was neither better nor worse than idolatry. The coachman was exceedingly terrified, not knowing what to do. However, at length, he made a shift to turn aside into a narrow way. The Pope was in an open landau. He waved his hands, as if he had been swimming: and frequently repeated these words, ' God bless you all! ' Mr. Fletcher's spirit was greatly stirred, and he longed to bear a public testimony against anti-christ. And he would undoubtedly have done it had he been able to speak Italian. He could hardly refrain from doing it in Latin, till he considered that only the priests could have understood him. One, to whom he related this, saying, if he had done this, the multitude would have torn him to pieces; he answered, ' I believe the Pope himself would have prevented it; for he was a man of sense and humanity '.

A GERMAN IN LONDON IN 1782

Source: Travels of Carl Philipp Moritz in 1782, reprint of English translation of 1795, London, Humphrey Milford, 1924.

(a) *Source:* the same, pp. 29-31.

The footway paved with large stones on both sides of the streets, appears to a foreigner exceedingly convenient and plea-sant; as one may there walk in perfect safety, in no more danger from the prodigious crowd of carts and coaches, than if one was in one's own room; for no wheel dares come a finger's breadth upon the curb-stone. However, politeness requires you to let a lady, or any one to whom you wish to show respect, pass, not, as we do, always to the right, but on the side next the houses or the wall, whether that happens to be on the right, or on the left, being deemed the safest and most convenient. You seldom see a person of any understanding or common sense walk in the middle of the streets in London, excepting when they cross over; which at Charing Cross and other places, where several streets meet, is sometimes really dangerous.

It has a strange appearance, especially in the Strand where there is a constant succession of shop after shop; and where, not unfrequently, people of different trades inhabit the same house, to see their doors, or the tops of their windows, or boards expressly for the purpose, all written over from top to bottom, with large painted letters. Every person, of every trade or occupation, who owns ever so small a portion of an house, makes a parade with a sign at his door; and there is hardly a cobbler, whose name and profession may not be read in large golden characters, by every one that passes. It is here not at all uncommon to see on doors in one continued succession, ' *children educated here* '; ' *shoes mended here* '; ' *foreign spirituous liquors sold here* '; and ' *Funerals furnished here* '. Of all these inscriptions, I am sorry to observe, that ' *Dealer in foreign spirituous liquors* ' is by far the most frequent. And indeed it is allowed by the English themselves, that the propensity of the common people to the drinking of brandy or gin, is carried to a great excess: and I own it struck me as a peculiar phraseology, when, to tell you, that a person is intoxicated or drunk, you hear them say, as they generally do, that *he is in liquor*. In the late riots,[1] which even yet, are hardly quite subsided, and which are still the general topic of conversation, more people have been found dead near empty brandy-casks in the streets, than were killed by the musket balls of regiments, that were called in. As much as I have seen of London, within these two days, there are on the whole I think not very many very fine streets and very fine houses, but I met

[1] The Gordon Riots.

everywhere a far greater number, and handsomer people, than one commonly meets in Berlin. It gives me much real pleasure, when I walk from Charing Cross up the Strand, past St. Paul's to the Royal Exchange, to meet, in the thickest crowds, persons, from the highest to the lowest ranks, almost all well-looking people and cleanly and neatly dressed. I rarely see even a fellow with a wheelbarrow, who has not a shirt on; and that too such an one, as shows it has been washed; nor even a beggar, without both a shirt, and shoes and stockings. The English are certainly distinguished for cleanliness.

(*b*) the same, p. 227.

Nothing in London makes so disgusting an appearance to a foreigner, as the butchers' shops; especially in the environs of the Tower. Guts and all the nastiness are thrown into the middle of the street, and cause an insupportable stench.

(*c*) Vauxhall Gardens in Lambeth were fashionable at this time. They had been opened about 1661, but were developed especially after 1732. In 1859 they were finally closed.

Source: the same, pp. 39–41.

Vauxhall is, properly speaking, the name of a little Village in which the garden, . . . is situated. You pay a shilling on entrance.

On entering it, I really found, or fancied I found, some resemblance to our Berlin Vauxhall. . . . The walks at least, with the paintings at the end, and the high trees, which, here and there, form a beautiful grove or wood, on either side, were so similar to those of Berlin that often as I walked along them, I seemed to transport myself, in imagination, once more to Berlin. . . . Here and there (particularly in one of the charming woods which art has formed in this garden) you are pleasingly surprised by the sudden appearance of the statues of the most renowned English poets and philosophers; such as Milton, Thomson and others. But, what gave me most pleasure, was the statue of the German composer, Handel, which, on entering the garden, is not far distant from the orchestra.

This orchestra is among a number of trees situated as in a little wood, and is an exceedingly handsome one. As you enter the garden, you immediately hear the sound of vocal and instrumental music. There are several female singers constantly hired here to sing in public.

On each side of the orchestra are small boxes, with tables and benches, in which you sup. The walks before these, as well as in every other part of the garden, are crowded with people of all ranks. . . .

Latish in the evening, we were entertained with a sight, that is indeed singularly curious and interesting. In a particular part of the garden, a curtain was drawn up, and by means of some mechanism, of extraordinary ingenuity, the eye and the ear are so completely deceived, that it is not easy to persuade oneself it is a deception; and that one does not actually see and hear a natural waterfall from an high rock. As every one was flocking to this scene in crowds, there arose all at once, a loud cry of, ' Take care of your pockets '. This informed us, but too clearly, that there were some pick-pockets among the crowd; who had already made some fortunate strokes. . . .

THE EXECUTION OF KING LOUIS XVI OF FRANCE

Monday, January 21st, 1793

Source: The narrative of the Abbé Edgeworth in J. M. Thompson *English Witnesses of the French Revolution*, Basil Blackwell, 1938.

The Abbé Edgeworth (1745–1807) was an Irishman brought up in France. He was ordained priest and ministered especially to English and Irish Catholics in Paris. In 1791 he became confessor to the Princess Elizabeth, who recommended him to her brother, Louis XVI. The Abbé escaped to England in 1795. He was sent to Germany with messages for the future Louis XVIII, and died there of a fever contracted while ministering to some French prisoners of war.

. . . The King finding himself seated in the carriage, where he could neither speak to me nor be spoken to without witness, kept a profound silence. I presented him with my breviary, the only book I had with me, and he seemed to accept it with pleasure; he appeared anxious that I should point out to him the psalms that were most suited to his situation and he recited them attentively with me. The gendarmes, without speaking, seemed astonished and confounded at the tranquil piety of their monarch, to whom they doubtless never had before approached so near.

The procession lasted almost two hours; the streets were lined with citizens, all armed, some with pikes and some with guns, and the carriage was surrounded by a body of troops, formed of the most desperate people of Paris. As another precaution, they had placed before the horses a number of drums, intended to drown any noise or murmur in favour of the King; but how could they be heard? Nobody appeared either at the doors or windows, and in the street nothing was to be seen, but armed citizens—citizens, all rushing towards the commission of a crime, which perhaps they detested in their hearts.

The carriage proceeded thus in silence to the Place de Louis XV, and stopped in the middle of a large space that had been left round the scaffold: this space was surrounded with cannon, and beyond, an armed multitude extended as far as the eye could reach. As soon as the King perceived that the carriage stopped, he turned and whispered to me, ' We are arrived, if I mistake not '. My silence answered that we were. One of the guards came to open the carriage door, and the gendarmes would have jumped out, but the King stopped them, and leaning his arm on my knee, ' Gentlemen,' said he, with the tone of majesty, ' I recommend to you this good man; take care that after my death no insult be offered to him—I charge you to prevent it '. . . . As soon as the King had left the carriage, three guards surrounded him, and would have taken off his clothes, but he repulsed them with haughtiness; he undressed himself, untied his neckcloth, opened his shirt, and arranged it himself. The guards, whom the determined countenance of the King had for a moment disconcerted, seemed to recover their audacity. They surrounded him again, and would have seized his hands. ' What are you attempting?' said the King, drawing back his hands. ' To bind you', answered the wretches. ' To bind *me*,' said the King, with an indignant air. ' No! I shall never consent to that: do what you have been ordered, but you shall never bind me. . . .'

The path leading to the scaffold was extremely rough and difficult to pass; the King was obliged to lean on my arm, and from the slowness with which he proceeded, I feared for a moment that his courage might fail; but what was my astonishment, when arrived at the last step, I felt that he suddenly let go my arm, and I saw him cross with a firm foot the breadth of the whole scaffold; silence by his look alone, fifteen or twenty drums that were placed opposite to me; and in a voice so loud that it must have been heard at the Pont Tournant, I heard him pronounce distinctly these memorable words: ' I die innocent of all the crimes laid to my charge: I pardon those who have occasioned my death; and I pray to God that the blood you are going to shed may never be visited on France.'

He was proceeding, when a man on horseback, in the national uniform, and with a ferocious cry, ordered the drums to beat. Many voices were at the same time heard encouraging the executioners. They seemed reanimated themselves, in seizing with violence the most virtuous of Kings, they dragged him under the axe of the guillotine, which with one stroke severed his head from his body. All this passed in a moment. The youngest of the guards, who seemed about eighteen, immediately seized the head, and showed it to the people as he walked round the scaffold; he accompanied this monstrous ceremony with the most atrocious and indecent gestures. At first an awful silence prevailed; at length some cries of ' Vive la Republique! ' were heard. By degrees the voices multiplied, and in less than ten minutes this cry, a thousand times repeated, became the universal shout of the multitude, and every hat was in the air. . . .

OPINION IN ENGLAND

Source: Diary and Letters of Madame d'Arblay, Colburn, 1843, vol. v, p. 393. This extract is taken from a letter written by Dr. Burney to his daughter.

From a letter dated Monday, January 28th, 1793.

. . . I have been wholly without spirit for writing, reading, working, or even walking or conversing, ever since the first day of my arrival: the dreadful tragedy [execution of Louis XVI] acted in France has entirely absorbed me. Except the period of the illness of our own estimable King, I have never been so overcome with grief and dismay, for any but personal and family calamities. . . . We are all here expecting war every day. . . .

From a letter written by Dr. Burney. Thursday, January 31st, 1793.

. . . The cry of Charles Fox and his adherents, against a war on the French wild beasts, is so loud and clamorous, that I fear it will dismay honest men and real lovers of their country and constitution. He [Fox] has published a pamphlet, which furnishes plenty of words, though not one new argument. He has merely dilated his late Whig and Parliamentary speeches; . . . and urges stronger than ever the necessity of treating with France. . . .

At the Club [the Literary Club] on Tuesday, the fullest I ever knew, consisting of fifteen members, fourteen seemed all of one mind, and full of reflections on the late transaction in France; but, when about half the company was assembled, who should come in but Charles Fox! There were already three or four bishops arrived, hardly one of whom could look at him, I believe, without horror. After the first bow and cold salutation, the conversation stood still for several minutes.

LIFE IN THE NAVY

Source: Sir A. Phillimore, *Life of Admiral Sir William Parker:* 3 vols., 1876–80, and, a condensed version of the same book, Sir A. Phillimore: *The Last of Nelson's Captains.* Harrison.

William Parker entered the service when he was eleven years old; this was his first letter home.

Further Reading: The article in the *Dictionary of National Biography.* D. Mathew: *British Seamen,* Collins, 1947.

' Orion ', Spithead
Sunday Morn
February 24th 1793

My dearest Mother,

It gave me great pleasure to receive your kind letter, for which I thank you, and I have begun upon a large sheet the moment I received it. . . . I am very happy and as comfortable as if I was at home, and like it of all things; and I think I have every prospect of doing well, particularly under the care of so good a gentleman as Captain Duckworth, who is like a father to us all. Mr. Nevill and all on board are extremely kind to me. I have not yet gone higher than the maintop. We are to sail to the West Indies, and I have my things on shore being altered and made cooler for me. Pray tell Patty that I do not sleep in a hammock, but a cot, which is a much more comfortable thing, and that is not swung yet, so I manage very well. . . .

Sir John Jervis[1] has told Mr. Nevill (who he knows very well) to take care of me, and I assure you he does, and is by far the best friend I have on board (Captain Duckworth excepting); tells me to ask him anything I want, and often asks me questions in those rules of navigation I have gone through; . . . Captain Duckworth says, I shall not do any service of any kind before two years. But a Mr. Gray is so good as to say he will take me to watch with him in a year, and if he has a little sloop and goes with Captain Duckworth, he will take me with him, but do not mention a word about it to anybody, or in any of your letters. I am very glad to hear that Admiral Gardner is Admiral of our Fleet. Captain Duckworth is so good as to send for some plums, and other good things, for Messrs. Lane, Baker, and me.

My father has furnished me with a box of colours, drawing-books, and everything that could possibly amuse me. He sends me music and more drawings from town by Admiral Gardner. Captain Duckworth very often asks me to breakfast, dine, and drink tea with him. He desires his compliments to all our family. Nobody ever looks at our letters. I intend to get Sir John Jervis to forward this. . . . My paper being by this time filled, and I suppose I must have worn out your patience, I must conclude with desiring you to give my best love to all our family, and friends, and the servants.

And believe me, dearest Mother,

Your dutiful son,

W. Parker.

THE BATTLE OF THE GLORIOUS FIRST OF JUNE. Sunday June 1st, 1794

Rear-Admiral Villaret Joyeuse had been told by Robespierre that he would be guillotined if he did not escort safely to harbour the ships bringing American grain. The Rear-Admiral got the grain-ships

[1] Sir John Jervis was W. Parker's uncle.

through, but he lost seven of his battleships in doing it. England, hungry for victory, went wild over ' Black Dick ' Howe's achievement.

Source: Sir A Phillimore: *Life of Admiral Sir William Parker* and Sir A. Phillimore: *The Last of Nelson's Captains,* (condensed version of above). Harrison.

From a letter written by William Parker, who was 12 years old, to his father from *Orion.*

Further Reading: G. Callender: *Sea Kings of Britain,* vol. iii, Longmans, 1909. D. Mathew: *British Seamen,* Collins, 1947.

. . . on the 28th, about eight o'clock in the morning, we saw a large strange fleet to windward. . . . Lord Howe then made the signal to prepare for battle. At half-past eleven we could perceive them pretty distinctly formed in one line consisting of 30 sail, 26 of which were of the line of battle, and three three-deckers. We carried a great press of canvas, notwithstanding it blew very hard, to get to windward of them. We kept bearing up for them, and at four in the evening the signal was made for Admiral Paisley and his squadron to attack the enemy's rear. At eight o'clock Admiral Paisley got within gunshot and gave them a very warm and fierce reception, which the enemy returned with great vivacity. The whole of our fleet were now carrying all the sail they could get up with, and bring the French Fleet to action. At nine we beat to quarters and were in perfect readiness to pour a broadside into any of the enemy's ships we could bring our ships to bear on; the night being very dark it afforded a grand and awful sight from the flash of the guns. At half-past nine the firing ceased, owing to the wind blowing very hard and a rough sea preventing our ships from getting up with and bringing the enemy to action, which very much dissatisfied our officers and the ship's company.

·   ·   ·   ·

[May 29] The enemy fired chiefly at our rigging trying to dismast us, and we at their hulls, which we thought the best way of weakening them. It was surprising to see with what courage our men behaved; there were even some of them so eager that they jumped up in the rigging to huzza, and Captain Duckworth hauled them down by the legs. . . . We had not fired two broadsides before an unlucky shot cut a poor man's head right in two, and wounded Jno. Fane and four other youngsters like him very slightly. The horrid sight of this poor man I must confess did not help to raise my spirits. At twelve the bold and brave Admiral Gardner, according to custom, broke their line, upon which our ship's company gave three hearty cheers at their quarters; we then passed the whole of the French line, and were exposed to a very smart and close cannonading from the enemy, which we returned with very great warmth. We then lay-to to repair our rigging a little, when seeing their sternmost ship of 80 guns a little way ahead we bore up for her, and running close under her weather quarter let fly a broadside into her, which raked her fore and aft, and so effectually that it made the Frenchmen, according to custom, run from their quarters and huddle together down below, and the French captain was the only person seen upon deck, which he walked very resolutely and put every one of his men to sword whom he saw fly. . . .

[On the 30th and 31st foggy weather hid the enemy fleet]

Lord Howe always likes to begin in the morning and let us have a whole day at it. The next morning early the signal was made to form the line of battle. . . . At eight the action began, and the firing from the enemy was very smart before we could engage the ship that came to our turn to engage, as every ship is to have one because our line is formed ahead, and theirs is formed also. . . . I believe we were the ninth or tenth ship; our lot fell to an 80 gun ship, so we would not waste our powder and shot by firing at other ships, though I am sorry to say they fired very smartly at us and unluckily killed two men before we fired a gun, which so exasperated our men that they kept singing out, ' For God's sake, brave Captain, let us fire! Consider, sir, two poor souls are slaughtered already '. But Captain Duckworth would not let them fire till we came abreast of the ship we were to engage, when Captain Duckworth cried out, ' Fire, my boys, fire! ' upon which our enraged boys gave them such an extraordinary warm reception that I really believe it struck the rascals with the panic. . . . The smoke was so thick that we could not at all times see the ships engaging ahead and astern. Our main-top mast and main yard being carried away by the enemy's shot,

the Frenchmen gave three cheers, upon which our ship's company, to show they did not mind it, returned them the three
cheers, and after that, gave them a furious broadside. . . . At
about ten the ' Queen ' broke their line again, and we gave three
cheers at our quarters; and now we engaged which ever ship
we could best. A ship of 80 guns, which we had poured three
or four broadsides into on the 29th May, we saw drawing ahead
on our lee quarter to fire into us. . . . Their firing was not very
smart, though she contrived to send a red hot shot into the
Captain's cabin where I am quartered, which kept rolling about
and burning everybody, when gallant Mears, our first lieutenant,
took it up in his speaking trumpet and threw it overboard. At
last being so very close to her we supposed her men had left
their quarters. She bore down to leeward of the fleet being very
much disabled. . . . The ships that were not disabled still engaged
the enemy. . . . At two the firing ceased, but we did not know
whether the action was over or no. We were employed in getting
ready for engaging, and were very close to the Admiral and
perceived he had lost both his fore and main top masts in the
action, and two or three of our own ships totally dismasted.
There were seven of the Frenchmen also dismasted, but some
of them had still their colours flying. We saw one of them hoisting
a little small sail and egging down, and she would soon have
joined her own fleet had not Mr. Mears seen it, and let fly an
18-pounder right astern of her, which made her strike her colours
and hoist English, and strike her sail also. Captain Duckworth
ordered no more guns to be fired at her; and then we had it in
our power to say that she struck to the ' Orion '. The French
fleet then ran away like cowardly rascals, and we made all the
sail we could. Lord Howe ordered our ships that were not very
much disabled to take the prizes in tow. . . . But I forgot to tell
you that the ship which struck to us was so much disabled that
she could not live much longer upon the water, but gave a dreadful reel and lay down on her broadside. We were afraid to send
any boats to help them, because they would have sunk her by
too many poor souls getting into her at once. You could plainly
perceive the poor wretches climbing over to windward and crying
most dreadfully. She then righted a little, and then her head

went down gradually, and she sank. She after that rose again a little and then sunk, so that no more was seen of her. Oh, my dear father! when you consider of five or six hundred souls destroyed in that shocking manner, it will make your very heart relent. Our own men even were a great many of them in tears and groaning, they said God bless them. Oh, that we had come into a thousand engagements sooner than so many poor souls should be at once destroyed in that shocking manner. I really think it would have rent the hardest of hearts. We then bore away for England. . . .

AN ENCOUNTER WITH SMUGGLERS

Source: Recollections of James Anthony Gardner, Commander R.N., ed. Sir R. V. Hamilton and J. K. Laughton, Navy Records Society, 1906, pp. 258–259.

During part of the Napoleonic Wars, Gardner was stationed at the Signal Station, Fairlight, near Hastings.

Notwithstanding the many cruisers that were on the station and the unceasing look-out on the coast by the officers of the customs, the smugglers contrived to make several runs. One morning in the month of November the midshipman called me up a little before daylight, and reported that fifteen horses were in the field near the station, with Flushing jackets strapped on their backs, and made fast to the hedge, without anyone with them. As the day began to break, I went to the brow of the hill, and saw on the beach between two and three hundred people, and a boat a short way from the shore. The moment they got sight of me they set up a shout, and made use of horrible threats. However, I went down with the midshipman, and found some custom-house officers who had been up to their necks in water trying to get at the boat, but all to no purpose. The fellows on board seemed to be drunk, and held up some kegs which they stove; and making use of language the most vile, stood to the westward. I immediately dispatched the midshipman to give information to the custom-house and made the signal to the next station. A galley was soon after manned and armed, and after a long chase the smuggler was captured with several tubs of liquor. As I returned to my station the mob showed their heads just above the brow of the hill, and complimented me with three groans and then dispersed; and glad I was to see them clear off. They appeared to be all strangers, the custom-house officers declaring they had never seen one of them before. Some of them swore there would be a shot in our locker the first opportunity, and we expected they would have attacked us in the night; but we heard no more of them.

THE PRESS GANG

The great difficulty of the eighteenth-century navy was to get crews. Pay was low—a seaman could earn much more in the merchant navy; food was appalling; punishments were brutal. One of the chief methods of recruiting was impressment, and during the eighteenth century an official Impress Service was organised. Most pressed men were taken from merchant ships as they sailed into English waters at the end of a voyage, but the press also operated on shore.

Source: Landsman Hay, ed. M. D. Hay, Hart-Davis, 1953, pp. 216–220.

Robert Hay had run away to sea when he was 13. At the date of this incident (1811) he was 22. He had just landed from his ship when he was press-ganged. He was transferred to the *Ceres*, moored six miles from land at the Great Nore. With the help of inflated bladders he managed to swim ashore and thus to escape.

Further Reading: M. Lewis: *The Navy of Britain*, Allen and Unwin, 1948, pp. 307–32.

I was when crossing Towerhill accosted by a person in seamen's dress who tapped me on the shoulder enquiring in a familiar and technical strain 'What ship?' I assumed an air of gravity and surprise and told him I presumed he was under some mistake as I was not connected with shipping. The fellow, however, was too well acquainted with his business to be thus easily put off. He gave a whistle and in a moment I was in the hands of six or eight ruffians who I immediately dreaded and soon found to be a press gang. They dragged me hurriedly along through several streets amid bitter execrations bestowed on them, expressions of sympathy directed towards me and landed me in one of their houses of rendezvous. I was immediately carried into the presence of the Lieutenant of the gang, who questioned me as to my profession, . . . I made some evasive answers to these interrogations . . . but my hands being examined and found hard with work, and perhaps a little discoloured with tar . . . I was remanded for further examination.

Some of the gang then offered me spirits and attempted to comfort me. . . . The very scoundrel who first laid hold of me put on a sympathising look and observed what a pity it was to be pressed. . . . Such sympathy from such a source was well calculated to exasperate my feelings, but to think of revenge was folly. . . .

In a short time I was reconducted for further examination before the Lieutenant, who told me as I was in his hands and would assuredly be kept I might as well make a frank confession of my circumstances, it would save time and insure me better treatment. . . . I therefore acknowledged that I had been a voyage to the West Indies and had come home Carpenter of a ship. His eye seemed to brighten at this intelligence. ' I am glad of that, my lad,' said he, ' we are very much in want of Carpenters. Step along with these men and they will give you a passage on board.' I was then led back the way I came by the fellow who first seized me, put aboard of a pinnace at Tower Wharf and by midday was securely lodged on board the Enterprise.

As soon as the boat reached the ship I was sent down into the great cabin, in various parts of which tables were placed covered with green cloth, loaded with papers and surrounded with men well dressed and powdered. Such silence prevailed and such solemn gravity was displayed in every countenance that I was struck with awe and dread. . . . No sooner did I enter the cabin door than every eye was darted on me. . . .

A short sketch of what had passed between the press officer and myself had been communicated to the examining officer, for when I was ushered into his presence he thus addressed me:

' Well, young man, I understand you are a carpenter by trade.'

' Yes, sir.'

'And you have been at sea? '

' One voyage, sir.'

'Are you willing to join the King's Service? '

' No, sir.'

' Why? '

' Because I get much better wages in the merchant service and should I be unable to agree with the Captain I am at liberty to leave him at the end of the voyage.'

'As to wages,' said he, ' the chance of prize money is quite an equivalent and obedience and respect shown to your officers are all that is necessary to insure you good treatment. . . . Take my advice, my lad,' continued he, ' and enter the service cheerfully, you will then have a bounty, and be in a fair way for promotion. If you continue to refuse, remember you are aboard . . ., you will be kept as a pressed man and treated accordingly.'

I falteringly replied that I could not think of engaging in any service voluntarily when I knew of a better situation elsewhere. He said no more, but making a motion with his hand I was seized by two marines, hurried along towards the main hatchway with these words thundered in my ears, 'A pressed man to go below '. What injustice and mockery thought I . . . but my doom was fixed and I was thrust down among five or six score of miserable beings, who like myself had been kidnapped, and immured in the confined and unwholesome dungeon of a press room.

AN OFFICER AT SPITHEAD

Bad conditions and low pay caused the two mutinies in the Fleet in 1797, at the Nore and at Spithead.

Source: Recollections of James Anthony Gardner, Commander R.N., ed. Sir R. V. Hamilton and J. K. Laughton, Navy Records Society, 1906, pp. 192–3.

Further Reading: A. Bryant: The Years of Endurance, Collins, 1942, pp. 181–99. G. E. Manwaring and B. Dobrée: The Floating Republic, 1935.

On our arrival at Spithead, the latter end of April 1797, we found the fleet in a high state of mutiny. We had orders to fit for foreign service, and I had directions to go with a party of seamen and marines to the dockyard for new cables and stores. The mutiny, which in some measure had been suppressed, broke out afresh on board the London, 98, Vice-Admiral Colpoys, and some of the mutineers were killed; but the officers were overpowered and the admiral's flag struck by the scoundrels, and the bloody flag of defiance hoisted in its room. I went with my party to the yard in the morning, and began to get off the stores, when a marine said he would not assist in rousing the cable into the lighter and advised the others to knock off; upon which I told him if he did not immediately take hold of the cable with the rest I would cut him down (which was my intention). This had the effect and he went to work with the others. When I got on board our men were in a state of mutiny, and every ship at Spithead and St. Helen's the same. I had the first watch that night, and the master relieved me at twelve, and everything seemed quiet; but about three bells in the morning watch I was sent for by the captain, and on my coming on deck I found the ship's company assembled there and the captain, in the most impressive manner, requesting them to return to their duty, but all to no purpose. Had we been the only ship, we should soon have driven the scoundrels to the devil; but as we were situated, surrounded by line-of-battle ships acting in the same disgraceful manner, it would have been of little use to resist. About six a paper was handed up to the captain with the following order in writing:—

'It is the unanimous opinion of the ship's company that Captain Bazeley, Lieutenants Hickey and Gardner, Mr. White the purser, and Messrs. Kinneer and Allen, midshipmen, are to quit the ship by 6, or violent measures will be taken to enforce the order.'

Soon after 6 the barge was manned and armed; every vagabond had a cutlass, and our trunks were handed in, with orders from the delegates not to carry them anywhere for us. I had a brace of pistols with a double charge which I put in my greatcoat pockets in case I should want their assistance. It was blowing a gale of wind at N E when we left the ship, and near ten o'clock before we landed on Point Beach; our things were handed out, and I desired the bowman and one or two more, who I knew to be great scoundrels, to take them to Turner's (living on the beach, and only a step from the boat) shewing them at the same time my pistols and saying, ' You understand me '. They then most reluctantly took our things to the place I directed. This was all I wanted, as I heard some of the ringleaders say as we were quitting the ship that if any of the boat's crew assisted in taking our things to any place after landing they should be severely

K

ducked on their return; and they were as good as their word; for those fellows got a fine ducking the moment they got on board, the others having reported them.

LORD NELSON'S WAY OF LIFE

Son of the rector of Burnham Thorpe in Norfolk, he entered the Navy in 1770. On the outbreak of war in 1793 he was appointed to the *Agamemnon* of sixty-four guns, to proceed to the Mediterranean. In 1796 he became Commodore. He played a conspicuous part in the victory of Cape St. Vincent in 1797, became a rear-admiral, won the battle of the Nile in 1798 and was then created Baron Nelson of the Nile. In 1801 he played the chief part in the bombardment of Copenhagen and was made a viscount. In 1805 he gained the decisive battle of Trafalgar; but, being struck by a musket ball from the mizzen top of the *Redoubtable*, he died three hours later just as victory was assured. He was buried in St. Paul's.

This description of Nelson's way of life comes towards the end of the *Narrative* of Dr. Beatty, the surgeon on the *Victory*.

Source: Despatches and Letters of Vice-Admiral Lord Viscount Nelson, ed. Nicolas, Murray, 1846, vol. vii, pp. 260–1.

Further Reading: Carola Oman: *Nelson,* Hodder and Stoughton, 1947. D. Mathew: *British Seamen,* Collins, 1947.

His Lordship used a great deal of exercise, generally walking on deck six or seven hours in the day. He always rose early, for the most part shortly after daybreak. He breakfasted in summer about six, and at seven in winter; and if not occupied in reading or writing despatches, or examining into the details of the Fleet, he walked on the quarter-deck the greater part of the forenoon; going down to his cabin occasionally to commit to paper such incidents or reflections as occurred to him during that time, and as might be hereafter useful to the service of his country. He dined generally about half-past two o'clock. At his table there were seldom less than eight or nine persons, consisting of the different officers of the ship. . . . At dinner he was alike affable and attentive to every one; he ate very sparingly himself; the liver and wing of a fowl, and a small plate of macaroni, in general composing his meal, during which he occasionally took a glass of champagne. He never exceeded four glasses of wine after dinner, and seldom drank three; and even those were diluted with either Bristol or common water.

. . . He possessed such a wonderful activity of mind, as even prevented him from taking ordinary repose, seldom enjoying two hours of uninterrupted sleep; and on several occasions he did not quit the deck during the whole night. At these times he took no pains to protect himself from the effects of wet, or the night air, wearing only a thin great coat; and he has frequently, after having his clothes wet through with rain, refused to have them changed, saying that the leather waistcoat which he wore over his flannel one would secure him from complaint. He seldom wore boots, and was consequently very liable to have his feet wet. When this occurred he has often been known to go down to his cabin, throw off his shoes, and walk on the carpet in his stockings for the purpose of drying the feet of them. He chose rather to adopt this uncomfortable expedient, than to give his servants the trouble of assisting him to put on fresh stockings; which, from his having only one hand, he could not himself conveniently effect.

THE BATTLE OF THE NILE
Wednesday, August 1st, 1798

(a) *Source:* Narrative of Midshipman the Hon. George Elliot on board the *Goliath* quoted Fraser: *Sailors whom Nelson Led*, Methuen, 1913, pp. 86 et sqq.

Further Reading: D. Mathew: *The Naval Heritage*, Collins, 1945. *British Seamen*, Collins, 1947.

I, as signal-midshipman, was sweeping round the horizon ahead with my glass from the royal-yard, when I discovered the French fleet at anchor in Aboukir Bay. The *Zealous* was so close to us that, had I hailed the deck, they must have heard me. I therefore slid down by the backstay and reported what I had seen. We instantly made the signal, but the under-toggle of the upper flag at the main came off, breaking the stop, and the lower flag came down. The compass-signal, however, was clear at the peak; but before we could recover our flag, *Zealous* made the signal for the enemy's fleet; whether from seeing our compass-signal or not I never heard. But we thus lost the little credit of first signalling the enemy, which, as signal-midshipman, rather affected me. . . .

When we were nearly within gunshot, standing as A.D.C. close to Captain Foley, I heard him say to the Master that he wished he could get inside the leading ship of the enemy's line (the *Guerrier*). I immediately looked for the buoy or her anchor, and saw it apparently at the usual distance of a cable's length—i.e. 200 yards—which I reported. They both looked at it, and agreed there was room to pass between the ship and her anchor (the danger was the ship being close up to the edge of the shoal), and it was decided to do it. The Master then had orders to go forward and drop the anchor the moment it was a ship's breadth inside the French ship, so that we should not actually swing on board of her. All this was exactly executed.

I also heard Foley say he should not be surprised to find the Frenchman unprepared for action on the inner side; and as we passed her bow I saw he was right. Her lower-deck guns were not run out, and there was lumber, such as bags and boxes, on the upper-deck ports, which I reported with no small pleasure. We first fired a broadside into the bow. Not a shot could miss at the distance. The *Zealous* did the same, and in less than a quarter of an hour this ship was a perfect wreck, without a mast, or a broadside gun to fire.

. . . The French captains were all on board their Admiral's ship, and did not expect us to come in that night. They had sent for their boats to return from the shore where they were procuring water. The senior officer of the van division, seeing us stand on under all sail, got anxious, and sent his own boat to hasten off the boats of his division without waiting to fill with water. She had not got back when we were getting very close, and as his own launch was passing the flag-ship, half-laden with water, he got into her, but she pulled up slowly against the fresh sea-breeze and did not reach his ship till we had passed her. I saw him waving his hat, and evidently calling to his ship, when still at a considerable distance. An officer was leaning against his ensign staff listening. At last this officer ran forward to the poop and down to the lower deck. We knew what was coming, and off went their whole broadside, but just too late to hit us, and passed harmlessly between us and *Zealous*, and before he could give a second broadside *Zealous* was past his range. We therefore both got up to our places without injury of any sort, and were able to take up the exact positions we wished, neither ship returning a single shot. . . . *Zealous* exactly followed *Goliath's* example, but the enemy being occupied, she furled her sails, and anchoring a little more to windward, veered into the place just left by the *Goliath*. From this moment the *Guerrier* never fired a shot, except from her stern guns; she had been practically destroyed in five minutes by her two opponents. As the *Goliath* passed her quarter the *Guerrier's* foremast fell by the deck, and five minutes after the main and mizen fell, and also the main of the *Conquérant*. . . . As the *Theseus* passed the *Goliath* in getting to her station, she gave her three tremendous cheers. Returned by the *Goliath's* crew and an attempt made by the French to copy, but the effort was ridiculous, and caused shouts of laughter in our ships, loud enough to be heard by both sides. The French admitted that the enthusiastic cheers were very disheartening to them.

(*b*) *Source:* Narrative of Captain Sir Edward Berry in *Vanguard* from *Despatches and Letters of Vice-Admiral Lord Viscount Nelson*, ed. Nicolas, vol. iii, pp. 48 et sqq.

The enemy appeared to be moored in a strong and compact Line of Battle, close in with the shore, their line describing an obtuse angle in its form, flanked by numerous Gun-boats, four Frigates, and a battery of guns and mortars, on an Island in their Van. This situation of the enemy seemed to secure to them the most decided advantages, as they had nothing to attend to but their artillery, in their superior skill in the use of which the French so much pride themselves, and to which indeed their splendid series of land victories are in a great measure to be imputed.

The position of the enemy presented the most formidable obstacles; but the Admiral viewed these with the eye of a seaman determined on attack, and it instantly struck his eager and penetrating mind, that where there was room for an enemy's ship to swing, there was room for one of ours to anchor. No further signal was necessary than those which had already been made. The Admiral's designs were as fully known to his whole squadron, as was his determination to conquer or perish in the attempt. The *Goliath* and *Zealous* had the honour to lead inside, and to receive the first fire from the van ships of the enemy. . . . These two ships, with the *Orion*, *Audacious* and *Theseus*, took their stations inside of the enemy's line, and were immediately in close action. The *Vanguard* anchored the first on the outer side of the enemy, and was opposed within half pistol-shot to *Le Spartiate*, the third in the enemy's line. In standing in, our leading ships were unavoidably obliged to receive into their bows the whole fire of the broadsides of the French line; until they could take their respective stations. . . . At this time the necessary number of our men were employed aloft in furling sails, and on deck, in hauling the braces, etc., preparatory to our casting anchor. As soon as this took place, a most animated fire was opened from the *Vanguard*, which ship covered the approach of those in the rear, which were following in a close line. The *Minotaur*, *Defence*, *Bellerophon*, *Majestic*, *Swiftsure*, and *Alexander*, came up in succession, and passing within hail of the *Vanguard*, took their respective stations opposed to the enemy's line. . . . Captain Thompson, of the *Leander*, of 50 guns, . . . advanced towards the enemy's line on the outside, and most judiciously dropped his anchor athwart hause of *Le Franklin*, raking her with great success, the shot from the *Leander's* broadside which passed that ship all striking *L'Orient*, the flag-ship of the French Commander-in-Chief.

The action commenced at sun-set which was at thirty-one minutes past six p.m., with an ardour and vigour, which it is impossible to describe. At about seven o'clock total darkness had come on, but the whole hemisphere was, with intervals, illuminated by the fire of the hostile fleets. Our ships, when darkness came on, had all hoisted their distinguishing lights, by a signal from the Admiral. The van ship of the enemy, *Le Guerrier*, was dismasted in less than twelve minutes, and, in ten minutes after, the second ship, *Le Conquérant*, and the third, *Le Spartiate*, very nearly at the same moment were almost dismasted. *L'Aquilon* and *Le Souverain Peuple*, the fourth and fifth ships of the enemy's line, were taken possession of by the British at half-past eight in the evening. Captain Berry, at that hour, sent Lieutenant Galwey, of the *Vanguard*, with a party of marines, to take possession of *Le Spartiate*, and that officer returned by the boat the French captain's sword, which Captain Berry immediately delivered to the Admiral, who was then below, in consequence of the severe wound which he had received in the head during the heat of the attack. At this time it appeared that victory had already declared itself in our favour, for although *L'Orient*, *L'Heureux*, and *Tonnant* were not taken possession of, they were considered as completely in our power, which pleasing intelligence Captain Berry had likewise the satisfaction of communicating in person to the Admiral. At ten minutes after nine, a fire was observed on board *L'Orient*, the French admiral's ship, which seemed to proceed from the after part of the cabin, and which increased with great rapidity, presently involving the whole of the after part of the ship in flames. This circumstance Captain Berry immediately communicated to the Admiral, who, though suffering severely from his wound, came up on deck, where the first consideration that struck his mind was concern for the danger of so many lives, to save as many as possible of whom he ordered Captain Berry to make every practicable exertion. A boat, the only one that could swim, was instantly despatched from the *Vanguard*, and other ships that were in a condition to do so immediately followed the example; by which means, from the best possible information the lives of about seventy Frenchmen were saved. The light thrown by the fire of *L'Orient* upon the surrounding objects, enabled us to perceive with more certainty the situation of the two fleets, the colours of both being clearly distinguishable. The cannonading was partially kept up to leeward of the centre till about ten o'clock, when *L'Orient* blew up with a most tremendous explosion. An awful pause and death-like silence for about three minutes ensued, when the wreck of the masts, yards etc. which had been carried to a vast height, fell down into the water, and on board the surrounding ships. A port fire from *L'Orient* fell into the main royal of the *Alexander*, the fire occasioned by which was, however, extinguished in about two minutes, by the active exertions of Captain Ball.

After this awful scene, the firing was recommenced with the ships to leeward of the centre, till twenty minutes past ten, when there was a total cessation of firing for about ten minutes, after which it was revived till about three in the morning when it again ceased. . . . The whole of the 2nd was employed in securing the French ships that had struck. . . . The Admiral, knowing that the wounded of his own ships had been well taken care of, bent his first attention to those of the enemy. He established a truce with the Commandant of Aboukir, and through him made a communication to the Commandant of Alexandria, that it was his intention to allow all the wounded Frenchmen to be taken ashore to proper hospitals.

(c) *Source:* Narrative of John Nichol, one of the gunner's crew on board the *Goliath*, quoted E. Fraser, *Sailors whom Nelson Led*, pp. 103–5.

The sun was just setting as we went into the bay, and a red and fiery sun it was. I would, if I had had my choice, been on deck; there I would have seen what was passing, and the time would not have hung so heavy; but every man does his duty with spirit, whether his station be in the slaughter-house or in the magazine. (The seamen call the lower deck, near the main-mast, ' the slaughter-house ', as it is amidships, and the enemy aim their fire principally at the body of the ship.) My station was in the powder-magazine with the gunner. As we entered the bay we stripped to our trousers, opened our ports, cleared, and every ship we passed gave them a broadside and three cheers. Any information we got was from the boys and women who carried the powder. They behaved as well as the men, and got a present for their bravery from the Grand Signior. When the French Admiral's ship blew up, the *Goliath* got such a shake we thought the after-part of her had blown up until the boys told us what it was. They brought us every now and then the cheering news of another French ship having struck, and we answered the cheers on deck with heartfelt joy. In the heat of the action, a shot came right into the magazine, but did no harm, as the carpenters plugged it up, and stopped the water that was rushing in. I was much indebted to the gunner's wife, who gave her husband and me a drink of wine every now and then, which lessened our fatigue much. There were some of the women wounded, and one woman belonging to Leith died of her wounds, and was buried on a small island in the bay. One woman bore a son in the heat of the action; she belonged to Edinburgh.

When we ceased firing, I went on deck to view the state of the fleets, and an awful sight it was. The whole bay was covered with dead bodies, mangled, wounded, and scorched, not a bit of clothes on them except their trousers. There were a number of French, belonging to the French Admiral's ship, the *L'Orient*, who had swam to the *Goliath*, and were cowering under her forecastle. Poor fellows! they were brought on board, and Captain Foley ordered them down to the steward's room, to get provisions and clothing. One thing I observed in these Frenchmen quite different from anything I had before observed. In the American War, when we took a French ship, the *Duc de Chartres*, the prisoners were as merry as if they had taken us, only saying, ' Fortune de guerre—you take me today, I take you tomorrow '. Those we now had on board were thankful for our kindness, but were sullen and downcast as if each had lost a ship of his own.

. . . The only incidents I heard of are two. One lad who was stationed by a salt-box, on which he sat to give out cartridges, and keep the lid close—it is a trying berth—when asked for a cartridge, he gave none, yet he sat upright; his eyes were open. One of the men gave him a push; he fell all his length on the deck. There was not a blemish on his body, yet he was quite dead, and was thrown overboard. The other, a lad who had the match in his hand to fire his gun. In the act of applying it, a shot took off his arm; it hung by a small piece of skin. The match fell to the deck. He looked to his arm, and seeing what had happened, seized the match in his left hand, and fired off the gun before he went to the cockpit to have it dressed. They were in our mess, or I might never have heard of it. Two of the mess were killed, and I knew not of it until the day after. Thus terminated the glorious first of August, the busiest night in my life.

A FRENCH ACCOUNT

Source: Translation of the French Rear-Admiral Blanquet's Account of the Battle of the Nile. *Despatches and Letters of Vice-Admiral Lord Viscount Nelson*, ed. Nicolas, Murray, 1846, vol. iii, p. 67.

At half-past five, the headmost ships of our line, being

within gun-shot of the English, the Admiral made the signal to engage, which was not obeyed until the enemy were within pistol shot and just doubling us. The action then became very warm. . . .

All the van were attacked on both sides by the enemy who ranged close along our line. . . . At a quarter past six, the *Franklin* opened her fire upon the enemy from the starboard side: at three-quarters past six, she was engaged on both sides. *L'Orient* at the same time began firing her starboard guns, and at 7 o'clock, the *Tonnant* opened her fire. All the ships, from the *Guerrier* to the *Tonnant* were now engaged against a superior force: this only redoubled the ardour of the French who kept up a very heavy and regular fire. At 8 o'clock at night, the ship which was engaging *L'Orient*, on the starboard quarter, notwithstanding her advantageous position, was dismasted and so roughly treated, that she cut her cables, and drove rather far from the Line. This event gave the *Franklin* hopes that *L'Orient* would now be able to assist her by attacking one of the ships opposed to her; but, at this very moment, the two ships that had been perceived astern of the fleet, and were quite fresh, steered right for the centre. One of them anchored on *L'Orient*'s starboard bow, and the other cut the line, astern of *L'Orient*, and anchored on her larboard quarter. The action in this part then became extremely warm. Admiral de Brueys. . . very soon received a shot in the belly, which almost cut him in two. He desired not to be carried below, but to be left to die upon deck. He only lived a quarter of an hour. Rear Admiral Blanquet . . . received a severe wound in the face which knocked him down. He was carried off the deck, senseless. . . . At a quarter past 9 o'clock *L'Orient* caught fire in the cabin; it soon afterwards broke out upon the poop. Every effort was made to extinguish it, but without effect. . . . At half-past nine, Citizen Gillet, Capitaine de Pavillon of the *Franklin*, was very severely wounded, and carried off the deck. At three quarters past nine, the arm chest, filled with musket-cartridges, blew up, and set fire to several places on the poop and quarter-deck but was fortunately extinguished. Her situation, however, was still very desperate, surrounded by enemies, and only eighty fathoms to windward of *L'Orient*, (entirely on fire) there could not be any other expectation than falling a prey to the enemy or the flames. . . . Those of the . . . ship's company of *L'Orient* who had escaped death, convinced of the impossibility of extinguishing the fire . . . endeavoured to save themselves. . . . The Adjutant-General Motard, although badly wounded, swam to the ship nearest *L'Orient*, which proved to be English. Commodore Casabianca and his son, only ten years old, who during the action gave proofs of bravery and intelligence far above his age, were not so fortunate. They were in the water, upon the wreck of *L'Orient*'s mast (not being able to swim) seeking each other, until three-quarters past ten, when the ship blew up, and put an end to their hopes and fears. The explosion was dreadful, and spread the fire all round to a considerable distance. The *Franklin*'s decks were with red-hot pincers, pieces of timber, and rope, on fire. . . . Immediately after the tremendous explosion, the action ceased everywhere, and was succeeded by the most profound silence. The sky was obscured by thick clouds of black smoke, which seemed to threaten the destruction of the two fleets. It was a quarter of an hour before the ships' crews recovered from the kind of stupor they were thrown into. Towards eleven o'clock, the *Franklin*, anxious to preserve the trust confided to her, recommenced the action with a few of her lower-deck guns; all the rest were dismounted, two-thirds of her ship's company being killed or wounded and those who remained much fatigued. She was surrounded by enemy's ships, some of which were within pistol shot and who mowed down the men every broadside. At half past 11 o'clock, having only three lower-deck guns that could defend the honour of the flag, it became necessary to put an end to so disproportioned a struggle; and Citizen Martinet, captain of a frigate, ordered the Colours to be struck. . . .

THE BATTLE OF COPENHAGEN
Thursday, April 2nd, 1801

In 1800 Russia, Prussia, Sweden and Denmark formed the Armed Neutrality to resist the British policy of preventing neutral trade with France. The Danish fleet was the most powerful force at the disposal of this new organisation. It was essential for England to act vigorously against this threat, and a fleet, under the command of Sir Hyde Parker, was sent against the Danes. The new First Lord of the Admiralty, Earl St. Vincent, insisted on the appointment of Nelson as second-in-command.

(a) *Source:* At a Council of War held on March 31st in the *London. Despatches and Letters of Vice Admiral Lord Nelson,* Vol. IV, p. 303. Narrative of Colonel Stewart, who commanded the troops with the fleet.

During this Council of War, the energy of Lord Nelson's character was remarked: certain difficulties had been started by some of the members, relative to each of the three Powers we should either have to engage, in succession or united, in those seas. The number of the Russians was, in particular, represented as formidable. Lord Nelson kept pacing the cabin, mortified at everything which savoured either of alarm or irresolution. When the above remark was applied to the Swedes, he sharply observed, ' The more numerous the better ': and when to the Russians, he repeatedly said, ' So much the better, I wish they were twice as many, the easier the victory, depend on it '. He alluded, as he afterwards explained in private, to the total want of tactique among the Northern Fleets; and to his intention, whenever he should bring either the Swedes or Russians to action, of attacking the head of their line, and confusing their movements as much as possible. He used to say, ' Close with a Frenchman, but out-manoeuvre a Russian '.

(b) *Source:* the same, Vol. IV, p. 304. Narrative of Stewart.

On board the *Elephant,* the night of the 1st of April was an important one. As soon as the Fleet was at anchor, the gallant Nelson sat down to table with a large party of his comrades in arms. He was in the highest spirits, and drank to a leading wind, and to the success of the ensuing day. Captains Foley, Hardy, Fremantle, Riou, Inman, his Lordship's second-in-command, Admiral Graves, and a few others to whom he was particularly attached, were of this interesting party; from which every man separated with feelings of admiration for their great leader, and with anxious impatience to follow him to the approaching battle. The signal to prepare for action had been made early in the evening. All the captains retired to their respective ships, Riou excepted, who with Lord Nelson and Foley arranged the order of battle, and those instructions that were to be issued to each ship on the succeeding day. These three officers retired between nine and ten, to the after-cabin, and drew up those orders that have been generally published. . . . From the previous fatigue of this day, and of the two preceding, Lord Nelson was so much exhausted while dictating his instructions, that it was recommended to him by us all, and indeed, insisted upon by his old servant, Allen, who assumed much command on these occasions, that he should go to his cot. It was placed on the floor, but from it he still continued to dictate. . . . The orders were completed about one o'clock, when half a dozen clerks in the foremost cabin proceeded to transcribe them. Lord Nelson's impatience again showed itself; for instead of sleeping undisturbedly, as he might have done, he was every half hour calling from his cot to these clerks to hasten their work, for that the wind was becoming fair: he was constantly receiving a report of this during the night. Their work being finished about six in the morning, his Lordship, who was previously up and dressed, breakfasted, and about seven made the signal for all captains. The instructions were given to each by eight o'clock. . . .

(c) *Source:* the same, vol. iv, pp. 308–10. Narrative of Stewart.

Lord Nelson was at this time, as he had been during the whole action, walking the starboard side of the quarter-deck; sometimes much animated, and at others heroically fine in his observations. A shot through the mainmast knocked a few splinters about us. He observed to me, with a smile, ' It is warm work, and this day may be the last to any of us at a moment '; and then stopping short at the gangway, he used an expression never to be erased from my memory, and said with emotion, ' but mark you, I would not be elsewhere for thousands '. When the signal, No. 39[1] was made, the Signal Lieutenant reported it to him. He continued his walk, and did not appear to take notice of it. The Lieutenant meeting his Lordship at the next turn asked, whether he should repeat it. Lord Nelson answered, ' No, acknowledge it '. On the Officer returning to the poop, his

[1] To discontinue the engagement.

Lordship called after him, 'Is No. 16[1] still hoisted?' The Lieutenant answering in the affirmative, Lord Nelson said, 'Mind you keep it so'. He now walked the deck considerably agitated, which was always known by his moving the stump of his right arm. After a turn or two, he said to me, in a quick manner, 'Do you know what's shown on board of the Commander-in-Chief, No. 39?' On asking him what that meant, he answered, 'Why, to leave off action'. 'Leave off action!' he repeated, and then added, with a shrug, 'Now, damn me if I do'. He also observed, I believe, to Captain Foley, 'You know, Foley, I have only one eye—I have a right to be blind sometimes'; and then with an archness peculiar to his character, putting the glass to his blind eye, exclaimed, 'I really do not see the signal'. This remarkable signal was, therefore, only acknowledged on board the *Elephant*, not repeated. Admiral Graves did the latter, not being able to distinguish the *Elephant's* conduct: either by a fortunate accident, or intentionally, No. 16 was not displaced. The squadron of frigates obeyed the signal, and hauled off. That brave officer, Captain Riou, was killed by a raking shot, when the *Amazon* showed her stern to the *Trekoner*. He was sitting on a gun, was encouraging his men, and had been wounded in the head by a splinter. He had expressed himself grieved at being thus obliged to retreat, and nobly observed, 'What will Nelson think of us?' His clerk was killed by his side; and by another shot, several of the Marines, while hauling on the main-brace, shared the same fate. Riou then exclaimed, 'Come then, my boys, let us die all together!' The words were scarcely uttered, when the fatal shot severed him in two. . . .

The action now continued with unabated vigour. About 2 p.m. the greater part of the Danish line had ceased to fire; some of the lighter ships were adrift, and the carnage on board of the enemy, who reinforced their crews from the shore, was dreadful. The taking possession of such ships as had struck was, however, attended with difficulty; partly by reason of the batteries on Anak Island protecting them, and partly because an irregular fire was made on our boats, as they approached, from the ships themselves. The *Dannebrog* acted in this manner, and fired at our boat, although that ship was not only on fire and had

[1] 'For close action' which had been flying from the beginning.

struck, but the Commodore, Fischer, had removed his Pendant and had deserted her. A renewed attack on her by the *Elephant* and *Glatton*, for a quarter of an hour, completely silenced and disabled the *Dannebrog*. . . . On our smoke clearing away, the *Dannebrog* was found to be drifting in flames before the wind, spreading terror throughout the enemy's line. The usual lamentable scene then ensued; and our boats rowed in every direction, to save the crew, who were throwing themselves from her at every port-hole; few, however, were left unwounded in her after our last broadsides, or could be saved. She drifted to leeward, and about half-past three blew up. . . . After the *Dannebrog* was adrift, and had ceased to fire, the action was found to be over, along the whole of the line astern of us; but not so with the ships ahead and with the Crown batteries. Whether from ignorance of the custom of war, or from confusion on board the Prizes, our boats were, as before mentioned, repulsed from the ships themselves, or fired at from Anak Island. Lord Nelson naturally lost temper at this, and observed: ' That he must either send on shore, and stop this irregular proceeding, or send in our fire-ships and burn them.' He accordingly retired into the stern galley, and wrote, with great dispatch, that well-known letter addressed to the Crown Prince, with the address,—' To the Brothers of Englishmen, the brave Danes ' etc.: and this letter was conveyed on shore through the contending fleets.

THE BATTLE OF TRAFALGAR
Monday, October 21st, 1805

When Nelson joined the Fleet watching off Cadiz, Codrington wrote: ' Lord Nelson is arrived, and a sort of general joy has been the consequence.' The victory which followed was overwhelming. Of the 33 ships in the Combined Fleet, 18 were captured, four which escaped surrendered two weeks later to Sir Richard Strachan, eleven reached Cadiz never to put to sea again, and 20,000 prisoners were taken. As Collingwood said: ' There never was so complete an annihilation of a fleet.'

(a) *Source:* Surgeon Beatty in the *Victory*. His narrative quoted in *Dispatches and Letters of Lord Nelson*, ed. Nicholas, pp. 137–139.

Further Reading: A. Bryant, *The Years of Victory*, Collins, 1944, pp. 154–75. J. S. Corbett, *The Campaign of Trafalgar*, Longmans, 1910. D. Mathew: *British Seamen*, Collins, 1947, and *The Naval Heritage*, 1945.

Soon after daylight, Lord Nelson came upon deck; he was dressed as usual in his Admiral's frock-coat, bearing on the left breast four stars of different orders, which he always wore with his common apparel. . . . He displayed excellent spirits, and expressed his pleasure at the prospect of giving a fatal blow to the naval power of France and Spain; and spoke with confidence of obtaining a signal victory, notwithstanding the inferiority of the British Fleet, declaring to Captain Hardy that he would not be contented with capturing less than twenty sail of the Line. . . . The wind was now from the west, but the breezes were very light, with a long, heavy swell running. The signal being made for bearing down upon the enemy in two lines, the British Fleet set all possible sail. The Lee Line, consisting of thirteen ships, was led by Admiral Collingwood in the *Royal Sovereign*, and the Weather Line, composed of fourteen ships, by the Commander-in-Chief in the *Victory*.

His Lordship ascended the poop, to have a better view of both Lines of the British Fleet, and while there gave particular directions for taking down from his cabin the different fixtures. . . .

Immediately after this he quitted the poop, and retired to his cabin for a few minutes. [Here Nelson composed a prayer and added a codicil to his will.]

(*b*) *Source:* Second-Lieutenant Ellis of the Marines of the *Ajax* quoted in *Sailors whom Nelson Led*—Edward Fraser, London 1913, pp. 215–216.

I was sent below with orders, and was much struck with the preparations made by the bluejackets, the majority of whom were stripped to the waist; a handkerchief was tightly bound round their heads and over the ears, to deaden the noise of the cannon, many men being deaf for days after an action. The men were variously occupied; some were sharpening their cutlasses, others polishing the guns, as though an inspection were about to take place instead of a mortal combat, whilst three or four, as if in mere bravado, were dancing a horn-pipe; but all seemed deeply anxious to come to close-quarters with the enemy. Occasionally they would look out of the ports; and speculate as to the various ships of the enemy, many of which had been on former occasions engaged by our vessels. . . .

(c) *Source:* Midshipman Badcock of the *Neptune.* The same, p. 218.

In our fleet Union Jacks and ensigns were made fast to the fore and fore-topmast-stays, as well as to the mizen rigging, besides one at the peak, in order that we might not mistake each other in the smoke, and to show the enemy our determination to conquer. Towards eleven our two lines were better formed, but still there existed long gaps in Vice-Admiral Collingwood's division. Lord Nelson's van was strong: three three-deckers— *Victory, Temeraire,* and *Neptune*—and four seventy-fours, their jib-booms nearly over the others' taffrails. The bands playing: 'God Save the King', 'Rule Britannia', and 'Britons Strike Home'. The crews stationed on the forecastles of the different ships, cheering the ship ahead of them when the enemy began to fire, sent those feelings to our hearts that ensured victory.

(d) *Source:* Captain Blackwood: Nicholas, *Letters and Despatches* vol. vii, p. 149.

I was walking with him [Lord Nelson] on the poop when he said, 'I'll now amuse the fleet with a signal', and he asked me if I did not think there was one yet wanting. I answered that I thought the whole of the Fleet seemed very clearly to understand what they were about, and to vie with each other who should first get nearest to the *Victory* or *Royal Sovereign.* These words were scarcely uttered when his last well known signal was made: 'England expects every man will do his duty'. The shout with which it was received throughout the fleet was truly sublime. 'Now,' said Lord Nelson, 'I can do no more. We must trust to the Great Disposer of all Events, and the justice of our cause. I thank God for this great opportunity of doing my duty.'

(e) Second-Lieutenant Ellis. *Sailors whom Nelson Led,* 226–227.

I was desired to inform those on the main-deck of the Admiral's signal. Upon acquainting one of the quarter-masters of the order, he assembled the men with 'Avast there, lads, come and hear the Admiral's words'. When the men were mustered, I delivered with becoming dignity the sentence, rather anticipating that the effect on the men would be to awe them by its grandeur. Jack, however, did not appreciate it, for there were murmurs from some, whilst others in an audible whisper, mur-

L

mured, ' Do our duty! Of course we'll do our duty! I've always done mine, haven't you? Let us come alongside of 'em, and we'll soon show whether we'll do our duty '. Still the men cheered vociferously—more, I believe, from love and admiration of their Admiral and leader than from a full appreciation of this well-known signal.

(*f*) *Source:* Surgeon Beatty. *Sailors whom Nelson Led,* pp. 230–234.

At fifty minutes past eleven the enemy opened their fire on the Commander-in-Chief. . . . In a very short time afterwards Mr. Scott, Public Secretary to the Commander-in-Chief, was killed by a cannon-shot while in conversation with Captain Hardy. Lord Nelson being then near them; Captain Adair, of the Marines, with the assistance of a seaman, endeavoured to remove the body from his Lordship's sight: but he had already observed the fall of his secretary; and now said with anxiety, ' Is that poor Scott that is gone? ' and on being answered in the affirmative by Captain Adair, he replied, ' Poor fellow! '

Lord Nelson and Captain Hardy walked the quarter-deck in conversation for some time after this, while the enemy kept up an incessant raking fire.

A double-headed shot struck one of the party of Marines drawn up on the poop and killed eight of them. When his Lordship, perceiving this, ordered Captain Adair to disperse his men round the ship, that they might not suffer so much from being together.

In a few minutes afterwards a shot struck the fore-brace bits on the quarter-deck, and passed between Lord Nelson and Captain Hardy; a splinter from the bits bruising Captain Hardy's foot, and tearing the buckle from his shoe. They both instantly stopped, and were observed by the officers on deck to survey each other with inquiring looks, each supposing the other to be wounded. His Lordship then smiled, and said: ' This is too warm work, Hardy, to last long ', and declared that through all the battles he had been in, he had never witnessed more cool courage than was displayed by the *Victory's* crew on this occasion.

The *Victory* by this time, having approached close to the enemy's van, had suffered very severely without firing a single gun: she had lost about twenty men killed, and had about thirty wounded. . . .

At four minutes past twelve o'clock, she opened her fire, from both sides of her decks upon the enemy; when Captain Hardy represented to his Lordship, that it appeared impracticable to pass through the enemy's Line without going on board some of their ships, Lord Nelson answered, ' I cannot help it: it does not signify which we run on board of; go on board which you please, take your choice '.

[During the battle the *Victory* lay on board the *Redoubtable* for some time.]

The *Redoubtable* commenced a heavy fire of musketry from the tops, which was continued for a considerable time with destructive effect to the *Victory*'s crew. . . . It was from this ship that Lord Nelson received his mortal wound. About fifteen minutes past one o'clock, which was in the heat of the engagement, he was walking in the middle of the quarter-deck with Captain Hardy, and in the act of turning near the hatchway, with his face towards the stern of the *Victory*, when the fatal ball was fired from the enemy's mizen top. . . . The ball struck the epaulette on his left shoulder and penetrated his chest. He fell with his face on the deck. Captain Hardy, who was on his right, and had advanced some steps before his Lordship, on turning round, saw the serjeant-major of the Marines with two seamen raising him from the deck. . . .

Captain Hardy expressed a hope that he was not severely wounded, to which the gallant Chief replied, ' They have done for me at last, Hardy '.

' I hope not ', answered Captain Hardy.

' Yes ', replied his Lordship, ' my backbone is shot through '.

Captain Hardy ordered the seamen to carry the Admiral to the cockpit. . . . While the men were carrying him down the ladder from the middle-deck, his Lordship observed that the tiller ropes were not yet replaced; and desired one of the midshipmen stationed there to go upon the quarter-deck and remind Captain Hardy of that circumstance, and request that new ones should be immediately rove. Having delivered this order, he took his handkerchief from his pocket and covered his face with it, that he might be conveyed to the cockpit at this crisis unnoticed by the crew.

Source: A letter from a Marine on board *Victory: Letters of English Seamen,* ed. Moorhouse, 1910, pp. 299–301.

Victory, Spithead
Dec. 5, 1805.

Dear Sister,

Comes with my kind love to you are in good health so thank God I am; for I am very certain that it is by his mercy that me and my country is, and you and your religion is kept up; for it has pleased the Almighty God for to give us a complete victory of the combined fleets of France and Spain; for there was a signal for them being out of Cadiz the 19th of October, but we did not see them till the 21st, in the morning, and about 12 o'clock we gave three cheers, and then the engagement began very hot on both sides, but about five o'clock the victory was ours, and twenty sail-of-the-line struck to us. They had 34 sail-of-the-line and we had 27 of the line, but the worst of it was, the flower of the country, Lord Nelson, got wounded at twelve minutes past one o'clock, and closed his eyes in the midst of victory. Dear Sister, it pleased the Lord to spare my life, and my brother Thomas his, for he was with the same gentleman. It was very sharp for us, I assure you, for we had not a moment's time till it was over, and the 23rd of the same instant we got a most shocking gale of wind, and we expected to go to the bottom, but, thanks be to God, He had mercy on us, every ship of ours got safe into harbour, and all the French but four got knocked to pieces on the rocks. . . . We had 125 killed and wounded, and 1500 in the English fleet killed and wounded, and the enemy 12,000; so I shall leave you to judge how your country fight for the religion you enjoy, the laws you possess, and on the other hand how Bounaparte has trampt them causes down in the places he has had concern with, for nothing but torment is going forward. So never think it a disgrace to having brothers in service. . . . My dear, I shall just give you a description of Lord Nelson. He is a man about five feet seven, very slender, of an affable temper; but a rare man for his country, and has been in 123 actions and skrimmages, and got wounded with a small ball, but it was mortal. It was his last words, that it was his lot for me to go, but I am going to heaven, but never haul down your colours to France, for your men will stick to you. These words was to Captain Hardy, and so we did, for we came off victorious, and they have behaved well to us, for they wanted to take Lord Nelson from us, but we told Captain as we brought him out we would bring him home; so it was so, and he was put into a cask of spirits. So I must conclude. Your loving brother,

James Bagley.

Source: a letter from a seaman present at Trafalgar in *Letters of English Seamen* 1587–1808, ed. Moorhouse, 1910, pp. 302–3.

Royal Sovereign.

Honoured Father,

This comes to tell you I am alive and hearty except three fingers; but that's not much, it might have been my head. I told brother Tom I should like to see a greatly battle, and I have seen one, and we have peppered the Combined rarely: and for the matter of that, they fought us pretty tightish for French and Spanish. Three of our mess are killed, and four more of us winged. But to tell you the truth of it, when the game began, I wished myself at Warnborough with my plough again; but when they had given us one duster, and I found myself snug and tight, I set to in good earnest, and thought no more about being killed than if I were at Murrell Green Fair, and I was presently as busy and as black as a collier. How my fingers got knocked overboard I don't know, but off they are, and I never missed them till I wanted them. You see, by my writing, it was my left hand, so I can write to you, and fight for my King yet. We have taken a rare parcel of ships, but the wind is so rough we cannot bring them home, else I should roll in money, so we are busy smashing ' em, and blowing 'em up wholesale.

Our dear Admiral Nelson is killed! So we have paid pretty sharply for licking 'em. I never sat eyes on him, for which I am both sorry and glad; for, to be sure, I should like to have seen him—but then, all the men in our ship who have seen him are such soft toads, they have done nothing but blast their eyes and cry, ever since he was killed. God bless you! chaps that fought like the devil, sit down and cry like a wench. I am still in the *Royal Sovereign*, but the Admiral [Collingwood] has left her, for she is like a horse without a bridle, so he is in a frigate that he may be here and there and everywhere for he's as *cute* as here and there one; and as bold as a lion, for all he can cry!—I saw his tears with my own eyes, when the boat hailed and said my Lord was dead. So no more at present from your dutiful son,

Sam.

THE DEATH OF NELSON

Source: Surgeon Beatty's Narrative in *Despatches and Letters*, ed. Nicolas, vol. vii, pp. 247-52.

The Surgeon then examined the wound, assuring his Lordship that he would not put him to much pain in endeavouring to discover the course of the ball; which he soon found had penetrated deep into the chest, and had probably lodged in the spine. This being explained to his Lordship, he replied he was confident his back was shot through. The back was then examined externally, but without any injury being perceived; on which his Lordship was requested by the surgeon to make him acquainted with all his sensations. He replied that he felt a gush of blood every minute within his breast: that he had no feeling in the lower part of his body: and that his breathing was difficult, and attended with very severe pain about that part of the spine where he was confident that the ball had struck; ' for ', said he, ' I felt it break my back '. These symptoms . . . indicated to the surgeon the hopeless situation of the case; but till after the victory was ascertained and announced to his Lordship, the true nature of his wound was concealed by the surgeon from all on board except only Captain Hardy, Doctor Scott, Mr. Burke, and Messrs. Smith and Westemburg, the Assistant Surgeons.

The *Victory's* crew cheered whenever they observed an enemy's ship surrender. On one of these occasions, Lord Nelson anxiously inquired what was the cause of it; when Lieutenant Pasco, who lay wounded at some distance from his Lordship, raised himself up, and told him that another ship had struck; which appeared to give him much satisfaction. He now felt an

ardent thirst; and frequently called for drink, and to be fanned with paper, making use of these words; ' Fan, fan ', and ' drink, drink '. This he continued to repeat when he wished for drink or the refreshment of cool air, till a very few minutes before he expired. Lemonade, and wine and water, were given to him occasionally. He evinced great solicitude for the event of the battle, and fears for the safety of his friend Captain Hardy. Doctor Scott and Mr. Burke used every argument they could suggest, to relieve his anxiety. Mr. Burke told him the enemy were decisively defeated, and that he hoped his Lordship would still live to be himself the bearer of the joyful tidings to his country. He replied, ' It is nonsense, Mr. Burke, to suppose I can live; my sufferings are great, but they will all be soon over '.
. . .

Many messengers were sent to Captain Hardy by the surgeon, requesting his attendance on his Lordship; who became impatient to see him, and often exclaimed: ' Will no one bring Hardy to me? He must be killed: he is surely destroyed.' The Captain's aide-de-camp, Mr. Bulkeley, now came below, and stated that circumstances respecting the fleet required Captain Hardy's presence on deck, but that he would avail himself of the first favourable moment to visit his Lordship. On hearing him deliver this message to the surgeon, his Lordship inquired who had brought it. Mr. Burke answered, ' It is Mr. Bulkeley, my Lord ', —' It is his voice ', replied his Lordship: he then said to the young gentleman, ' Remember me to your father '.

An hour and ten minutes, however elapsed, from the time of his Lordship's being wounded, before Captain Hardy's first subsequent interview with him; the particulars of which are nearly as follows. They shook hands affectionately, and Lord Nelson said: ' Well, Hardy, how goes the battle? How goes the day with us? '—' Very well, my Lord ', replied Captain Hardy: ' we have got twelve or fourteen of the enemy's ships in our possession; but five of their van have tacked, and show an intention of bearing down upon the *Victory*. I have therefore called two or three of our fresh ships around us, and have no doubt of giving them a drubbing.' ' I hope ', said his Lordship, ' none of *our* ships have struck, Hardy '. ' No, my Lord ',

replied Captain Hardy; ' there is no fear of that '. Lord Nelson
then said: ' I am a dead man, Hardy, I am going fast: it will
be all over with me soon. Come nearer to me. Pray, let my dear
Lady Hamilton have my hair, and all other things below belonging to me.' . . . Captain Hardy observed that he hoped Mr.
Beatty could yet hold out some prospect of life.—' Oh, no,'
answered his Lordship, ' it is impossible. My back is shot
through, Beatty will tell you so.' Captain Hardy then returned
on deck, and at parting shook hands again with his revered friend
and commander.

His Lordship now requested the surgeon . . . to return to
the wounded, and give his assistance to such of them as he could
be useful to; ' for ', said he, ' you can do nothing for me '. The
surgeon assured him that the assistant surgeons were doing
everything that could be effected for those unfortunate men; but
on his Lordship's several times repeating his injunctions to that
purpose, he left him, surrounded by Doctor Scott, Mr. Burke,
and two of his Lordship's domestics. After the surgeon had been
absent a few minutes attending Lieutenants Peake and Reeves
of the Marines, who were wounded, he was called by Doctor
Scott to his Lordship, who said: 'Ah, Mr. Beatty! I have sent
for you to say, what I forgot to tell you before, that all power
of motion and feeling below my breast are gone; and *you*',
continued he, ' very well *know* I can live but a short time '. . . .
The surgeon answered, ' My Lord, you told me so before: '
but he now examined the extremities, to ascertain the fact; when
his Lordship said, 'Ah, Beatty! I am too certain of it. . . . *You*
know* I am gone '. The surgeon replied: ' My Lord, unhappily
for our Country, nothing can be done for you '; and having
made this declaration he was so much affected, that he turned
round and withdrew a few steps to conceal his emotions. . . .
Drink was recommended liberally, and Doctor Scott and Mr.
Burke fanned him with paper. He often exclaimed, ' God be
praised, I have done my duty '; and upon the surgeon's inquiring
whether his pain was still very great, he declared, it continued
so very severe, that he wished he was dead. ' Yet ', said he in
a lower voice, ' one would like to live a little longer, too '; and
after a pause of a few minutes, he added in the same tone, ' What

would become of poor Lady Hamilton, if she knew my situation!'

... Captain Hardy now came to the cockpit to see his Lordship a second time, which was after an interval of about fifty minutes from the conclusion of his first visit. . . . Lord Nelson and Captain Hardy shook hands again, and while the Captain retained his Lordship's hand, he congratulated him, even in the arms of death, on his brilliant victory; which, said he, was complete; though he did not know how many of the enemy were captured, as it was impossible to perceive every ship distinctly. He was certain however of fourteen or fifteen having surrendered. His Lordship answered, ' That is well, but I bargained for twenty ': and then emphatically exclaimed, '*Anchor*, Hardy, *anchor*!' To this the Captain replied: ' I suppose, my Lord, Admiral Collingwood will now take upon himself the direction of affairs:— ' Not while I live, I hope, Hardy!' cried the dying Chief; and at that moment endeavoured ineffectually to raise himself from the bed. ' No,' added he; ' do *you* anchor, Hardy'. Captain Hardy then said: ' Shall *we* make the signal, sir?'—' Yes ', answered his Lordship, ' for if I live, I'll anchor '. . . . He then told Captain Hardy he felt that in a few minutes he should be no more, adding in a low tone, ' Don't throw me overboard, Hardy'. The Captain answered: ' Oh! no, certainly not '. ' Then ', replied his Lordship, ' you know what to do, and ', continued he , ' take care of my dear Lady Hamilton, Hardy: take care of poor Lady Hamilton. Kiss me, Hardy '. The Captain now knelt down, and kissed his cheek; when his Lordship said, ' Now I am satisfied. Thank God I have done my duty '. Captain Hardy stood for a minute or two in silent contemplation: he knelt down again, and kissed his Lordship's forehead. His Lordship said, ' Who is that? '. The Captain answered: ' It is Hardy '; to which his Lordship replied, ' God bless you, Hardy! ' After this affecting scene Captain Hardy withdrew and returned to the quarter-deck, having spent about eight minutes in this his last interview with his dying friend.

Lord Nelson now desired Mr. Chevalier, his steward, to turn him upon his right side; which being effected, his Lordship said: ' I wish I had not left the deck, for I shall soon be gone '.

He afterwards became very low; his breathing was oppressed, and his voice faint. He said to Doctor Scott, ' Doctor, I have *not* been a *great* sinner '; and after a short pause, ' Remember, that I leave Lady Hamilton and my daughter Horatia as a legacy to my country: and,' added he, ' never forget Horatia '. His thirst now increased; and he called for ' drink drink ', ' fan, fan ' and ' rub, rub ', addressing himself in the last case to Doctor Scott, who had been rubbing his Lordship's breast with his hand, from which he found some relief. These words he spoke in a very rapid manner, which rendered his articulation difficult: but he every now and then with evident increase of pain, made a greater effort with his vocal powers, and pronounced distinctly these last words: ' Thank God, I have done my duty '; and this great sentiment he continued to repeat as long as he was able to give it utterance.

His Lordship became speechless in about fifteen minutes after Captain Hardy left him. Doctor Scott and Mr. Burke, who had all along sustained the bed under his shoulders (which raised him in nearly a semi-recumbent posture, the only one that was supportable to him), forbore to disturb him by speaking to him; and when he had remained speechless about five minutes, his Lordship's steward went to the surgeon, who had been a short time with the wounded in another part of the cockpit, and stated his apprehensions that his Lordship was dying. The surgeon immediately repaired to him, and found him on the verge of dissolution. He knelt down by his side, and took up his hand; which was cold, and the pulse gone from the wrist. On the surgeon's feeling his forehead which was likewise cold, his Lordship opened his eyes, looked up, and shut them again. The surgeon again left him, and returned to the wounded who required his assistance; but was not absent five minutes before the steward announced to him that he believed his Lordship had expired. The surgeon returned, and found that the report was but too well founded: his Lordship had breathed his last at thirty minutes past four o'clock; at which period Doctor Scott was in the act of rubbing his Lordship's breast, and Mr. Burke supporting the bed under his shoulders.

THE RETREAT TO CORUNNA, 1808-9

The two men sentenced to death had been caught robbing a Spaniard. These extracts show the demoralisation of the British Army on Moore's retreat from Spain. The weather was appalling and the troops suffered incredible privations.

Source: A Boy in the Peninsular War: Services, Adventures and Experiences of Robert Blakeney, ed. J. Sturgis, Murray, 1899.

Blakeney joined the 28th Regiment in 1804 when he was 15.

Early on the morning of the 3rd the reserve marched up towards the crown of a low hill, in front of Calcabellos on the Bembibre side. Here we halted, leaving so much of it above us as served to screen us from the view of an approaching foe. No enemy having as yet advanced, the General of division ordered a hollow square to be formed, facing inwards. A drumhead court-martial sat in rear of every regiment, and within the square were placed the triangles. The culprits seized in the town, as soon as tried and sentenced, were tied up, and a general punishment took place along the four faces of the square; and this continued for several hours. During this time our vedettes came in frequently to report to the general that the enemy were advancing. His only reply was, ' Very well '. The punishment went on. The two culprits whom I have mentioned as having been seized in the act of committing a robbery stood with ropes round their necks. Being conducted to an angle of the square, the ropes were fastened to the branches of a tree which stood there, and at the same time the delinquents were lifted up and held on the shoulders of persons attached to the provost-marshal. In this situation they remained awaiting the awful signal for execution, which would instantly be carried into effect by a mere movement from the tree of the men upon whose shoulders they were supported. At this time (between twelve and one o'clock, as well as I can remember) a cavalry officer of high regimental rank galloped into the square and reported to General Paget that the piquets were engaged and retiring. ' I am sorry for it, Sir,' said the general; ' but this information is of a nature which would induce me to expect a report rather by a private dragoon than from you. You had better go back to your fighting piquets, sir, and animate your men to a full discharge of their duty'. General Paget was then silent for a few moments, and apparently suffering under great excitement. He at length addressed the square by saying: 'My God! is it not lamentable to think that, instead of preparing the troops confided to my command to receive the enemies of their country, I am preparing to hang two robbers? But though *that* angle of the square should be attacked I shall execute these villains in *this* angle.' The General again became silent for a moment, and our piquets were heard retiring up the opposite side of the hill and along the road which flanked it on our left. After a moment's pause he addressed the men a second time in these words: 'If I spare the lives of these two men will you promise to reform?'.

Not the slightest sound, not even breathing, was heard within the square. The question was repeated: 'If I spare the lives of these men, will you give me your word of honour as soldiers that you will reform?' The same awful silence continued until some of the officers whispered to the men to say 'Yes', when that word loudly and rapidly flew through the square. The culprits were then hastily taken away from the fatal tree, . . . even as the men gave the cheers customary when condemned criminals are reprived, our piquets appeared on the summit of the hill above us, intermixed with the enemy's advanced guard.

(*b*) The same.

Some of the divisions in front, instead of keeping together on the road during a halt, which took place on the approach of the night of the 9th, were permitted to separate and go into buildings; and on their divisions marching off, immense numbers were left behind, so that when the reserve came up we were halted to rouse up the stragglers. In many instances we succeeded, but generally failed; we kicked, thumped, struck with the butt ends of the firelocks, pricked with swords and bayonets, but to little purpose. There were three or four detached buildings in which some wine was found, and which also contained a large quantity of hay; and between the effects of the wine and the inviting warmth of the hay it was totally impossible to move the men.

And here I must confess that some even of the reserve, absolutely
exhausted from the exertions they used in arousing the slothful
of other divisions to a sense of their duty . . . could not resist
the temptation; and in the partial absence of the officers, who
were rousing up other stragglers, sat and from that sunk down
probably with the intention of taking only a few minutes' repose;
yet they too remained behind.

SIR JOHN MOORE AT CORUNNA
Monday, January 16th, 1809

The son of a distinguished Glasgow physician and man of letters,
he was educated chiefly on the Continent and entered the army in
1776. On the conclusion of the American war he was put on half pay
and entered Parliament. He distinguished himself at the storming of
Calvi in the Corsican expedition, and became Adjutant-General in 1794.
He again distinguished himself in the expedition against St. Lucia and
was appointed Governor of the island. In 1799, after seeing service in
Ireland, he was seriously wounded in Holland. In 1800 he fought in
Egypt and was again wounded. He was sent to the Peninsula and was
appointed Commander-in-Chief in October 1808. On January 16th,
1809, he won the victory of Corunna, but was killed in the battle
and buried at midnight in the citadel.

Source: Life of Sir Charles Napier, by Sir William Napier, Macmillan,
1894, vol. i, pp. 94–6.

He came at speed, and pulled up so sharp and close he seemed
to have alighted from the air, man and horse looking at the
approaching foe with an intenseness that seemed to concentrate
all feeling in their eyes. The sudden stop of the animal, a cream-
coloured one, with black tail, and mane, had cast the latter streaming forward, its ears were pushed out like horns, while its eyes
flashed fire, and it snorted loudly with expanded nostrils, expressing terror, astonishment, and muscular exertion. My first
thought was, it will be away like the wind, but then I looked at
the rider and the horse was forgotten. Thrown on its haunches,
the animal came, sliding and dashing the dirt up with its fore
feet, thus bending the General forward almost to its neck;
but his head was thrown back and his look more keenly piercing
than I ever before saw it. He glanced to the right and left,
and then fixed his eye intently on the enemy's advancing column,

at the same time grasping the reins with both his hands, and pressing the horse firmly with his knees. His body thus seemed to deal with the animal, while his mind was intent on the enemy, and his aspect was one of searching intentness beyond the power of words to describe. For a while he looked, and then galloped to the left without uttering a word.

TAKEN PRISONER AT CORUNNA

Sir Charles Napier (1782–1853) was wounded five times at Corunna while leading 1st Battalion 50th Regiment and captured. The French released him on condition that he would not serve again until officially exchanged; the exchange took place in Jan. 1810 and Napier returned to the Peninsula to fight at Busaco and Fuentes d'Onoro. In 1813 he fought in the war against the United States; in 1815 he was in Belgium. After the war his great gifts as administrator found some scope when he became Resident of Cephalonia. In 1839 he commanded troops in the north of England when Chartist disturbances were feared. The climax of his career was reached in 1843 when he won the battles of Miani and Hyderabad, which prepared the way for the annexation of Scinde, and his famous despatch—'Peccavi, I have Scinde.'

His brother William was the historian of the Peninsular War.

Source: An account by Sir Charles Napier of his capture, quoted in W. Butler: *Sir Charles Napier*, Macmillan, 1894, pp. 38–40.

[Charles Napier has been surrounded during the fighting.]

I said to the four soldiers [Irish privates of the Fiftieth and Forty-Second] 'Follow me and we will cut through them!' Then with a shout I rushed forward. The Frenchmen had halted, but now ran on to us, and just as my spring was made the wounded leg failed, and I felt a stab in the back; it gave me no pain, but felt cold, and threw me on my face. Turning to rise, I saw the man who had stabbed me making a second thrust. Whereupon, letting go my sabre, I caught his bayonet by the socket, turned the thrust, and raising myself by the exertion, grasped his firelock with both hands, thus in mortal struggle regaining my feet. His companions had now come up, and I heard the dying cries of the four men with me, who were all instantly bayoneted. We had been attacked from behind by men not before seen, as we stood with our backs to a doorway, out of which must have rushed several men, for we were all stabbed in an instant, before the two parties coming up the road reached us. They did so, however, just as my struggle with the man who had wounded me was begun. That was a contest for life, and being the strongest I forced him between myself and his comrades, who appeared to be the men whose lives I had saved when they pretended to be dead on our advance through the village. They struck me with their muskets, clubbed and bruised me much, whereupon, seeing no help near, and being overpowered by numbers, and in great pain from my wounded leg, I called out ' *Je me rend* ', remembering the expression correctly from an old story of a fat officer whose name being James called out ' *Jemmy round* '. Finding they had no disposition to spare me, I kept hold of the musket, vigorously defending myself with the body of the little Italian who had first wounded me; but I soon grew faint, or rather tired. At that moment a tall dark man came up, seized the end of the musket with his left hand, whirled his brass-hilted sabre round, and struck me a powerful blow on the head, which was bare, for my cocked hat had fallen off. Expecting the blow would finish me, I had stooped my head in hopes it might fall on my back, or at least on the thickest part of the head, and not on the left temple. So far I succeeded, for it fell exactly on the top, cutting me to the bone but not through it. Fire sparkled from my eyes. I fell on my knees, blinded but not quite losing my senses, and holding still on to the musket. Recovering in a moment I saw a florid, handsome young French drummer holding the arm of the dark Italian, who was in the act of repeating the blow. Quarter was then given; but they tore my pantaloons in tearing my watch and purse from my pocket and a little locket of hair which hung round my neck. But while this went on two of them were wounded, and the drummer, Guibert, ordered the dark man who had sabred me to take me to the rear. When we began to move, I resting on him because hardly able to walk, I saw him look back over his shoulder to see if Guibert was gone; and so did I, for his rascally face made me suspect him. Guibert's back was towards us; he was walking off, and the Italian again drew his sword, which he had before sheathed. I called out to the drummer, ' This rascal is going to kill me; brave Frenchmen don't kill prisoners '. Guibert ran back, swore furiously at the

Italian, shoved him away, almost down, and putting his arm round my waist supported me himself. Thus the generous French man saved me twice, for the Italian was bent upon slaying. . . . We had not proceeded far up the lane, when we met a soldier of the Fiftieth walking at a rapid pace. He instantly halted, recovered his arms, and cocked his piece, looking fiercely at us to make out how it was. My recollection is that he levelled at Guibert, and that I threw up his musket, calling out, ' For God's sake, don't fire. I am a prisoner, badly wounded, and can't help you; surrender '.—' For why should I surrender? ' he cried aloud, with the deepest of Irish brogues. ' Because there are at least twenty men upon you.'—' Well, if I must surrender—there ', said he, dashing down his firelock across their legs and making them jump, ' there's my firelock for yez '. Then coming up close he threw his arm round me, and giving Guibert a push that sent him and one or two more reeling against a wall, he shouted out, ' Stand back, ye bloody spalpeens, I'll carry him myself; bad luck to the whole of yez '. My expectation was to see them fall upon him, but John Hennessey was a strong and fierce man, and he now looked bigger than he was, for he stood upon higher ground. Apparently they thought him an awkward fellow to deal with. He seemed willing to go with me, and they let him have his way.

[Hennessey later escaped and rejoined the British troops.]

THE EXPEDITION TO THE ISLAND OF WALCHEREN, 1809

The object of this expedition was to seize islands in the Scheldt as a preliminary to the closing of that river and the capture of Antwerp.

Source: Recollections of Rifleman Harris, edited by Captain Curling, 1848, pp. 172, et sqq.

. . . A fair wind soon carried us off Flushing, where one part of the expedition disembarked; the other made for South Beveland, among which latter I myself was. The five companies of Rifles immediately occupied a very pretty village, with rows of trees on either side of its principal streets, where we had plenty of leisure to listen to the cannonading going on amongst the companies we had left at Flushing. The appearance of the country (such as it was) was extremely pleasant, and for a few days the men enjoyed themselves much.

But at the expiration of (I think) less time than a week, an awful visitation came suddenly upon us. The first I observed of it was one day as I sat in my billet, when I beheld whole parties of our Riflemen in the street shaking with a sort of ague, to such a degree that they could hardly walk; strong and fine young men who had been but a short time in the service seemed suddenly reduced in strength to infants, unable to stand upright—so great a shaking had seized upon their whole bodies from head to heel. The company I belonged to was quartered in a barn, and I quickly perceived that hardly a man there had stomach for the bread that was served out to him, or even to taste his grog, although each man had an allowance of half-a-pint of gin per day. In fact I should say that about three weeks from the day we landed, I and two others were the only individuals who could stand upon our legs. They lay groaning in rows in the barn, amongst the heaps of lumpy black bread they were unable to eat.

This awful spectacle considerably alarmed the officers, who were also many of them attacked. The naval doctors came on shore to assist the regimental surgeons, who, indeed, had more upon their hands than they could manage; Dr. Ridgeway of the Rifles, and his assistant, having nearly five hundred patients prostrate at the same moment. In short, except myself and three or four others, the whole concern was completely floored.

Under these circumstances, which considerably confounded the doctors, orders were issued (since all hopes of getting the men upon their legs seemed gone) to embark them as fast as possible, which was accordingly done with some little difficulty. The poor fellows made every effort to get on board; those who were a trifle better than others crawled to the boats; many supported each other; and many were carried helpless as infants. . . . On shipboard the aspect of affairs did not mend; the men beginning to die so fast that they committed ten or twelve to the deep in one day. It was rather extraordinary that myself, and Brooks, and a man named Bowley, who had all three been at Corunna, were at this moment unattacked by the disease, and

M

notwithstanding the awful appearance of the pest-ship we were in, I myself had little fear of it, I thought myself so hardened that it could not touch me. It happened, however, that I stood sentinel (men being scarce) over the hatchway, and Brooks, who was always a jolly and jeering companion (even in the very jaws of death) came past me, and offered me a lump of pudding, it being pudding-day on board. At that moment I felt struck with a deadly faintness, shaking all over like an aspen, and my teeth chattering in my head so that I could hardly hold my rifle. Brooks looked at me for a moment with the pudding in his hand, which he saw I could not take, ' Hullo ', he said, ' why Harris, old boy, you are not going to begin are you? ' I felt unable to answer him, but only muttered out as I tumbled, ' For God's sake get me relieved, Brooks! '. . . . In fact I was now sprawling upon the forecastle, amongst many others, in a miserable state, our knapsacks and our great-coats over us, . . . and thus we arrived at Dover. . . . The Warwickshire Militia were at this time quartered at Dover. They came to assist in disembarking us, and were obliged to lift many of us out of the boats like sacks of flour. If any of those militiamen remain alive, they will not easily forget that piece of duty; for I never beheld men more moved than they were at our helpless state. Many died at Dover and numbers in Deal. . . .

BEFORE THE LINES OF TORRES VEDRAS

Hostilities were tacitly suspended on this front during the winter of 1810-11.

Source: J. Kincaid, Adventures in the Rifle Brigade, Boone, 1838.

I used to be much amused at seeing our naval officers come up from Lisbon riding on mules, with huge ships' spy-glasses, like six-pounders, strapped across the backs of their saddles. Their first question invariably was, ' Who is that fellow there? ', pointing to the enemy's sentry, close to us, and, on being told that he was a Frenchman, ' Then why the devil don't you shoot him! '

Repeated acts of civility passed between the French and us during this tacit suspension of hostilities. The greyhound of an officer followed a hare, on one occasion, ran into their lines, and they very politely returned him.

I was one night on piquet, at the end of the bridge, when a ball came from the French sentry, and struck the burning billet of wood round which we were sitting, and they sent in a flag of truce, next morning, to apologise for the accident, saying that it had been done by a stupid fellow of a sentry, who imagined that people were advancing upon him. . . .

THE STORMING OF CIUDAD RODRIGO,
Sunday, January 19th, 1812

Source: J. Kincaid, *Adventures in the Rifle Brigade* 1809–15, Boone, 1838, pp. 101 et sqq.

Kincaid was in the storming party of 3 officers and 100 volunteers from each regiment.

The advantage of being on a storming party is considered as giving the prior claim to be *put out of pain*, for they receive the first fire, which is generally the best, not to mention that they are also expected to receive the earliest salutation from the beams of timber, hand-grenades, and other missiles, which the garrison are generally prepared to transfer from the top of the wall, to the tops of the heads of their foremost visitors. . . .

We had some difficulty at first in finding the breach, as we had entered the ditch opposite to a ravelin, which we mistook for a bastion. I tried first one side of it and then the other, and seeing one corner of it a good deal battered, with a ladder placed against it, I concluded that it must be the breach, and calling to the soldiers near me, to follow, I mounted with the most ferocious intent, carrying a sword in one hand and a pistol in the other; but, when I got up, I found nobody to fight with, except two of our own men, who were already laid dead across the top of the ladder. I saw, in a moment, that I had got into the wrong box, and was about to descend again, when I heard a shout from the opposite side, that the breach was there; and, moving in that direction, I dropped myself from the ravelin, and landed in the ditch, opposite to the foot of the breach, where I found the head of the storming party just beginning to fight their way into it. The combat was of short duration, and, in less than half an hour from the commencement of the attack, the place was in our possession.

After carrying the breach, we met with no further opposition, and moved round the ramparts to see that they were perfectly clear of the enemy, previous to entering the town. I was fortunate enough to take the left hand circuit, by accident, and thereby escaped the fate which befel a great portion of those who went to the right, and who were blown up, along with some of the third division, by the accidental explosion of a magazine. . . .

. . . finding the current of soldiers setting towards the centre of the town, I followed the stream, which conducted me into the great square, on one side of which the late garrison were drawn up as prisoners, and the rest of it was filled with British and Portuguese intermixed, without any order or regularity. I had been there but a very short time, when they all commenced firing, without any ostensible cause; some fired in at the doors and windows, some at the roofs of houses, and others at the clouds; and, at last, some heads began to be blown from their shoulders in the general hurricane, when the voice of Sir Thomas Picton, with the power of twenty trumpets, began to proclaim damnation to every body, while Colonel Barnard, Colonel Cameron, and some other active officers, were carrying it into effect with a strong hand; for, seizing the broken barrels of muskets, which were lying about in great abundance, they belaboured every fellow most unmercifully about the head, who attempted either to load or fire, and finally succeeded in reducing them to order.

THE STORMING OF BADAJOZ
Monday, April 6th, 1812

Source: A Boy in the Peninsular War: The Services, Adventures and Experiences of Robert Blakeney, edited by J. Sturgis, Murray, 1899, pp. 263–99.

The dreadful strife now commenced. The thundering cheer of the British soldiers as they rushed forward through the outer ditch, together with the appalling roar of all arms sent forth in defiance from within, was tremendous. Whenever an instant pause occurred it was filled by the heart-rending shrieks of the trodden-down wounded and by the lengthened groans of the dying. Three times were the breaches cleared of Frenchmen, driven off at the point of the bayonet by gallant British soldiers to the very summit, when they were by the no less gallant foe each time driven back, leaving their bravest officers and foremost soldiers behind, who, whether killed or wounded, were tossed down headlong to the foot of the breaches. Throughout this dreadful conflict our bugles were continually sounding the advance. The cry of ' Bravo! Bravo! ' resounded through the ditches and along the foot of the breaches; but no British cry was heard from within the walls of Badajoz save that of despair, uttered by the bravest, who despite of all obstacles forced their way into the body of the place, and there through dire necessity abandoned, groaned forth their last stabbed by unnumbered wounds. Again and again were the breaches attacked with re-doubled fury and defended with equal pertinacity and stern resolution, seconded by every resource which science could adopt or ingenuity suggest. Bags and barrels of gunpowder with short fuses were rolled down, which, bursting at the bottom or along the face of the breaches, destroyed all who advanced. Thousands of live shells, hand-grenades, fireballs and every species of destruc-tive combustible were thrown down the breaches and over the walls into the ditches, which, lighting and exploding at the same instant, rivalled the lightning and thunder of heaven. This at intervals was succeeded by an impenetrable darkness as of the infernal regions. Gallant foes laughing at death met, fought, bled and rolled upon earth; and from the very earth destruction burst, for the exploding mines cast up friends and foes together, who in burning torture clashed and shrieked in the air. Partly burned they fell back into the inundating water, continually lighted by the incessant bursting of shells. . . .

At length the bugles of the 4th and light divisions sounded the recall. . . . I galloped off to where Lord Wellington had taken his station. This was easily discerned by means of two fireballs shot out from the fortress at the commencement of the attack, which continued to burn brilliantly along the water-cut. . . . Near the end of this channel, behind a rising mound, were Lord Wellington and his personal staff, screened from the enemy's direct fire, but within the range of shells. One of his staff sat down by his side with a candle to enable the general to read and write all his communications and orders. . . . I stood not far from his lordship. But due respect prevented any of us bystanders from approaching so near as to enable us to ascertain the import of the reports which he was continually receiving; yet it was very evident that the information which they conveyed was far from flattering; and the recall on the bugles was again and again repeated. But about half-past eleven o'clock an officer rode up at full speed on a horse covered with foam, and announced the joyful tidings that General Picton had made a lodgment within the castle by escalade, and had withdrawn the troops from the trenches to enable him to maintain his dearly purchased hold. Lord Wellington was evidently delighted. . . . I mounted my horse . . . and then made the best of my way to the walls of the castle; their height was rather forbidding, and an enfilading fire still continued. The ladders were warm and slippery with blood and brains of many a gallant soldier.

THE CAPTURE OF A DESERTER FROM THE ROYAL WELCH FUSILIERS, 1813

Source: MS. records of Royal Denbigh Militia, quoted H. A. Tipping, *The Royal Welch Fusiliers,* Country Life, 1916, p. 249.

As the regiment were crossing Westminster Bridge on the march to Portsmouth for embarkation to Bordeaux, the goat which marched in front of the band suddenly darted on the pavement, butted a man in plain clothes against the parapet, keeping him there fixed, until he was recognised as one of the deserters and made a prisoner.

THE BATTLE OF WATERLOO
Sunday, June 18th, 1815

(*a*) *Source:* C. Mercer, *Journal of the Waterloo Campaign,* 1870.

On the ridge opposite to us dark masses of troops were stationary, or moving down into the intervening plain. Our own advancing infantry were hid from view by the ground. We therefore recommenced firing at the enemy's masses, and the cannonade, spreading, soon became general again along the line. Whilst thus occupied with our front, we suddenly became sensible of a most destructive flanking fire from a battery which had come, the Lord knows how, and established itself on a knoll somewhat higher than the ground we stood on, and only about 400 or 500 yards a little in advance of our left flank. The rapidity and precision of this fire were quite appalling. Every shot, almost, took effect, and I certainly expected we should all be annihilated. Our horses and limbers, being a little retired down the slope, had hitherto been somewhat under cover from the direct fire in front; but this plunged right amongst them, knocking them down by pairs, and creating horrible confusion. The drivers could hardly extricate themselves from one dead horse ere another fell, or perhaps themselves. The saddle-bags, in many instances, were torn from the horses' backs, and their contents scattered over the field. One shell I saw explode under the two finest wheel-horses in the troop—down they dropped. In some instances the horses of a gun or ammunition waggon remained, and all their drivers were killed. The whole livelong day had cost us nothing like this. Our gunners too—the few of them left fit for duty were so exhausted that they were unable to run the guns up after firing, consequently at every round they retreated nearer to the limbers; and as we had pointed our two left guns towards the people who were annoying us so terribly, they soon came altogether in a confused heap, the trails crossing each other, and the whole dangerously near the limbers and ammunition waggons, some of which were totally unhorsed, and others in sad confusion from the loss of their drivers and horses, many of them lying dead in their harness attached to their car-riages. I sighed for my poor troop—it was already but a wreck.

I had dismounted, and was assisting at one of the guns to encourage my poor exhausted men, when through the smoke a black speck caught my eye, and I instantly knew what it was. The conviction that one never sees a shot coming towards you unless directly in its line flashed across my mind, together with the certainty that my doom was sealed. I had barely time to exclaim ' Here it is then '—much in that gasping sort of way one does when going into very cold water takes the breath— ' whush ' it went past my face, striking the point of my pelisse collar, which was lying open, and smash into a horse close behind me. I breathed freely again.

Whilst in position on the right of the second line, I had reproved some of my men for lying down when shells fell near them until they burst. Now my turn came. A shell, with a long fuse, came slop into the mud at my feet, and there lay fizzing and flaring, to my infinite discomfiture. After what I had said on the subject, I felt that I must act up to my own words, and, accordingly, there I stood, endeavouring to look quite composed until the cursed thing burst—and, strange to say, without injuring me, though so near. The effect on my men was good. We pointed our two left guns towards the people who were annoying us so terribly, but had scarcely fired many rounds at the enfilading battery when a tall man in the black Brunswick uniform came galloping up to me from the rear, exclaiming, 'Ah! mine Gott! —mine Gott! Vat is it you doose, sare? Dat is your friends de Proosiens; and you kills dem! Ah, mine Gott!—mine Gott! Vill you no stop, sare?—vill you no stop? Ah! mine Gott— mine Gott! vat for is dis? De Inglish kills dere friends de Proosiens! Vere is de Dook von Vellington? . . . etc. etc., and so he went on raving like one demented. I observed that if these were our friends the Prussians they were treating us very un-civilly; and that it was not without sufficient provocation we had turned our guns on them, pointing out to him at the same time the bloody proofs of my assertion. Apparently not noticing what I said, he continued his lamentations, saying, ' Vill you no stop, sare, I say?' Wherefore, thinking he might be right, to pacify him I ordered the whole to cease firing, desiring him to remark the consequences. Psieu, psieu, psieu, came our friends' shot, one after another; and our friend himself had a narrow escape from one of them. ' Now, sir ', I said, ' you will be convinced; and we will continue our firing, whilst you can ride round the way you came, and tell them they kill their friends —the English; the moment their fire ceases, so shall mine.' Still he lingered, exclaiming, ' Oh, dis is terreeble to see de Proosien and de Inglish kill von anoder!' At last darting off I saw no more of him.

(b) *Source:* Letter from Brevet-Major A. C. Mercer, Royal Horse Artillery. From H. T. Siborne, *Waterloo Letters*, Casssell, 1891.

Mercer is describing French cavalry attacks on infantry squares.

His troop is then moved up into the front line between two squares of Brunswickers.

. . . a heavy Column of Cavalry . . . was advancing upon us at a rapid pace, so that there scarcely appeared time even to get into action, and, if caught in column, of course we were lost.

However, the order was given to deploy, and each Gun as it came up immediately opened its fire; the two Infantry Squares at the same time commencing a feeble and desultory fire; for they were in such a state that I momentarily expected to see them disband.

Their ranks, loose and disjointed, presented gaps of several file in breadth, which the Officers and Sergeants were busily employed filling up by pushing and even thumping their men together; whilst these, standing like so many logs, with their arms at the recover, were apparently completely stupified and bewildered. I should add that they were all perfect children. None of the privates, perhaps, were above eighteen years of age. In spite of our fire the Column of Cavalry continued advancing at a trot . . . but at the very moment when we expected to be overwhelmed, those of the leading Squadrons suddenly turning, and endeavouring to make way to the rear, confusion took place, and the whole broke into a disorderly crowd. The scene that ensued is scarcely to be described. Several minutes elapsed ere they succeeded in quitting the Plateau, during which our fire was incessant, and the subsequent carnage frightful, for each Gun (9 pounders) was loaded with a round and case shot; all of which, from the shortness of the distance, size of the object, and elevation of the ground on which they stood, *must* have taken effect.

Many, instead of seeking safety in retreat, wisely dashed through the intervals between our Guns . . . but the greater part, rendered desperate at finding themselves held, as it were, in front of the Battery, actually fought their way through their own ranks, and in the struggle we saw blows exchanged on all sides. . . .

At length the Column being reformed, again ascended the Plateau, and advanced to attack us. . . . Experience, having shown us the unerring and destructive effects of a close fire, we allowed the leading Squadrons to attain about half the distance between the brow of the slope and the road in our front before we com-

menced. It is scarcely necessary to say that the result was precisely similar to what has been already detailed. Again they fell
into confusion, and again for several minutes were exposed to a
deliberate fire of case shot within 20 yards, so that the heap of
killed and wounded left on the ground, before great, was now
enormous.

(c) *Source:* Letter from Major J. Luard of Vandeleur's Cavalry
Brigade. From ed. H. T. Siborne, *Waterloo Letters*, Cassell, 1891.

Describes the action following the attack of the 2nd Column of the
Imperial Guard on the British infantry.

The fire now became tremendous, particularly of musketry.
I had at this moment my horse shot in the head by a musket-ball,
and Lieutenant Phillips of the 11th, while condoling with me on
seeing me mounted on a troop horse, had his head shot off by
a cannon-shot. The fire became every moment hotter, and from
the rapid way in which it approached us, appeared as if the enemy
was carrying the hill by which we were partially covered, and I
confess I thought at that moment the day was going hard with
us, that the Infantry were beaten, and that we (the Cavalry), by
desperate charges, were to recover what they had lost.

The foreign troops in our front appeared to think so also,
but certainly had not resolved to recover the day, for they began
to give way rapidly. We closed our squadron intervals, and
would not let them pass through, and by the persuasion of Sir
John Vandeleur, other Officers, and myself, they again formed
to the front. The fire now rapidly slackened, the Duke of
Wellington appeared in our front in great spirits, and we moved
to the front at a smart trot, in a Column. . . .

We passed the scene of carnage where our Line had been
formed, moved down the hill with great rapidity, passed our
own Infantry as well as broken Columns of the French, and
pursued Cavalry of all arms mixed, the ground strewed with
cuirasses thrown away to lighten the Cuirassiers in their flight.
About a mile and a half from our position, a road runs through
the valley, on the opposite side of which a Column of French
Infantry formed square to oppose us. We instantly wheeled into
line, received their fire and charged, taking or destroying the
whole. . . . We continued to pursue the Enemy until we came

upon some huts, which had been the Enemy's bivouac the preceding night. . . .

Having taken some waggons laden with provisions and brandy, I, as Adjutant, collected a number of canteens of each Troop, and filled them, to be divided equally amongst all the men. . . .

(*d*) *Source:* Captain H. W. Powell, First Foot Guards, in Maitland's Infantry Brigade, ed. Siborne: *Waterloo Letters.*

Between five and six the Emperor was so much pressed by the Prussian advance on his right that he determined to make a last grand effort, and as he had tried every other Corps without effect there only remained to him the ' Garde Imperiale '. With these he resolved to play his last stake and to ensure success. His Artillery were ordered to concentrate their whole fire on the intended point of attack. That point was the rise of our position about half-way between Hougoumont and La Haye Sainte.

. . . There ran along this part of the position a cart road, on one side of which was a ditch and bank, in and under which the Brigade sheltered themselves during the cannonade, which might have lasted three-quarters of an hour. Without the protection of this bank every creature must have perished.

The Emperor probably calculated on this effect, for suddenly the firing ceased, and as the smoke cleared away a most superb sight opened on us. A close Column of Grenadiers . . . of la Moyenne Garda, about 6,000 strong, led, as we have since heard, by Marshall Ney, were seen ascending the rise *au pas de charge* shouting ' Vive l'Empereur '. They continued to advance till within fifty or sixty paces of our front, when the Brigade were ordered to stand up. Whether it was from the sudden and un-expected appearance of a Corps so near them, which must have seemed as starting out of the ground, or the tremendous heavy fire we threw into them, *La Garde*, who had never before failed in an attack *suddenly* stopped. Those who from a distance and more on the flank could see the affair, tell us that the effect of our fire seemed to force the head of the Column bodily back.

In less than a minute above 300 were down. They now wavered, and several of the rear divisions began to draw out as if to deploy, whilst some of the men in their rear beginning to fire over the heads of those in front was so evident a proof of their confusion, that Lord Saltoun . . . holloaed out ' Now's the time, my boys '. Immediately the Brigade sprang forward. La Garde turned and gave us little opportunity of trying the steel. We charged down the hill till we had passed the end of the orchard of Hougoumont. . . .

(*e*) *Source: Autobiography and Journals of Benjamin Robert Haydon*, ed. Elwin (Macdonald 1950), pp. 255–8.

B. R. Haydon, born at Plymouth in 1786, was an artist notable for his huge paintings of historical subjects. Financial difficulties, against which he had struggled for most of his life, finally overwhelmed him and he committed suicide in 1846.

Sammons, my old corporal, whom I had lost sight of, now appeared again. Wilkie, and I, and Scott had got up several of the wounded to my room, and Sammons brought a genuine letter from the field and gave it to me to read, if I could, for the benefit of the company. Here it is.

[1]Brussels, June 23rd, 1815.

Respected Friend,

I take this opportunity of sending these few lines hoping they will find you in good health, as this: only I received a wound on my left arm by a cannon ball which has took off part of the flesh, but missed the bone. Dear friend I witnessed the most dreadful slaughter what was ever known by the oldest soldier in the army.

From Friday we advanced, and Saturday we retreated by being overpowered, but the first regiment was engaged, and got great applause, but thunder lightning and rain prevented us from being engaged till Sunday. The French kept advancing till ten o'clock, then we opened our fire with our cannon and infantry, and hard fighting till three, when our artillery retreated with infantry, and then we was forced to charge them though five to one, and some say eleven to one, but they turned for bold Life Guards to pursue. The slaughter is more than I can describe. They run like a hare before the hounds, but our horses getting faint, and troops of French coming up with cannon, cut our men off very fast, and still they fought like lions more than

[1] Spelling of letter corrected.

men, determined to conquer or die to a man. I saw many of my comrades fall, before I got the wound, but we got three eagles, and Lord Wellington said that gained the applause of the whole of the British. The numbers of killed and wounded is more than can at present be told on both sides. Our regiment mounted twenty-five to go on with, the rest is wounded and missing. Shaw is no more; Hornwood, and many that I cannot insert;—there will be many widows in our regiment—you will hear when the returns come—and many wounded. Shepherd is billeted with me, and wounded with a ball in his arm, and with a lance in his side. . . . Shepherd was took prisoner on the plains of Waterloo, and drove to a large town called Shalligarow [Charleroi], and which is twenty-four miles from where we was engaged; the blood was running from his wounds in torrents, and used like a dog, but he made his escape from them, and got here on Monday and came to Brussels; his horse was shot, then mounted a French one, and that was shot: he was forced to yield prisoner, being wounded in three places in his side, and in his arm. . . . We took 154 pieces of cannon, and all the waggons for miles, and our army is now passing a hill without firing a gun; and they will soon be in Paris; the French was only nine miles off and Boney said he would ' dine by four o'clock. ' The town was to be plundered, and now he is 100 miles off and we have his brother safe prisoner. . . .

I hope you have got the money from the colonel. Please remember me to Jane, and I shall be glad to see you safe again; give my love to brother and sister, and tell them to write to my father.

I have no more to say at present.

I remain, your obedient friend,
William Chapman,
2nd Life Guards.

Sammons was a favourite model . . . a good soldier;—had been through the war in Spain, and was very angry he had not been at Waterloo.

Whilst the wounded were describing the battle, Sammons explained what was military, and thereby kept up his command,

he being a corporal and they being privates. . . . The description
of the men was simple, characteristic, and poetical. They said
when the Life Guards and Cuirassiers met, it was like the ringing
of ten thousand blacksmith's anvils. One of them knew my
models, Shaw and Dakin. He saw Dakin, while fighting on foot
with two Cuirassiers, also on foot, divide both their heads with
cuts five and six. He said Dakin rode out foaming at the mouth,
and cheered on his troop. In the evening he saw Dakin lying
dead, cut in pieces. Dakin sat to me for the sleeping groom on
his knees in Macbeth. . . .

AFTER THE BATTLE OF WATERLOO

Source: Creevey Papers: Letter to Charles Ord dated Bruxelles,
Sunday, June 25th. The standard edition of the Creevey Papers is
that edited by Sir H. Maxwell, 1903. There is also *Creevey's Life
and Times*, ed. John Gore, John Murray, 1934, from pages 80–1 of
which this extract is taken.

Thomas Creevey was born in Liverpool on March 5, 1768. He
was educated at Queens' College, Cambridge, was called to the Bar in
1794, and later practised as a barrister. He entered Parliament in 1802
for the pocket borough of Thetford, became Secretary to the Board of
Control in the Ministry of All the Talents 1806, and in 1830 became
Treasurer of Ordnance. He died in 1838.

. . . In the course of that morning (Monday) Wellington
came over here to write his dispatch, and . . . he beckoned
to me out of his windows to come up to him, and having shook
hands, he very gravely told me how very *critical* the battle had
been, and with what incredible gallantry our troops had conducted
themselves. He walked about uttering expressions of astonishment at our men's courage and particularly at the Guards keeping
their position in a Chateau and garden in front of the left of his
position.

On Tuesday morning, nothing would serve Barnes and
Hamilton but I must ride over and see their positions, so I was
mounted on your old friend the *Curate*, accompanied by Barnes's
groom on a Boss Coach Horse. Two miles on this side Waterloo
Wellington overtook me in his curricle with Harvey, so we went
on together and he said Harvey would mount his horse at
Waterloo and shew me over the field of battle, and all about it,

which he did with Lord Arthur Hill . . . and others. Terrible as this sight was in prospect and in fact, it was most interesting, and I would not have missed it for the world. I talked with various French soldiers lying among the dead, but not dead or dying themselves. They were very gay, and Lord Arthur got off and gave three or four of them some gin and water out of a bottle he had, and they all called him ' Mon Général ' and said he was ' bien honnête '. Harvey told me in riding home he thought the French left on the field were 15,000. . . .

PEACE ANNOUNCED AT WELLINGTON'S HEADQUARTERS

Source: Private Journals of Francis Seymour Larpent, London, 1853, vol. iii. pp. 138–40.

F. S. Larpent (1776–1845) was at headquarters with Wellington from 1812 to 1814 as deputy Judge-Advocate.

Just as we were sitting down to dinner—about forty of us, General Frere and several Spaniards, General Picton, and Baron Alten, the principal French, etc.—in came Cooke with the dispatches (the peace). The whole was out directly, champagne went round, and after dinner Lord Wellington gave ' Louis XVIII ', which was very cordially received with three times three, and white cockades were sent for to wear at the theatre in the evening. In the interim, however, General Alava got up, and with great warmth gave Lord Wellington's health, as *El Liberador de Espana*. Everyone jumped up, and there was a sort of general exclamation from all the foreigners—French, Spanish, Portuguese, Germans, and all—*El Liberador de Espana! Liberador de Portugal! Le Liberateur de la France! Le Liberateur de l'Europe!* And this was followed, not by a regular three times three, but a cheering all in confusion, for nearly ten minutes. Lord Wellington bowed, confused, and immediately called for coffee.

We then all went to the play. The public were quite in the dark as to what had just arrived, but Lord Wellington was received in the stage box (where he sat supported by Generals Picton, Frere, and Alava etc., and also the Maire) with no little applause, I can assure you. At the door the people would scarcely take the money from us; and in the opposite stage box the

French left the box themselves and made room for us. We had our white cockades on the breast. The English officers in the house stared, and did not know what to make of it. Some thought it a foolish, giddy trick. In about ten minutes Lord Wellington turned his hat outwards to the front of the box; it was seen, and a shout ensued immediately. The play was *Richard, oh mon Roi* fixed upon really before the news came. The *Henri IV* was played, and then the new French Constitution was read aloud from one of the boxes. The people most anxious, in general pleased; in some things not. This was followed by ' God Save the King ', which was received with great applause.

WITH NAPOLEON TO ST. HELENA

After the battle of Waterloo Napoleon abdicated and, apparently with the idea of going to the United States, proceeded to the Atlantic coast at Rochefort. He found, however, that it was impossible to evade the English fleet and on July 15th he surrendered to Admiral Hotham of H.M.S. *Bellerophon.* By the Convention of August 2, 1815, the four great Powers declared that Napoleon was their prisoner and that his custody was especially entrusted to the British Government. Napoleon was taken to St. Helena, where he spent his time fabricating the fantastic Napoleonic legend which was to be so largely responsible for restoring the crown to his dynasty. Napoleon died at Longwood on St. Helena, 5th May, 1821.

Source: With Napoleon to St. Helena by Rachel Leighton in the *Cornhill Magazine* for March 1933 (from the commonplace book of T. N. Parker, of Sweeney Hall, Oswestry).

The writer of the letters, an officer of the 82nd Foot attached for this voyage to H.M.S. *Northumberland,* is unknown, and the identity of the lady to whom they were addressed is uncertain.

Further Reading: H. A. L. Fisher, *Bonapartism,* Oxford University Press, 1928. Lord Rosebery: *Napoleon: The Last Phase,* Humphreys, 1900.

My dear Harriet,—

I am not paying you a very high compliment in saying I only write to keep myself awake, . . . it is my Guard and I have to sit in the antichamber of Napoleon to prevent communication between him and the ship's crew and also to be a check on his domestics, 'tis now about one o'clock and I must keep awake till six, here I am surrounded by five of the Imperial Guards of the present day who lie snoring on the floor, the most trustworthy sleeps across the entrance of his room I suppose fearful that he might be assassinated. I assure you I am heartily sick of his presence for this duty is very severe and disagreeable there are only four of us to do it, an officer of the Royal Artillery, one of the Fifty-third and two of us, so that we have three nights in bed and one up. It would be nothing if it was only a common Guard but being obliged to keep awake is the disagreeable part of it, there is one consolation it will not last long. Napoleon gets very sulky if he is not treated with that deference and respect he has been accustomed to and sometimes appears quite peevish and sullen, his followers the Generals pay him just the same respect as though he was still Emperor, whenever he is on deck they stand uncovered and approach him with the same respect as if he were still Emperor. Beattie my Captain was at Acre, Bonaparte learnt this in conversation with him, seemed quite pleased caught hold of his ear and gave it a good pinch which is his custom when pleased and seems to have taken a great liking to him—he breakfasts at eleven, instead of tea takes half a pint of claret, dines at five and immediately after comes on deck for an hour (he eats very heartily and drinks about a pint of claret) then he goes to cards, Vingt-un is the game that is always played, he always stakes two napoleons d'or on a card and generally loses. He is sometimes very communicative, to-day he mentioned the project he had formed for invading England 1815 (sic) declared it to have been his intention to have led the expedition himself and said he thought it might have succeeded, the plan was this, he sent his fleet to the West Indies for the purpose of drawing our fleet there, which it did, Lord Nelson and Sir M. Calder both following Villeneuve there. He was to return immediately to the Channel, Napoleon said he calculated upon Villeneuve's arrival in the Channel at least a fortnight before our troops would get back which would give him a naval superiority for a short time, his army was embarked (200,000 he says) but the plan was disconcerted by Villeneuve's going into Cadiz instead of coming to the Channel, his words were ' He might as well have been in the East Indies as at Cadiz ' . . . . Bertrand is the only one that seems to feel his situation, he talks of Napoleon often with tears, and is always extremely agitated when conversing on the state of France, he says Napoleon did

N

not calculate upon fighting the English and Prussians at Waterloo, the Prussians were beat on the 16th and they did not suppose they could have been up to take part in the battle of the 18th, he thinks they would have gained the victory if Prussians had not come up, but *circumstances were not favourable*, the French soldiers fought very well, the generals did not. . . . Yet notwithstanding these admissions, they break out gasconading about their victories and Napoleon's great generalship, blame Wellington for making mistakes at Waterloo and many other things equally absurd. . . . Augt. 20th.

. . . . I know not how to describe the life we live here, though a little more settled than at first, 'tis still one of great confusion, the mess place crowded from morning to night, we sit down 24 to dinner in the place intended for 12, the weather begins to get very warm as we approach the tropics, I keep on the lower deck on which there are 800 men (troops and all) the heat is dreadful, but I am in very good health; the day is passed at backgammon, chess, and cards, it is impossible to read or write in the daytime, I therefore leave it till my guard at night.

The Admiral behaves very well, there is refreshment and generally a bottle of madeira left out for the officer of the Guard, there is now one of champagne but I have not attacked it yet. I believe the object of the Guard is to prevent communication with the crew. Napoleon told the Admiral that he did not doubt that he could get many to join him if he tried and indeed they are as mutinous a set of rascals as I ever heard of, though I don't think they would assist him to escape, what I am going to state (for the credit of the country) must be a secret, they mutinied and refused to get anchor up at Portsmouth, the Artillery Coy 33rd and ourselves were under arms for three hours, that is until they had sailed, about 20 of the principal seamen were seized and confined and sent away from the ship and the conduct and language of the sailors is now beyond everything, they think nothing of striking the midshipmen. The *professed* intention of the guard is lest he and his followers should get out from his cabin window into a boat which hangs close to them, and lower it down, which is barely possible. . . .

[From a letter dated St. Helena, Oct. 16, 1815].

We arrived at this barren horrid looking Island yesterday after a tedious passage of ten weeks during which we experienced no bad weather or disagreeable heat, so far fortunate. . . .

For the last week we have had nothing but salt rations, and no vegetables, we shall now get vegetables but for fresh meat it is out of the question, there being only five bullocks on the Island, a ship sails tomorrow for the Cape of Good Hope to procure Bullocks and other necessaries. . . . I have dined three times with Napoleon and always sat directly opposite to him at table, I cannot say I think his manners have much of that elegance you would expect from one of his ci-devant high rank, they are rather vulgar than otherwise and he has a particular disagreeable grunt when he does not quite understand what you say which answers to our interjection ' ha ! ' desiring a repetition. He converses without the least reserve, but not at table with the Frenchmen and takes no more notice of the ladies than if they were a hundred miles off (as good a comparison as I dare make) I have only seen him speak once to Madame Bertrand at table, and seldom elsewhere. Bertrand is a good kind of man but I think credulously disposed. Montholon is a man of whom one can give no character he is like the common run. Gourgaud is a vain boasting Frenchman. Napoleon landed here on the 17th he is at a house in the country until the one he is to inhabit is ready for his reception. The expense of his establishment will not be very trifling, his yesterday's dinner cost eighty pounds and it cannot be expected that he can get one hereafter at a cheaper rate.

WITH NAPOLEON AT ST. HELENA

Source: Diary of William Kershaw, quoted in A. Ponsonby, *More English Diaries*, Methuen, 1927, p. 185 et sqq.

William Kershaw was a purser in the Merchant Service; he was returning home from the East.

On entering the grounds at Longwood the officer on guard demands your pass, which I delivered. I rode round the house in hopes of a glimpse but seeing the officer who had charge of Bonaparte's person, he requested me to dismount and walk into his tent which is placed at the bottom of the garden, here I found two or three gentlemen on the same errand as myself. The officer advised us to wait till the carriage was ordered, however my object was to see Lascassas and get introduced. I walked into the garden and turning short on a path came within a yard of two persons in close conversation, this was unexpected, and I observed one of them uncovered, and the other having a star on his breast, I made no doubt it was Bonaparte, but so widely different even at first sight, did he appear, from the representations and portraits I had seen and formed in my mind, that I could not forbear the vacant stare, however to prevent intrusion I moved my hat and passed, Bonaparte took his hat off and bowed *rather politely* (this in general he is not given credit for). Just as I had reached the end of the path I observed the gentleman who was in conversation running after me, I stopped, and when he came up, asked me who I was, and what, and that His Majesty the Emperor would see me should I desire it. This gentleman was Lascassas, and I apologised for having intruded. He spoke very good English, and we walked up the path together where General Bonaparte was standing, when we came within a yard of him, I bowed and uncovered, Lascassas doing the same, and introducing me to him. Bonaparte took his hat off to his knee, and immediately replaced it, holding it by the top—I remained uncovered. The General with a sort of half smile on his countenance began by asking if I have made my fortune and how much, this being answered, he placed his hands behind him and commenced asking questions without selection, and as quick as answers could be given—sometimes scarcely waiting for them, before he proposed something else of quite a different nature; he appeared to anticipate the answers of every question asked. . . . [Bonaparte asked many questions—most about the Chinese—as Kershaw was on his way home from the Far East]. . . . We now hoped we had not detained him and bowed to him as we retired. Bonaparte took his hat off, saying ' Good day, gentlemen ', after we had gone a few steps, he said, 'A good voyage to you '. His carriage had been waiting at the door some time, for him to take his usual evening ride, the distance of which is confined to about a mile round and round, in fact there is not much more level ground for a carriage to travel on. He was dressed in a plain green coat with silver buttons (each having a different device on) with an upright green velvet collar, on his left side was a large emblazoned star, the imperial eagle in the centre. Nankeen breeches and white silk stockings with large gold buckles in his shoes. He wears a large cocked hat not mounted —the picture of Isabey with a full length portrait of Napoleon in the gardens of Malmaison with his arms folded has some resemblance, the best of any I have seen certainly, but this is not half stout enough for him, unless since the painting of that, he has greatly increased in corpulency—he is what we generally say of such a stature a little thick set man with a corporation—a most inactive appearance, with a large head, large mouth, the eyes deeply arched and his teeth apparently very good. On approaching him he surveys you from head to foot and then fixes his eyes sternly at you for a few moments—while speaking he takes his snuff box from his coat pocket and at every pause, takes a copious pinch.

THE BOMBARDMENT OF ALGIERS AND THE RESCUE OF CHRISTIAN SLAVES 1816

In 1816 Admiral Lord Exmouth was ordered to visit the north African powers and demand the release of all British subjects kept by them as slaves. This demand was granted, but when the Dey of Algiers was further requested to abolish Christian slavery he refused to do so. Exmouth returned to England with this answer and was sent out to north Africa again to enforce the British demand by bombarding Algiers. The bombardment was entirely successful, and the Dey freed 3,000 slaves, mostly Spaniards and Italians.

A member of Exmouth's family (the Pellews) had been a captive for 24 years in north Africa in the first half of the eighteenth century.

Source: A letter printed in *Young Gentlemen* by C. F. Walker, Longmans, 1938, pp. 232–6.

The writer was a fifteen-year-old midshipman of the frigate *Severn*.

H.M.S. *Severn*
Algiers Bay.

Dear Father,

Knowing how very anxious you will be to hear from me after so long silence I cannot possibly let this ship go to England without tipping you a bit of a stave at least if it is only to tell you that I am one of those lucky fellows who escaped unhurt. On the 24th of July we sailed from Portsmouth for Plymouth where we arrived on the 28th, and sailed for Gibraltar on the following morning. Nothing happened during the voyage worthy of notice, only that we made a very quick one for we were moored in Gibraltar bay on the 9th of August, when we cleared for action and returned all our useless stores. On the 14th we sailed for Algiers and owing to a foul wind all the way did not make the bay until the 27th, when we all hove to, within about four miles of the town. The Admiral then made the signal for our Captain and ordered him to go in with the flag of truce to present our terms to the Dey, consequently we stood close under the town and sent a boat on shore with the white flag, on which was a Lieutenant belonging to the *Queen Charlotte*, and an interpreter, whom Lord Exmouth had previously sent on board of us, this was about 8 o'clock in the morning; the moment the boat attempted to land, they snatched the paper out of the boat and never gave them any answer. When, at about 3 in the evening, Lord Exmouth hoisted the preparative flag and stood in in the most noble manner that you can imagine, the *Leander* frigate followed him and then came the *Severn*, as to the stations of the other ships I am not able to inform you for they were a good way astern of us when we went in, so that it was impossible to see them afterwards for the smoke. The *Queen Charlotte* engaged a battery of three tiers of guns on the right-hand side of the mole head, and the *Leander* engaged a battery just ahead of us so that these three ships were almost touching one another. They never fired a shot at us till the *Queen Charlotte* let go her anchor, when one shot was fired from the battery she was going to engage, which was immediately returned by her whole broadside and three cheers throughout the whole fleet. About half past 3 the action became general. The first broadside that our battery fired into us carried away the whole of our main lower rigging, and struck our main mast in two places. We were so very close that the upper tiers of our battery could not bear upon us, but presently we were obliged to haul off to make room for six frigates[1]

[1] These were ships of Algiers.

which were on fire to drift out of the mole, during which time they raked us in a dreadful manner, but soon after we got into our station again and played upon them in a noble manner. We had scarcely one man left in our tops about 9 o'clock, and about $\frac{1}{2}$ past 8 a shot came through the fore top sail into the foretop and took two men's legs off and sprung our main top mast, about $\frac{3}{4}$ past ten our battery began to slacken and at about 12 it was completely silenced for they had every gun dismounted. Almost the first shot that was fired struck the muzzle of my gun and hove the breech right off forward, but luckily did no other damage, presently after a shot came between the port and took a man's thigh off, and as I was standing close by one poor fellow a musket ball struck him in the stomach and he never spoke again. After the action which was about 12 we literally had not one whole rope in the ship. Our sides, masts, yards, sails and rigging, were as completely riddled as anything you ever saw, but notwithstanding we had next to the *Queen Charlotte* the very worst situation there I suppose we have fewer men killed than any ship in the fleet, only 5 killed and 33 wounded. At 12 after we had expended every grain of powder in the ship we were obliged to haul off and luck it was that the Admiral had just made the signal to that effect, so we all anchored again within about 4 miles of the Town. The next morning, what a sight there was, boat loads of dead going to be hove overboard and we could distinguish the dead piled up in heaps on shore. About ten o'clock the next day the Admiral intended to have gone in again but they sent off to say that they had had quite enough of it, and they would agree to our terms so tomorrow we land and destroy the town.[1] In the *Impregnable* they had 100 killed and 140 wounded. Lord Exmouth received two slight wounds in the heat of the action. Capn. Coode of the *Albion* received 5 wounds, and our friend Capn. Elkins [Ekins] is wounded severely, but how or where I don't know. I heard one of his midshipmen say so but had not time to speak to him. It must have been a beautiful sight from a distance for after seven o'clock it was quite dark, but the ships on fire made such a light that we could see a great way round us. I don't think that in Algiers which is—was the

[1] This was not done, as the Dey submitted completely.

strongest place next to Gibraltar in the world there are three guns left mounted upon the whole place and this time tomorrow there won't be so many stones one upon another. We are now all as busy as bees repairing our damages which are very great. One of our midshipmen had his arm shot off. I suppose we shall return to England again soon or else get new masts at Minorca. I have been as deaf as a post ever since the action, but I hope it will soon go off. I shall soon write again. Pray let me hear from you at the first opportunity. Our Captain has just received the Admiral's thanks for the noble manner in which he behaved. Give my love to all. And believe me

> Ever your affectionate son,
> Edward Trevor.

LORD CASTLEREAGH: A WOMAN'S POINT OF VIEW

Robert Stewart, Viscount Castlereagh (1769–1822), succeeded his father as Marquis of Londonderry in 1821. He was Chief Secretary for Ireland 1799–1801, President of the Board of Control in 1802, Secretary for War and the Colonies in 1805 and again in 1807–9. As Foreign Secretary from 1812 to 1822 he was one of the leaders in the struggle against Napoleon, and was largely responsible for the arrangements concluded at the Congress of Vienna. In 1822 he suffered a mental breakdown and committed suicide at his home at North Cray Farm in Kent on August 12, 1822.

Source: The Journal of Mrs. Arbuthnot, ed. F. Bamford and Duke of Wellington, vol. i, Macmillan, 1950, pp. 180–3.

Further Reading: H. Nicolson, *The Congress of Vienna,* Constable, 1948. Marriott, *Castlereagh,* Methuen, 1936. Webster: *The Foreign Policy of Castlereagh,* Bell, 1931.

Aug. 29th—

Such has been the untimely end of this great and amiable man, respected for his private virtues by his bitterest political enemies (private ones he had none) and loved to adoration by his family and friends. He was in the 54th year of his age, and retained all the personal beauty which had distinguished him in early youth. He was above six feet high and had a remarkably fine commanding figure, very dark eyes, rather a high nose and a mouth whose smile was sweeter than it is possible to describe. It was impossible to look at him and see the benevolent and amiable expression of his countenance without a disposition to like him, and over his whole person was spread an air of dignity and nobleness such as I have never seen in any other person. His manners were perfect as those of a high-born polished gentleman, and nothing could be more graceful and easy than his reception of people who attended the assemblies constantly given by Lady Londonderry. He was excessively agreeable, a great favourite amongst women, and used occasionally to excite Lady Londonderry's jealousy; but he was the kindest and most affectionate of husbands, paid her the greatest possible attention and had unbounded confidence in her. In discussing matters of business I used to remark that he was slow in finding words and had an involved way of explaining a subject, but it was always plain that the idea was right and clear in his mind, and nothing could exceed his strong good sense.

. . . He had a natural slowness of constitution of which he was himself quite aware, for he has often told me he required the goading and violence of the House of Commons to rouse him, and that he was determined never to go into the House of Lords as they were too quiet and sleepy for him. The consequences of his temperament, and of his not having had a classical education, which rendered his language involved and often incorrect, were that, when he had to make a statement or an opening speech, he was generally flat and dull and scarcely commanded the attention of the House; but in reply, and particularly when the Opposition had been violent or ungentlemanlike, he was very powerful. Nothing, too, could exceed his tact and judgement in dwelling on the strong points of his own arguments or the weak ones of his antagonists; and his management was so good, and he was himself so gentlemanlike and so high minded, that he was one of the most popular leaders the Government ever had.

In private life it is not possible to conceive anything more amiable, his tastes were simple, he was passionately fond of music, fond of flowers, of his farm, full of kindness for his servants and of charity for the poor, adored by his whole family, of which he was the affectionate protector. . . .

On the 16th the Duke, who was gone to the Netherlands

and who had been sent for express, arrived in town and on the 17th he called on us. He told me that, though he had seen Lord L[ondonderry] in such a state and felt convinced that it was a species of insanity under which he was labouring, the idea of the Catastrophe never once entered his mind. He said that he had suffered more than he could describe from his interview with him. Lord Londonderry had been in such a state of dreadful agitation, had cried so bitterly when the consciousness of his own delusions forced themselves upon his mind, and had appeared altogether to be suffering under such severe bodily and mental sickness that he had been unable to drive it out of his mind. He had wished much to stay with Lord L[ondonderry] who would not allow him to do so; but, having obtained from him a promise that he would see a physician and having himself written to the physician stating his belief that Lord L[ondonderry] was under a mental delusion, he never imagined that *nothing* would be done for him, that, with the exception of one cupping, he would be left without restraint for his mind to prey upon itself.

It appears Lord L[ondonderry] had had an interview with the King, on the same day he saw the Duke and had talked in so strange a way that the King sent for Lord Liverpool in the middle of the night and told him Lord Castlereagh was mad. . . .

GEORGE IV

George IV when he was Prince of Wales.

Son of George III, he was brought up in seclusion at Kew with his brothers, and received a good education. He came of age in 1783 and established himself at Carlton House. He became a close friend of Charles James Fox and the other Whig leaders. In 1782 he married Mrs. Fitzherbert, but he subsequently denied the marriage in order to conciliate Parliament. The marriage was valid, though illegal owing to the Royal Marriage Act, the Prince's minority and the bride's Catholicism. In 1784 he built Brighton Pavilion, where he spent much of his time. In 1795 in order to conciliate his father he married Caroline of Brunswick, but in a few months he openly separated from her. In 1811 he was compelled to accept the Regency on terms which he found highly unsatisfactory. He attempted to divorce his wife and thereby ensured her a popularity which she did not deserve. Spencer Walpole's summary: ' he was a bad son, a bad husband, a bad father, a bad subject, a bad monarch and a bad friend ', if severe, is not undeserved.

(a) *Source:* A letter from Dr. Burney in *Diary and Letters of Madame d'Arblay*, Colburn, 1846, vol. vi, pp. 333–4.

Further Reading: R. Fulford, *George IV*, Duckworth, 1935. Sir Shane Leslie, *George IV*, Benn, 1926.

July 12, 1805.

. . . Your brother, Dr. Charles, and I, have had the honour last Tuesday of dining with the Prince of Wales at Lord Melbourne's, at the particular desire of H.R.H. He is so good-humoured and gracious to those against whom he has no party prejudice, that it is impossible not to be flattered by his politeness and condescension. I was astonished to find him, amidst such constant dissipation, possessed of so much learning, wit, knowledge of books in general, discrimination of character, as well as original humour. He quoted Homer in Greek to my son as readily as if the beauties of Dryden or Pope had been under consideration. And as to music, he is an excellent critic; has an enlarged taste—admiring whatever is good in its kind, of whatever age or country the composers or performers may be; without, however, being insensible to the superior genius and learning necessary to some kinds of music more than others.

The conversation was general and lively, in which several of the company, consisting of eighteen or twenty, took a share, till towards the heel of the evening, or rather the *toe* of the morning; for we did not rise from table till one o'clock, when Lady Melbourne being returned from the opera with her daughters, coffee was ordered; during which H.R.H. took me aside and talked exclusively about music near half an hour, and as long with your brother concerning Greek Literature. He is a most excellent mimic of well-known characters; had we been in the dark any one would have sworn that Dr. Parr and Kemble were in the room.

HIS CORONATION

(b) *Source: The Journal of Mrs. Arbuthnot*, 1820–1832. ed. F. Bamford and Duke of Wellington, Macmillan, 1950, vol. i, pp. 7–8 and 14–16.

Harriet, daughter of the Hon. Henry Fane, married Charles Arbuthnot, M.P. After a period as Ambassador at Constantinople, he became Joint Secretary to the Treasury, and (a position which gave him great influence) Patronage Secretary. Mrs. Arbuthnot, a firm Tory, was passionately interested in politics, and she and her husband were at the heart of the political world. Her journal is a fascinating, and extremely well-informed document. She died of cholera in August, 1834.

1821

[July] 19th. . . . The King came into the Hall at ten o'clock, the procession having been previously partly arranged. He looked at first excessively pale and tired but soon recovered and, after giving the Regalia to the different persons who were to carry it, the procession moved to the Abbey. While it proceeded by the platform to the north door of the Abbey, we went by a narrow passage erected from the door of the House of Lords to Poets' Corner and were seated in the Abbey before the procession arrived. On the King's entrance into the Abbey he was received with the loudest cheers, which were repeated with increased vehemence when the crown was placed on his head and, particularly, when the D. of York did homage and kissed him. It was a magnificent sight, that fine building full of people as it could possibly hold, all magnificently dressed, peers, heroes and statesmen all joining in one unanimous hurra. The ceremony occupied till towards three o'clock when the King returned to the Hall and passing through it, retired to a private room to rest till dinner.

The Duke of Wellington and Mr. Arbuthnot then came to where we were and took us to Mr. Bankes' in Old Palace Yard, where we had something to eat. . . .

The King returned to the Hall about 5 o'clock, when the Earl Marshal, the D. of Wellington (High Constable) and Lord Anglesea (High Steward) rode up the Hall with the first course and backed out again. They came in again with the second course, and the two latter with the Champion. It was very well done; the Duke of Wellington rode a white Arabian who backed most perfectly. There were a great many services done, caps given and returned, falcons presented by the D. of Atholl. The peers drank to the King, and he in return to the peers and his good people, and the whole concluded with ' God save the King', sung by the choristers and chorused by the whole assembly.

After the riding was over, the people had been allowed to crowd into the body of the Hall and only a small space was kept open at the foot of the steps, and it is not possible to describe anything finer than the scene was, the galleries all standing up waving their hats and handkerchiefs and shouting, ' God bless the King!' Altogether it was a scene I would not have missed seeing for the world, and shall never see again so fine a one.

The King behaved very indecently; he was continually nodding and winking at Lady Conyngham and sighing and making eyes at her. At one time in the Abbey he took a diamond brooch from his breast, and, looking at her, kissed it, on which she took off her glove and kissed a ring she had on!!! Any body who could have seen his disgusting figure, with a wig the curls of which hung down his back, and quite bending beneath the weight of his robes and his 60 years would have been quite sick. . . .

IN OLD AGE

(c) Source: Greville *Memoirs.*

Charles Cavendish Greville (1794–1865) was educated at Eton and Christ Church. The influence of the Duke of Portland obtained for him first the sinecure Secretaryship of Jamaica, and then the reversion of the Clerkship to the Privy Council. Greville, who was Clerk to the Privy Council from 1821 to 1859 kept a diary which was, of course, meant for publication.

December 16th, 1828. I sent for Bachelor and had a long talk with him. He said the King was well, but weak, his constitution very strong. . . . He thinks the hot rooms and want of air and exercise do him harm, and that he is getting every day more averse to exercise and more prone to retirement, which, besides that it weakens his constitution, is a proof that he is beginning to break. Bachelor thinks he is in no sort of danger; I think he will not live more than two years. He says that his attendants are quite worn out with being always about him, and living in such hot rooms (which obliges them to drink) and seldom getting air and exercise. . . . His Majesty keeps everybody at a great distance from him, and all about him are afraid of him. . . . March 17th, 1829.

He leads a most extraordinary life—never gets up till six in the afternoon. They come to him and open the window curtains at six or seven o'clock in the morning; he breakfasts in bed, does whatever business he can be brought to transact in bed too, he reads every newspaper quite through, dozes three or four hours, gets up in time for dinner, and goes to bed between ten and eleven. He sleeps very ill, and rings his bell forty times in the night; if he wants to know the hour, though a watch hangs close to him, he will have his *valet de chambre* down rather than turn his head to look at it. The same thing if he wants a glass of water; he won't stretch out his hand to get it. His valets are nearly destroyed . . . on the days they are in waiting their labours are incessant, and they cannot take off their clothes at night, and hardly lie down. He is in good health, but irritable. . . .

THE DUKE OF WELLINGTON

THE ARMY'S OPINION DURING THE PENINSULAR WAR

Arthur Wellesley (1760-1852), the future Duke of Wellington, was called in his youth, 'the fool of the family.' His mother referred to him as 'my awkward son,' and his elder brother described him as 'the biggest ass in Europe '. But he won the Peninsular War; he defeated Napoleon at Waterloo; he was in Parliament for over 45 years and in the Cabinet for more than 30; he became Prime Minister, and in his old age he was revered by many of his fellow-countrymen as the greatest living Englishman.

(*a*) *Source:* J. Kincaid, *Adventures in the Rifle Brigade*, 1809–15, Boone, 1838.

Further Reading: Philip Guedalla: *The Duke*, Hodder and Stoughton, 1931. Sir John Fortescue: *Wellington*, Williams and Norgate, 1925.

As a general action seemed now inevitable, we anxiously longed for the return of Lord Wellington . . . as we would rather see his long nose in the fight than a reinforcement of ten-thousand men any day. Indeed, there was a charm not only about himself but all connected with him, for which no odds could compensate. The known abilities of Sir George Murray, the gallant bearing of the lamented Pakenham, of Lord Fitzroy Somerset [later Lord Raglan], of the present Duke of Richmond, Sir Colin

Campbell, with others, the flower of our young nobility and gentry, who, under the auspices of such a chief, seemed always a group attendant on victory; and I'll venture to say that there was not a heart in that army that did not beat more lightly, when we heard the joyful news of his arrival, the day before the enemy's advance.

SANG FROID AT WATERLOO

(b) Source: The Greville Memoirs.

November 18, 1838, Wolbeding: Came here to-day and brought Lord Fitzroy Somerset [afterwards Lord Raglan] with me, who told me a great deal about the Duke and their old campaigns. He never saw a man so cool and indifferent to danger, at the same time without any personal rashness or bravado, never putting himself in unnecessary danger, never avoiding any that was necessary. He was close to the Duke, his left arm touching the Duke's right, when he was shot in the arm at Waterloo, and so was Lord Anglesey when he received his wound in the leg. When Lord Anglesey was shot he turned to the Duke and said, 'By God! I have lost my leg'. The Duke replied, 'Have you, by God?'.

ANOTHER SIDE OF HIS CHARACTER

(c) Source: The Autobiography of B. R. Haydon, ed. Elwin, Macdonald 1950, p. 569. Haydon was staying at Walmer Castle to paint a portrait of the Duke.

12th [October 1839]. At ten we breakfasted—the Duke, Sir Astley [Sir Astley Cooper, the surgeon], Mr. Booth, and myself. He put me on his right. ' Which will ye have, black tea or green? ' ' Black, Your Grace '. ' Bring black '. Black was brought, and I ate a hearty breakfast. In the midst, six dear, healthy, noisy children were brought to the windows. ' Let them in,' said the Duke, and in they came, and rushed over to him saying, ' How d'ye do, Duke? How d'ye do, Duke? ' One boy, young Gray, roared, ' I want some tea, Duke '. ' You shall have it, if you promise not to slop it over me as you did yesterday '. Toast and tea were then in demand. Three got on one side and three on the other, and he hugged 'em all. Tea was poured out, and I saw little Gray try to slop it over the Duke's frock-coat. Sir Astley said, ' You did not expect to see this '. They all then rushed out on the leads, by the cannon, and after breakfast I saw the Duke romping with the whole of them, and one of them gave His Grace a devil of a thump.

THE DUKE AND THE PUBLIC

(d) Source: The Greville Memoirs

May 19, 1833 . . . I was marvellously struck (we rode together through St. James's Park) with the profound respect with which the Duke was treated, everybody we met taking off their hats to him, everybody in the Park rising as he went by, and every appearance of his inspiring great reverence. I like this symptom, and it is the more remarkable because it is not *popularity*, but a much higher feeling toward him.

June 5, 1842 . . . Last night I went to Hullah's choral meeting at Exeter Hall, where the Queen Dowager appeared. It was fine to see, . . . but the finest thing was when the Duke of Wellington came in, almost at the end. The piece they were singing stopped at once; the whole audience rose, and a burst of acclamation and waving of handkerchiefs saluted the great old man, who is now the idol of the people. It was grand and affecting, and seemed to move everybody but himself.

July 13, 1847. . . . The Cambridge installation went off with prodigious éclat, and the Queen was enchanted at the enthusiastic reception she met with; but the Duke of Wellington was if possible received with even more enthusiasm. It is incredible what popularity environs him in his latter days; he is followed like a show wherever he goes, and the feeling of the people *for him* seems to be the liveliest of all popular sentiments; yet he does nothing to excite it, and hardly appears to notice it.

THE CATO STREET CONSPIRACY, February, 1820

Arthur Thistlewood was an extreme radical who wanted a violent revolution. He and his associates planned to blow up the Cabinet when the Ministers were dining at Lord Harrowby's house. A spy revealed the plot to the Government, and a force was sent to arrest the

conspirators in Cato Street, off the Edgware Road. They offered
resistance, a policeman was killed and Thistlewood and fourteen of
the conspirators escaped. They were later captured. The conspiracy
was an extreme manifestation of the discontent so deeply felt in the
country at this time.

Source: The Journal of Mrs. Arbuthnot, vol. i, pp. 7-8 and 14-16.
March 1820.

7th. . . . I went in the morning with Mr. Arbuthnot to see
the stable and loft in Cato Street, where the conspirators were
assembled the night they were apprehended. It is a most wretched
place, and the staircase up to the room where they were taken
so perpendicular I could hardly get up. Great crowds were
assembled round the door, and it was with some difficulty the
constables made way for us to go in. . . .

8th—Dined at Lord Cholmondeley's, very dull!! When we
came home we found the D. of Wellington, who had come after
the Cabinet dinner to spend the evening with us. He told us
they had issued the Commission for trying the conspirators and
said he was in hopes they should have evidence enough against
them without bringing forward the informer as one of the conspirators, by the name of John Monument, was anxious to
become King's evidence and tell all he knew. He said their plan
had been, after completing the murder of the Ministers, to attack
Coutts' and Child's banking houses to get money, to set fire to
several houses, to collect a mob, to break open the gun-smith's
shop to arm them, to seize six pieces of artillery which they
knew were in the artillery ground, and for which they had
provided ammunition, to seize on the Bank and Mansion House,
and to murder every body that attempted to leave London. It
makes me shudder to think of how near such a plot was to succeeding and what horrors we should have witnessed, and we may feel
shame and humiliation at the reflection of how changed must be
the character of Englishmen when a band of thirty and forty
men could be found willing and anxious to perpetrate such a
cowardly assassination. The Duke of Wellington, whom every
English person ought to worship, was singled out as particularly
obnoxious; and one of them declared that, after having murdered
him, he would publish that he had gone on his knees to beg for

o

mercy, ' in order that such a story might lower the pride of his family ' . . .

[March] 13th. The Duke told us that one of the Cato Street conspirators, whose bill of indictment was ignored by the Grand Jury, has since his release confessed all the plot, and his evidence tallies in a most remarkable manner with the story of Edwards, the informer; but, in consequence of the gross mismanagement of the Home Department, his evidence cannot be used in the trial as his name is not down among the witnesses.

May 3rd . . . I have omitted to mention the execution of the Cato Street conspirators, which took place on the 1st of this month. Thistlewood and 4 other of the leaders were hanged and beheaded, exhibiting to the last the most hardened and brutal want of religion or any proper feeling. One really ought to thank God that the world is rid of such monsters, for their avowals of guilt on the scaffold and when they were brought up for judgement were quite terrific. Six others, who pleaded guilty, were sent off the night before for transportation for life to Botany Bay.

My brother Cecil, who had never seen an execution, told me he had a great curiosity on this occasion and went. He wished very much to see how they would behave; but, when they were tied up, he felt so nervous and in fact *felt* so much more than they themselves did that he retired into a corner of the room and hid himself that he might not see the drop fall, which excited great contempt in the people who were in the room with him; amongst whom was one woman, young and pretty and very decent looking; who kept her eyes fixed on it all the time and, when they had hung a few seconds, exclaimed, ' there's two *on* them not dead yet ! '

GEORGE CANNING

He was the son of a barrister who died leaving his family in narrow circumstances. Canning's mother went on the stage. His uncle Stratford Canning, the father of the future Lord Stratford de Redcliffe, sent the boy to Eton where he did brilliantly. In 1787 he went up to Christ Church, and entered Lincoln's Inn in 1791. At Oxford he became a friend of the future Prime Minister, Lord Liverpool. He began as a Whig, but dislike of the French Revolution took him over to the Tories. In 1793 he entered Parliament as a follower of Pitt. In 1797 he took a leading part in publishing a satirical paper, *The Anti-Jacobin*, some of his contributions to which are remembered still. He supported Pitt over the Act of Union with Ireland, and resigned with his leader. In 1807 he became Foreign Secretary. His quarrel and duel with Castlereagh and his resignation helped to keep him out of office. In 1822 he was appointed by the East India Company to succeed Lord Hastings as Governor-General, when Castlereagh's suicide opened the way for him to become Foreign Secretary in Lord Liverpool's administration. On the death of Liverpool in February 1827 Canning became Prime Minister. He died on August 8th. His *Poems* were published in 1825 and his *Works* in 1828. Acton had no hesitation in placing Canning first in the roll of England's foreign ministers. Certainly a very great statesman, he had the vulgarity to use without mercy his splendid aptitude for ridicule. The lash of his tongue, as his friend Sir Walter Scott put it, ' fetched away both skin and flesh and would have penetrated the hide of a rhinoceros '. His victims remembered.

(*a*) *Source:* Redding, *Fifty Years' Recollections*, vol. i, pp. 177–8, quoted in *George Canning*, by Sir Charles Petrie, Eyre and Spottis-woode, 2nd edn., 1946, p. 129.

I met for the first time Canning, then in the prime of life, just before his departure for the election at Liverpool. In private society he fully sustained that superiority which he showed in the House of Commons . . . neat in dress . . . Canning had nothing of the stiffness, arrogance, or ordinary person of Pitt. He exhibited no extremes. His evening dress was in the plainer fashion of the time. There seemed to me about him, too, something of the character of his eloquence, classical, tasteful, candid, and conscious of innate power. A handsome man in feature, compact in person; moulded between activity and strength, although I fancied even then he exhibited marks of what care and ambition had done for him. His countenance indicated firmness of character, with a good-natured cast over all. He was bald as ' the first Caesar '.

In the dining-room or drawing-room little of that theatrical manner was visible which was perceptible in the delivery of his Parliamentary speeches. His gait as he paced the drawing-room I even now see, his well-fitted blue ribbed silk stockings and breeches with knee-buckles fitting well-turned limbs . . . he spoke with a full, clear intonation. . . .

    (*b*) *Source: Journal of Mrs. Arbuthnot*, i, pp. 258–9.

26th [Sept. 1823]

    The Duke [of Wellington] was greatly irritated against Mr. Canning, who he said knew no more of foreign politics than a child and had neither temper nor address to deal with foreigners; that he had so managed as to be completely in the dark about what was going on. None of the Foreign Ministers confide in him; the Emperors of Russia and Austria are on the point of meeting in Hungary, and Mr. Canning has not the least idea what the meeting is to arrange, and we none of us know and shall not unless the Duke finds it out from Madame de Lieven, who is in love with Metternich and will probably know from him what it is about. The Duke again and again repented having advised his having the Foreign seals and said, if it was to come over again, he would cut his hand off rather than recommend such a measure.

    (*c*) *Source: Journal of Mrs. Arbuthnot*, i, pp. 275–6.

18th [Nov. 1823].

    Mr. C[anning] has been making himself more ridiculous than enough by going round the country *speechifying* and discussing the acts and intentions of the Government. This is quite a new system *among us* and excites great indignation. He has made a sort of progress through the country, getting himself drawn through the towns and, as since he came into office he has done nothing but transact the common business of the Office, it is quite ludicrous. And he thinks it all very clever and is highly pleased with himself. The King has written to Lord Liverpool that he disapproves highly of this system of Mr. Canning's, and he took the opportunity of praising the Duke excessively. The Duke told Mr. A. yesterday that he positively would complain to Lord Liverpool of Canning's system of sending despatches without the Cabinet's knowledge, and that he will state everywhere, and in Parliament if it is necessary, that he is not responsible for measures to which he has not been a party.

(d) *Source: Journal of Mrs. Arbuthnot,* ii, p. 65.

1826 Dec.

15th . . . Mr. Arbuthnot saw Lord Liverpool yesterday and again to-day. He has been very ill and is only just recovering. He talks so habitually and constantly of going out of office that in general I pay no attention to it. This time, however, he at least speaks more seriously. He told Mr. Arbuthnot that he was perfectly aware that he had had a great shake, that if his life was spared a few years longer it must be by care and attention and, above all, *repose*, that he was wholly unfit for these troublesome times and that, indeed, independently of that, it was more than he could bear to be in office with Mr. Canning. ' I am,' he said, ' on the best possible terms with Mr. Canning; we are cordial and friendly to the greatest degree, but you must be aware that being in office with Mr. Canning is totally different to what it was with poor Londonderry. Then everything was calm and tranquil and nothing to worry one about trifles; but I have not strength and nerves to bear Mr. Canning's perpetual notes. He sends me a dozen of a day; every trifle, a remark from one of his secretaries, a pamphlet, a paragraph in a newspaper, is cause for his firing off a note; and I live in continual dread every time the door opens that it is to bring a note from Mr. Canning, till I am driven half distracted. Some people, whose nerves are less irritable, might not mind it, but I cannot bear it.'

It is all perfectly true; Mr. C[anning] has a mania for writing notes, the Duke gets sometimes a dozen a day, and formerly Mr. Pitt used to say that Mr. C[anning] was like a mistress, always affronted and always writing notes, and he used to end by putting them into the fire without reading them.

(e) *Source: The Greville Memoirs.*

August 10th, 1827.

. . . The Duke of Wellington talked of Canning the other day a great deal at my mother's. He said his talents were astonishing, his compositions admirable, that he possessed the art of saying exactly what was necessary and passing over those topics on which it was not advisable to touch, his fertility and resources inexhaustible. He thought him the finest speaker he had ever heard; though he prided himself extremely upon his compositions, he would patiently endure any criticisms upon such papers as he submitted for the consideration of the Cabinet, and would allow them to be altered in any way that was suggested; he (the Duke) particularly had often ' cut and hacked ' his papers, and Canning never made the least objection. . . . It was not so, however, in conversation and discussion. Any difference of opinion or dissent from his views threw him into ungovernable rage, and on such occasions he flew out with a violence which, the Duke said, had often compelled him to be silent that he might not be involved in bitter personal altercation. He said that Canning was usually very silent in the Cabinet, seldom spoke at all, but when he did he maintained his opinions with extraordinary tenacity. He said that he was one of the idlest of men. This I do not believe. . . .

LORD EGREMONT ENTERTAINS AT PETWORTH

Source: The Greville Memoirs.

May 23, 1834. . . . He had it arranged in the open air, and a fine sight it was; fifty-four tables, each fifty feet long were placed in a vast semi-circle on the lawn before the house. Nothing could be more amusing than to look at the preparations. The tables were all spread with cloths, and plates, and dishes; two great tents were erected in the middle to receive the provisions, which were conveyed in carts like ammunition. Plum puddings and loaves were piled like cannon balls, and innumerable joints of boiled and roast beef were spread out, while hot joints were prepared in the kitchen, and sent forth as soon as the firing of guns announced the hour of the feast. Tickets were given to the inhabitants of a certain district, and the number was about 4,000; but, as many more came, the old peer could not endure that there should be anybody hungering outside his gates, and he went out himself and ordered the barriers to be taken down and admittance given to all. They think 6,000 were fed. Gentlemen from the neighbourhood carved for them, and waiters were provided from among the peasantry. The food was distributed from the tents and carried off upon hurdles to all parts of the semicircle. A band

of music paraded around, playing gay airs. The day was glorious
—an unclouded sky and soft southern breeze. . . . At night there
was a great display of fireworks, and I should think that, at the
time they began, not less than 10,000 people were assembled. It
was altogether one of the gayest and most beautiful spectacles I
ever saw.

THE DUKE OF RUTLAND ENTERTAINS
AT BELVOIR

Source: The Greville Memoirs.

Belvoir Castle, January 4, 1838.

To-day (the cook told me) nearly four hundred people will
dine in the Castle. We all went into the servants' hall, where one
hundred and forty-five retainers had just done dinner and were
drinking the Duke's health, singing and speechifying with vociferous applause, shouting, and clapping of hands. I never knew
before that oratory had got down into the servants' hall, but
learned that it is the custom for those to whom the ' gift of the
gab ' has been vouchsafed to harangue the others, the palm of
eloquence being universally conceded to Mr. Tapps the head
coachman, a man of great abdominal dignity, and whose Ciceron-
ian brows are adorned with an ample flaxen wig, which is the
peculiar distinction of the functionaries of the whip. I should
like to bring the surly Radical here who scowls and snarls at ' the
selfish aristocracy who have no sympathies with the people ',
and when he has seen these hundreds feasting in the Castle, and
heard their loud shouts of joy and congratulation, and then
visited the villages around, and listened to the bells chiming all
about the vale, say whether ' the greatest happiness of the greatest
number ' would be promoted by the destruction of all the
feudality which belongs inseparably to this scene, and by the
substitution of some abstract political rights for all the beef and
ale and music and dancing with which they are made merry and
glad even for so brief a space. The Duke of Rutland is as selfish
a man as any of his class—that is, he never does what he does not
like, and spends his whole life in a round of such pleasures as
suit his taste, but he is neither a foolish nor a bad man, and

partly from a sense of duty, and partly from inclination, he devotes time and labour to the interest and welfare of the people who live and labour on his estate. He is a Guardian of a very large Union, and he not only attends regularly the meetings of Poor Law Guardians every week or fortnight . . . but he visits those paupers who receive out-of-door relief, sits and converses with them, invites them to complain to him if they have anything to complain of, and tells them that he is not only their friend but their representative at the assembly of Guardians, and it is his duty to see that they are nourished and protected. . . .

THE CONVICTION OF THE DORCHESTER LABOURERS

Spring Assizes, Western Circuit, Dorchester. Monday March 17th. Crown Court (before Baron Williams). Administering unlawful oaths.

The continual reduction of agricultural wages at Tolpuddle in Dorset caused the labourers there to get in touch with the Grand National Consolidated Trades Union, whose chief propagandist was Robert Owen. After two representatives of the Grand National had visited Tolpuddle, a Friendly Society of Agricultural Labourers was set up there. This society adopted the initiatory ceremonies common in the early Trade Unions. The local farmers persuaded the magistrates to take action, and George and James Lovelace, the leaders (who were Methodists) and some of their friends, were imprisoned. They were accused only of administering unlawful oaths—they had not called a strike nor even asked for higher wages. The accused were sentenced to seven years' transportation. The remainder of this savage sentence was remitted in 1836.

Source: The Times, March 20, 1834.

John Lock. I live at Half Puddle. I went to Toll Puddle a fortnight before Christmas. I know the prisoner James Brine. I saw him that evening at John Woolley's. He called me out and I went with him. He took me to Thomas Stanfield's, and asked me if I would go in with him. I refused and went away. I saw him in about a fortnight afterwards in a barn. He asked me if I would go to Toll Puddle with him. I agreed to do so. James Hammet was then with him. Edward Legg, Richard Peary, Henry Courtney, and Elias Riggs were with us. They joined us as we were going along. One of them asked if there would not be something to pay, and one said there would be 1 shilling to pay on entering, and 1d. a week after. We all went into Thomas Stanfield's house into a room upstairs. John Stanfield came to the door of the room. I saw James Lovelace and George Lovelace go along the passage. One of the men asked if we were ready. We said, yes. One of them said, ' Then bind your eyes ', and we took out handkerchiefs and bound over our eyes. They then led us into another room on the same floor. Someone then read a paper, but I don't know what the meaning of it was. After that we were asked to kneel down, which we did. Then there was some more reading; I don't know what it was about. It seemed to be out of some part of the Bible. Then we got up and took off the bandages from our eyes. I had then seen James Lovelace and John Stanfield in the room. Some one read again, but I don't know what it was, and then we were told to kiss the book, when our eyes were unblinded, and I saw the book, which looked like a little Bible. I then saw all the prisoners there. James Lovelace had on a white dress, it was not a smock-frock. They told us the rules, that we should have to pay 1 shilling then, and a 1d. a week afterwards, to support the men when they were standing out from their work. They said we were as brothers; that when we were to stop for wages we should not tell our masters ourselves, but that the masters would have a note or a letter sent to them.

SOCIAL INEQUALITY AND SOCIAL HARMONY IN OXFORDSHIRE

Source: Diary of a Country Parson (The Reverend James Woodforde) 1758–1781, ed. J. Beresford, Oxford University Press, 1924, pp. 29, 129.

James Woodforde (1740–1803) came of clerical and literary stock. His father was rector of Ansford and Castle Cary, Somerset. Woodforde was educated at Winchester and was a scholar and subsequently Fellow of New College. In 1773 he was Proctor. In 1774 he was presented to the college living of Weston in Norfolk where he lived until his death on January 1, 1803. He became famous only when his diary was published in 1924. The extracts illustrate the comparative ease with which, in a relatively static society, the different classes were able to mix ' in complete inequality and complete harmony '. The world of Jane Austen (1775-1817) is remote from that of the dinner-party at Chesterton. The essential division into ' two nations '—as Mr. G. M. Young pointed out—was not between Disraeli's (and Karl Marx's) the Rich and the Poor, but between the Respectable and those who were not.

1763

Aug. 3. Spent the evening at Rice's, my quondam Taylor, with himself and his wife, at High Street. They had provided a handsome supper for me (viz.) a neck of Lamb and Tarts, but I had supp'd at College. I smoaked a Pipe with Mr. Rice, and finished a Bottle of Wine between us, and his Wife, and then I departed. . . .

Aug. 21. Went to Chesterton again this morning and did the Duty of the day there. Dined at Mr. Pryor's again, and with him, his brother the Lawyer, his Sister and Niece and Mr. and Mrs. Weaver, Miss Goff, Mr. Payne a Baker at Brackley, an everlasting Spunger, but a droll Fellow, and Mr. Banks of our College. . . .

1774

Ap. 21. I supped and spent the evening at the Chequer. . . . At 11 this night was called out of the Chequer by Webber to go with him to quell a riot in George Lane, but when we came it was quiet, however we went to the Swan in George Lane, and unfortunately met with a Gownsman above stairs carousing with some low-life people. We conducted him to his College. He belongs to University College, is a scholar there, and his name is Hawkins, he was terribly frightened and cried almost all the way to his Coll. and was upon his knees often in the street, and bareheaded all the way. He is to appear again tomorrow before Webber. We returned to New College by 12 o'clock.

ELIZABETH FRY AT NEWGATE

Elizabeth Fry (1780–1845), sister of Joseph John Gurney and Daniel Gurney, was a member of the famous family of Quaker bankers. A Quaker minister at twenty-nine and a talented preacher, she married Joseph Fry, 1800. She formed an association for the improvement of female prisoners in Newgate, 1817, engaged in prison reform, and in improving the lot of tramps in London and Brighton. She started an order of nursing sisters.

Thomas Fowell Buxton (1786–1845) educated at Trinity College,

Dublin, he advocated prison reform, 1816–20; M.P. for Weymouth, 1818–37; advocated abolition of slavery in British dominions, 1822–33; pressed for abolition of African slave trade, 1839–40; and became a baronet, 1840. His monument is in Westminster Abbey.

The three following extracts illustrate the abominable conditions in one particularly abominable prison, the reaction to the situation by two outstanding examples of what may be broadly described as the Evangelical movement in English Christianity, and the immediate support which the *Edinburgh Review* was able to give.

Source: An Inquiry whether Crime and Misery are produced or prevented by our present System of Prison Discipline. Illustrated by Descriptions of the Borough Compter, Tothill Fields Prison, the Jail at St. Albans, the Jail at Guildford, the Jail at Bristol, the Jails at Bury and Ilchester, the Maison de Force at Ghent, the Philadelphia Prison, the Penitentiary at Millbank, and the Proceedings of the Ladies' Committee at Newgate. By Thomas Fowell Buxton, London 1818. Quoted by Jeffrey in ' Prison Discipline ', The *Edinburgh Review*, September, 1818.

Further Reading: Early Victorian England, ed. G. M. Young, vol. i, pp. 195–201. Janet Whitney: *Elizabeth Fry,* Harrap, 1938.

(i) About four years ago, Mrs. Fry was induced to visit Newgate, by the representations of its state made by some persons of the Society of Friends.

She found the female side in a situation which no language can describe. Nearly *three hundred women,* sent there for every gradation of crime, some untried, and some under sentence of death, were crowded together in the two wards and two cells, which are now quite appropriated to the untried, and which are found quite inadequate to contain even this diminished number with any tolerable convenience. Here they saw their friends, and kept their multitudes of children; and they had no other place for cooking, washing, eating and sleeping.

They all slept on the floor; at times one hundred and twenty in one ward, without so much as a mat for bedding; and many of them were very nearly naked. She saw them openly drinking spirits; and her ears were offended by the most dreadful imprecations. Every thing was filthy to excess, and the smell was quite disgusting. Every one, even the Governor, was reluctant to go amongst them. He persuaded her to leave her watch in the office, telling her that his presence would not prevent its being torn from her! She saw enough to convince her that every thing bad was going on. In short, in giving me this account, she repeatedly said 'All I tell thee, is a faint picture of the reality; the filth, the closeness of the rooms, the ferocious manners and expressions of the women towards each other, and the abandoned wickedness which everything bespoke, are quite indescribable!'

[She set to work immediately to do something for some seventy children who were wandering about in what Jeffrey accurately described as ' this scene of horror.']

(ii) The next day she commenced the school, in company with a young lady, who then visited a prison for the first time, and who since gave me a very interesting description of her feelings upon that occasion. The railing was crowded with half-naked women, struggling together for the front situations with the most boisterous violence, and begging with the utmost vociferation. She felt as if she was going into a den of wild beasts; and she well recollects quite shuddering when the door closed upon her, and she was locked in, with such a herd of novel and desperate companions. This day, however, the school surpassed their utmost expectations: their only pain arose from the numerous and pressing applications made by young women, who longed to be taught and employed. The narrowness of the room rendered it then impossible to yield to their requests: but they tempted these ladies to project a school for the employment of the tried women, for teaching them to read and to work.

When this intention was mentioned to the friends of these ladies, it appeared at first so visionary and unpromising, that it met with very slender encouragement. . . . But the noble zeal of these unassuming women was not to be repressed; and feeling that their design was intended for the good and the happiness of others, they trusted that it would receive the guidance and protection of Him, who often is pleased to accomplish the highest purposes by the most feeble instruments.

With these impressions, they had the boldness to declare, that if a committee could be found who would share the labour, and a matron who would engage never to leave the place, day or night, they would undertake to try the experiment, that is they would themselves *find employment* for the women, *procure the necessary money*, till the city could be induced to relieve them, and be answerable for the safety of the property committed into the hands of the prisoners.

The Committee *immediately presented itself*; it consisted of the wife of a clergyman, and eleven (female) members of the Society of Friends. They professed their willingness to suspend every other engagement and avocation, and to devote themselves to Newgate; and in truth, they have performed their promise. With no interval for relaxation, and with but few intermissions from the call of other and more imperious duties, they have since *lived* amongst the prisoners.

[The consequences are described and the impression made by them on qualified observers.]

(iii) Many of these knew Newgate; had visited it a few months before, and had not forgotten the painful impressions made by a scene exhibiting, perhaps, the very utmost limits, of misery and guilt.—They now saw, what, without exaggeration may be called a transformation. Riot, licentiousness, and filth, exchanged for order, sobriety, and comparative neatness in the chamber, the apparel, and the persons of the prisoners. They saw no more an assemblage of abandoned and shameless creatures, half-naked and half-drunk, rather demanding, than requesting charity. The prison no more resounded with obscenity, and imprecations, and licentious songs; and to use the coarse, but the just, expression of one who knew the prison well, " this hell upon earth " already exhibited the appearance of an industrious manufactory, or a well-regulated family.

A CURATE IN SHROPSHIRE

THOMAS JONES (1752–1845)

Educated at Ystrad Meurig under the famous scholar and poet Edward Richard (1714-77), he was ordained in 1774. He served a number of curacies, first in Wales and then in Shropshire. He finally became curate and then rector of Creaton and Spratton, Northamptonshire. A staunch churchman, he became a prominent figure among the clergy of the Evangelical party. His career at Creaton shows him as an exception to the perhaps too familiar generalisation that such men made little impression on rural parishes.

This extract shows an English Sunday still in its medieval pattern, as in Baxter's day, as well as the difficulties of such a man at the beginning of his career, and the influence of such men as Whitfield's friend, de Courcy at St. Alkmund's which linked with that of the Hills of Hawkestone who subsequently befriended Jones at Loppington.

Source: J. Owen, *Memoir of the Reverend Thomas Jones*, Seeleys, London, 1851, pp. 22–37.

1779–80: Leintwardine, near Ludlow.

Finding but very few people at Church on the Sundays, and not many in the streets, I was convinced that they had retired from the village for some purpose or other. I went one Sunday after service in quest of them, and at about a mile distant from the village, on entering a large secluded meadow, I found a company of at least three hundred persons, of all ages, engaged in all manner of diversions, such as cricket, foot-ball, etc. On seeing me entering the gate into the field, they all fled . . . so that in a few minutes not one was to be seen. This had no other good effect than to disperse them for that day. . . . During the year and a half I spent with them, no kind or degree of reformation appeared to have taken place. . . .

1780–1: Longnor, near Shrewsbury.

I went to Longnor in December, 1780. . . . Longnor is situated in the midst of a rich and delightful plain, not far distant from the foot of the classical and majestic hill, Caractacus . . . . Here again. . . I found myself placed in the midst of a people who knew not the Lord. They were very decent as to their outward conduct, and orderly in Church; but, as far as it appeared, destitute of spiritual religion, with the exception of one man, a Mr. Taylor, a Schoolmaster: he was a stated hearer of the Rev. Mr. De Courcy, at Shrewsbury, seven miles off. . . .

As my custom had always been to retire into solitude, out of doors, for devotion, I pursued the practice here, and went two or three times a week to the top of a very lofty hill, about three miles from my vicar's house where I lodged. And on this hill I generally spent about two hours, in meditation and earnest wrestling with heaven for divine blessings on my soul, which hungered after holiness and righteousness. . . . Whenever I travel through Shropshire, I never fail to turn my eyes toward that sacred hill (called the Lawley) and to gaze on it with reverence and delight, as my temple in the days of old.

OXFORD AND CAMBRIDGE IN THE EIGHTEENTH CENTURY: THE LIGHTER SIDE OF LEARNING

Source: Woodforde's *Diary of a Country Parson,* pp. 158–9.

John Scott, first Earl of Eldon (1751–1838), Fellow of University College, Oxford. Knighted and Solicitor-General, 1788; Attorney-General, 1793; Lord Chief Justice of Common Pleas, 1799; Lord Chancellor, 1801; Viscount Encombe and Earl of Eldon, 1821. In politics he was a strong opponent of parliamentary reform. His decrees were seldom appealed from, and hardly ever reversed.

Richard Watson (1737–1815), Scholar and Fellow of Trinity College, Cambridge. Professor, first of Chemistry and then of Divinity, to both of which subjects he made real contributions, he became Bishop of Llandaff in 1782. He was a Whig and a reformer. His *Apology for Christianity* which was directed against Gibbon is described by Mr. G. M. Young as ' too polite to provoke, and too dull to require, an answer '. Gibbon astutely described him as ' the most candid of my critics '. Both were men of brilliant achievement who rose from comparatively undistinguished origins to positions of the first importance.

The following extracts give in fact an unfairly poor impression of Oxford and Cambridge. Both universities stood in need of reform, but both produced an array of energy, learning and ability during the eighteenth century which was certainly not fortuitous.

Further Reading: C. Wordsworth: *Scholae Academicae,* 1877; and *Social Life at the English Universities in the Eighteenth Century,* 1874. Ward: *Georgian Oxford.* Oxford University Press, 1958. V. H. Green: *Oxford Common Room,* Arnold, 1957.

(i) LORD ELDON IS EXAMINED FOR HIS DEGREE AT OXFORD IN 1770

An examination for a degree at Oxford was a farce in my time. I was examined in Hebrew and History: " What is the Hebrew for the Place of a Skull? " said the Examiner. " Golgotha," I replied. " Who founded University College? " I answered " King Alfred ". " Very well, sir," said the Examiner, " then you are competent for your degree ".

(ii) RICHARD WATSON BECOMES PROFESSOR OF CHEMISTRY AT CAMBRIDGE IN 1764

At the time this honour was conferred upon me I knew nothing at all of Chemistry, had never read a syllable on the subject, nor seen a single experiment in it; but I was tired with mathematics and natural philosophy, and the *vehementissima gloriae cupido* stimulated me to try my strength in a new pursuit, and the kindness of the University (it was always kind to me) animated me to very extraordinary exertions.

(iii) RICHARD WATSON BECOMES REGIUS PROFESSOR OF DIVINITY AT CAMBRIDGE IN 1771

On being raised to this distinguished office, I immediately applied myself with great eagerness to the study of Divinity.

(iv) A FELLOW OF TRINITY ON HIS WAY TO DINE

Source: H. Gunning, *Reminiscences of Cambridge.* Cambridge University Press, 1932, pp. 135–136, 154–155.

Henry Gunning (1768–1854) senior esquire bedell of Cambridge University; scholar of Christ's College; sixth wrangler, 1788; esquire bedell, 1789 (senior, 1827–54). He had a tenacious memory and a reputation for wit. In consequence when, shortly after his death, his *Reminiscences* were published, there was an element of relief in the applause with which the book was greeted, since Gunning was found to have confined himself chiefly to giving a lively picture of the university at the end of the eighteenth century.

' When I was last in town,' said he, 'I was going to dine with a friend, and passed through a small court, just as a lad was hanging up a board, on which was this tempting inscription:

A roast pig this instant set upon the table.

' The invitation was irresistable—I ordered a quarter: it was *very delicate* and *very delicious.* I despatched a second and a third portion, but was constrained to leave one quarter behind, as my dinner hour was approaching, and my friend was remarkably punctual.'

(v)   'NEQUE ANGELI, NEQUE ANGLI'

Addresses were voted during this month by the University and Corporation, congratulating the King on the successful termination of the battle of the Nile. On the morning following the presentation, I called on a merchant in the city, who had taken his degree at the sister University. He told me that after their address had been presented, he remained with his friend Canning, to see the presentation of ours, and that they had a hearty laugh at our expense.

It unfortunately happened that several of our deputation were not particularly well calculated to make a good figure in a procession. The Vice-Chancellor was a martyr to gout, and so extremely deaf that he never knew whether he was speaking in a high or a low tone. Dr. Douglas had but one eye, and was a perfect skeleton. The Registrary (George Borlase) was afflicted with black jaundice; and Broderip, of King's, was just recovering from yellow jaundice. Another of the deputation was a cripple, but I cannot just now remember his name.

One of Canning's observations was—' What have we here? If Pope Gregory had seen this assemblage, he would not have said, " Haud Angli, sed Angeli "; his observation would probably have been, " Neque Angeli, neque Angli! ".

THE HOUSE OF COMMONS in 1782

Source: C. P. Moritz, *Travels in England in* 1782. London, Humphrey Milford, 1924, pp. 52–6.

And thus, I now, for the first time, saw the whole of the British nation assembled in its representatives, in rather a mean-looking building, that not a little resembles a chapel. The speaker, an elderly man, dressed in an enormous wig, with two knotted curls behind, and a black cloak, with his hat on his head, sat opposite to me on a lofty chair; before which stands a table, like an altar; and at this there sit two men, called clerks, dressed in black, with black cloaks. On the table, by the side of the great parchment acts, lies a huge, gilt sceptre, which is always taken away, and placed in a conservatory under the table, as soon as ever the speaker quits the chair. . . .

P

All round, on the sides of the house under the gallery, are benches for the members, covered with green cloth, always one above the other, in order that he who is speaking, may see over those who sit before him. The seats in the gallery are on the same plan. The members of parliament keep their hats on, but the spectators in the gallery are uncovered.

The members of the House of Commons have nothing particular in their dress; they even come into the house in their great coats, and with boots and spurs. It is not at all uncommon to see a member lying stretched out on one of the benches, while others are debating. Some crack nuts, others eat oranges, or what-ever else is in season. There is no end to their going in and out; and as often as anyone wishes to go out, he places himself before the speaker, and makes him his bow, as if, like a schoolboy, he asked his tutor's permission.

Those who speak seem to deliver themselves with but little, perhaps not always with even a decorous gravity. All that is necessary is to stand up in your place, take off your hat, turn to the speaker (to whom all the speeches are addressed) to hold your hat and stick in one hand, and with the other hand to make any such motions as you fancy necessary to accompany your speech.

If it happens that a member rises, who is but a bad speaker, or if what he says is generally deemed not sufficiently interesting, so much noise is made, that he can scarcely distinguish his own words. This must needs be a distressing situation; and it seems then to be particularly laughable, when the speaker, in his chair, like a tutor in a school, again and again endeavours to restore order, which he does, by calling out ' To Order! To Order! '

On the contrary, when a favourite member, and one who speaks well, and to the purpose, rises, the most perfect silence reigns: and his friends and admirers, one after another, make their approbation known by calling out ' Hear him '. . . .

The first day that I was at the House of Commons, an English gentleman, who sat next to me in the gallery, very obligingly pointed out to me the principal members; such as Fox, Burke, Rigby, etc., all of whom I heard speak. . . .

Fox was sitting to the right of the speaker, not far from the table on which the gilt sceptre lay. He now took his place so near it that he could reach it with his hand, and, thus placed, he gave it many a violent and hearty thump, either to aid, or to shew, the energy with which he spoke. . . . It is impossible for me to describe with what fire, and persuasive eloquence he spoke, and how the speaker in the chair incessantly nodded approbation, from beneath his solemn wig; and innumerable voices incessantly cried out ' Hear him! Hear him! ' and when there was the least sign that he intended to leave off speaking, they no less vociferously exclaimed, ' Go on ! ' and so he continued to speak in this manner for nearly two hours.

WESTMINSTER ELECTIONS
1782

Westminster was one of the few popular constituencies. Almost every householder had a vote.

Source: C. P. Moritz, *Travels in England in* 1782. London, Humphrey Milford, 1924, pp. 61–64.

The cities of London and Westminster send, the one four, and the other two members to parliament. Mr. Fox is one of the two members for Westminster; one seat was vacant; and that vacancy was now to be filled. Sir Cecil Wray, . . . was now publicly chosen. I was told, that at these elections, when there is a strong opposition party, there is often bloody work; but this election was, in the electioneering phrase, a hollow thing.

The election was held in Covent Garden, a large market-place, in the open air. There was a scaffold erected just before the door of a very handsome church. . . . A temporary edifice, formed only of boards and wood nailed together, was erected on the occasion. It was called the hustings: and filled with benches; and at one end of it, where the benches ended, mats were laid; on which those who spoke to the people stood. In the area before the hustings, immense multitudes of people were assembled; of whom the greatest part seemed to be of the lowest order. To this tumultuous crowd, however, the speakers often bowed very low, and always addressed them by the title of gentlemen. Sir Cecil

Wray was obliged to step forward, and promise these same
gentlemen, with hand and heart, that he would faithfully fulfil his
duties as their representative. He also made an apology, because,
on account of his journey and ill-health, he had not been able to
wait on them, as became him, at their respective houses. The
moment that he began to speak, even this rude rabble became all
as quiet as the raging sea after a storm . . . and as soon as he had
done speaking, they again vociferated a loud and universal huzza,
everyone at the same time waving his hat.

And now, being formally declared to have been legally
chosen, he again bowed most profoundly, and returned thanks
for the great honour done him: when a well-dressed man, whose
name I could not learn, stepped forward, and in a well-indited
speech, congratulated both the chosen and the choosers. ' Upon
my word,' said a gruff carter, who stood near me, ' that man speaks
well '.

Even little boys clambered up, and hung on the rails and the
lamp-posts; and, as if the speeches had also been addressed to
them, they too listened with the utmost attention; and they too
testified their approbation of it, by joining lustily in the three
cheers, and waving their hats.

. . . When the whole was over, the rampant spirit of liberty,
and the wild impatience of a genuine English mob were exhibited
in perfection. In a very few minutes, the whole scaffolding,
benches and chairs, and everything else, were completely
destroyed; and the mat, with which it had been covered, torn
into ten thousand long strips, or pieces, with which they encircled
multitudes of people of all ranks. These they hurried along
with them, and everything else that came in their way, as trophies
of joy; and thus, in the midst of exultation and triumph, they
paraded through many of the most populous streets of London.

LORD PERCY IS ELECTED IN PLACE OF FOX
1806

Source: Graham Wallas, *Life of Francis Place*, Allen and Unwin, 1918,
pp. 42–3.

My indignation was greatly increased when I saw the servants
of the Duke of Northumberland, in their showy dress liveries,

throwing lumps of bread and cheese among the dense crowd of vagabonds they had collected together. To see these vagabonds catching the lumps, shouting, swearing, fighting, and blackguarding in every possible way, women as well as men, all the vile wretches from the courts and alleys in St. Giles and Westminster . . . ; to see these people representing, as it was said, the electors of Westminster, was certainly the lowest possible step of degradation, except, indeed, if it be possible, to hear it said, as it was said, that ' the electors of Westminster had been treated by the bounty of the Duke '. Some who mingled in the mob were ashamed of the proceedings, and as the mob pressed round the butts which contained the beer, suggested that the best way would be to knock in the heads as they stood up on end. This was done immediately. The heads were beaten in, and the coal-heavers ladled the beer out with their long-tailed, broad-brimmed hats; but the mob pressing on, the butts were upset, and the beer flowed along the gutters, from whence some made efforts to obtain it. It may be possible to imagine something like the disgraceful scene, but it is not possible either to describe it or to excite in the reader the almost uncontrollable feelings of a spectator. I was not the only one who felt indignation.

1819

The successful candidate was the Whig William Lamb, afterwards Lord Melbourne. He had been opposed by Burdett and Hobhouse.

Source: E. Ashley, *Life of Lord Palmerston*, Bentley, 1879, vol i, p. 87. Extract from a letter written by Lord Palmerston.

Stanhope Street, March 2, 1819.

There was not much row till the last day. They meant to chair Lamb, and their infantry, consisting of some hundred bruisers and blackguards, were to have got possession of the ground, and then an escort of about sixty Whig equestrians were to have come up to have accompanied the procession through the streets to Brooks' and Burlington House. But, alas! how short-sighted are mortals. Crib, Gully, and Caleb Baldwin declared that to chair was impossible, that they and Lamb should all be murdered if it was attempted. On this the Committee gave it up, and sent to stop the cavalry. The messenger missed them, and at the appointed hour they arrived, found the avenues to Covent Garden blocked up by an immense crowd, cut their way through, found the chairing given up, and had to cut their way back again. They were covered with mud and dirt, and some received some severe blows with stones thrown at them. The mob chased them to Pall Mall, and some even to Grosvenor Square. Lady Cowper [Lamb's sister] had a very narrow escape. She was returning from the Ladies' Committee of Almack's at this time. Her coachman happened to have Lamb's colours in his hat, and in passing through St. James's Square to Pall Mall on her way to Melbourne House the mob began pelting the carriage, and one large stone nearly broke through the panel of the carriage, about three inches below the side glass. Lady Caroline Lamb's carriage was also attacked in St. James Street, and a boy who was in it cut on the forehead by something thrown. These brutal outrages are quite peculiar to the present day. Lamb himself would certainly have been demolished but for the protection of a detachment of Life Guards.

PETERLOO 1819

Between 50,000 and 60,000 people marched with banners to the Reform Meeting at St. Peter's Fields, Manchester, on Monday, August 16. Eleven were killed and perhaps 400 wounded when the soldiery, obeying the orders of the magistrates to arrest Henry Hunt, who was addressing the meeting, charged into the crowd.

Henry Hunt (1773–1835) was a Wiltshire farmer's son. While in the Wiltshire Yeomanry he had been imprisoned for refusing to apologise to his colonel, whom he had challenged to a duel. He became a well-known radical agitator. After his arrest at Peterloo he was sentenced to two years' imprisonment.

Source: Samuel Bamford, Passages in the Life of a Radical, 2 vols. London, 1893, pp. 166–8. First published in parts at Heywood, Lancs., 1839–1842.

Samuel Bamford (1788–1872). In his youth a weaver, a sailor in coastal vessels, then a warehouseman. Imprisoned for twelve months after Peterloo. Became a journalist in London and was a special constable during the Chartist agitation in 1848.

Further Reading: Two chapters on Peterloo in Humphry House: All in Due Time, Hart-Davis, 1955. Donald Read: Peterloo, Manchester Univ. Press, 1958.

The meeting was indeed a tremendous one. Hunt mounted the hustings; the music ceased. . . . Mr. Hunt, stepping towards the front of the stage, took off his white hat[1], and addressed the people.

Whilst he was doing so, I proposed to an acquaintance that, as the speeches and resolutions were not likely to contain anything new to us, and as we could see them in the papers, we should retire a while, and get some refreshment, of which I stood in much need, being in not very robust health. He assented, and we had got to nearly the outside of the crowd, when a noise and strange murmur arose towards the church. Some persons said it was the Blackburn people coming; and I stood on tiptoe, and looked in the direction whence the noise proceeded, and saw a party of cavalry in blue and white uniform, come trotting sword in hand, round the corner of a garden-wall, and to the front of a row of new houses, where they reined up in a line. . . .

On the cavalry drawing up they were received with a shout of goodwill, as I understood it. They shouted again, waving their sabres over their heads; and then, slackening rein, and striking spur into their steeds, they dashed forward, and began cutting the people.

' Stand fast,' I said, ' they are riding upon us, stand fast.' And there was a general cry in our quarter of ' stand fast '. The cavalry were in confusion: they evidently could not, with all the weight of man and horse, penetrate that compact mass of human beings; and their sabres were plied to hew a way through naked held-up hands, and defenceless heads; and then chopped limbs, and wound-gaping skulls were seen; and groans and cries were mingled with the din of that horrid confusion. 'Ah! ah!' 'For shame! For shame!' was shouted. Then, 'Break! break! they are killing them in front, and they cannot get away' ; and there was a general cry of ' Break! break '. For a moment the crowd held back as in a pause; then was a rush, heavy and resistless as a headlong sea; and a sound like low thunder, with screams, prayers, and imprecations from the crowd-moiled, and sabre doomed, who could not escape. . . .

[1] Hunt's white top hat was famous. To wear one became a sign of the holding of radical opinions.

On the breaking of the crowd, the yeomanry wheeled; and dashing wherever there was an opening, they followed, pressing and wounding. Many females appeared as the crowd opened; and striplings or mere youths also were found. Their cries were piteous and heart-rending; and would, one might have supposed, have disarmed any human resentment: but here their appeals were vain. Women, white-vested maids, and tender youths, were indiscriminately sabred or trampled. . . .

In ten minutes from the commencement of the havoc, the field was an open and almost deserted space. The sun looked down through a sultry and motionless air. The curtains and blinds of the windows within view were all closed. A gentleman or two might occasionally be seen looking out from one of the new houses . . . others were assisting the wounded, or carrying off the dead. The hustings remained, with a few broken and hewed flag-staves erect, and a torn and gashed banner or two dropping; whilst over the whole field, were strewed caps, bonnets, hats, shawls and shoes, and other parts of male and female dress; trampled, torn and bloody. The yeomanry had dismounted—some were easing their horses' girths, others adjusting their accoutrements; and some were wiping their sabres. Several mounds of human beings still remained where they had fallen, crushed down, and smothered. Some of these still groaning—others with staring eyes, were gasping for breath, and others would never breathe more. All was silent save those low sounds, and the occasional snorting and pawing of steeds. Persons might sometimes be noticed peeping from attics and over the tall ridgings of houses, but they quickly withdrew, as if fearful of being observed, or unable to sustain the full gaze, of a scene so hideous and abhorrent.

WILLIAM IV

William IV was the third son of George III. He entered the Navy at the age of 15, was present at the first Battle of Cape St. Vincent in 1780, and served in the West Indies.

When he was 57 he married Adelaide of Saxe-Meiningen. He became King in 1830 when he was 65, and died in 1837.

Source: The Greville Memoirs.

(*a*) William IV at the funeral of George IV.
July 18, 1830.

. . . At the late King's funeral he behaved with great in-
decency. That ceremony was very well managed and a fine
sight. . . . The attendance was not very numerous, and when
they had all got together in St. George's Hall a gayer company I
never beheld. . . . The King was chief mourner, and, to my
astonishment, as he entered the chapel directly behind the body,
in a situation in which he should have been apparently, if not
really, absorbed in the melancholy duty he was performing, he
darted up to Strathaven, who was ranged on one side below the
Dean's stall, shook him heartily by the hand, and then went on
nodding to the right and left.

(*b*)

July 20, 1830. . . . more affable, less dignified than the late
King; but when this [a meeting of the Privy Council] was over
. . . and he might very well have sat himself quietly down and
rested, he must needs put on his plainer clothes and start on a
ramble about the streets, alone too. In Pall Mall he met Watson
Taylor, and took his arm and went up to St. James's Street.
There he was soon followed by a mob making an uproar, and
when he got near White's a woman came up and kissed him.
Belfast (who had been sworn in Privy Councillor in the morning),
who saw this from White's, and Clinton thought it time to inter-
fere, and came out to attend upon him. The mob increased, and,
always holding W. Taylor's arm, and flanked by Clinton and
Belfast, who got shoved and kicked about to their inexpressible
wrath, he got back to the Palace amid shouting and bawling
and applause. When he got home he asked them to go in and
take a quiet walk in the garden, and said, ' Oh, never mind all
this; when I have walked about a few times they will get used to
it, and will take no notice.' . . . Belfast told me this in the Park,
fresh from the scene and smarting from the buffeting he had got.
. . .

July 21, 1830. . . . . Altogether he seems a kind-hearted, well-
meaning, not stupid, burlesque, bustling old fellow, and if he
doesn't go mad may make a very decent King.

A GERMAN VISITOR TO PARLIAMENT IN 1827

The debates which the German Prince heard arose out of the political situation which followed the death of Lord Liverpool. Canning had replaced Liverpool as Prime Minister, whereupon Wellington, Eldon, Peel, and four other members of the Tory Cabinet, distrusting Canning's policies, had resigned. The Whigs were divided in their attitude to the new Prime Minister: some, like Grey, disapproved of him; others, including Brougham, gave him their support.

Source: A Tour in Germany, Holland and England in the Years 1826, 1827 *and* 1828, by A German Prince (London 1832), vol. iv, pp. 17–24.

The author of this work was Prince von Pückler-Muskau (1785–1871). He had fought well in the War of Liberation; had inherited a fortune from his father, and had been created Prince by the King of Prussia. In 1866 he was with the Prussian army in the war with Austria.

May 1st [1827]

. . . From four o'clock in the afternoon till ten, I sat in the House of Commons; crowded, in horrible heat, most uncomfortably seated; and yet with such eager, excited attention, that the six hours passed like a moment.

There is something truly great in such a representative assembly! This simplicity of exterior; this dignity and experience; this vast power without, and absence of all pomp within!

The debate this evening was moreover of the highest interest. Most of the former Ministers have, as you know, resigned; among them, some of the most influential men in England, and (since Napoleon's and Blücher's death) the greatest Commander in Europe. Canning, the champion of the liberal party, has defeated this Ministry, and is, in spite of all their efforts, become head of the new one, the formation of which was left to him, according to the usual custom here. But the whole power of the exasperated ultra-aristocracy and their dependants presses upon him; and even one of his most particular friends, a commoner like himself, is among the resigning Ministers, and has joined the hostile party. This gentleman (Mr. Peel) today opened the attack, in a long and clever speech, though full of repetition. It would lead me too far, . . . were I to go into the details of the present political questions. My object is only to give you an idea of the tactic with which, on the one side, the leader of the new Opposition headed the attack, and was followed by several more obscure combatants, who planted a stroke here and there; while on the other, the old Opposition, the Whigs (who now support the liberal Ministry with all their might), more skilfully commenced with their musketry, and reserved the heavy fire of their great gun, Brougham. In a magnificent speech which flowed on like a clear stream, he tried to disarm his opponent; now tortured him with sarcasms; now taking a higher flight, wrought upon the sensibility, or convinced the reason of his hearers. . . .

I had heard and admired Brougham before. No man ever spoke with greater fluency,   hour after hour, in a clear unbroken stream of eloquence—with a fine and distinct organ,—riveting the attention,—without once halting, or pausing,—without repeating, recalling, or mistaking a word; defects which frequently deform Mr. Peel's speeches. Brougham speaks as a good reader reads from a book. Nevertheless, it seems to me that you perceive only extraordinary talent, formidable pungent wit, and rare presence of mind:—the heart-warming power of *genius*, such as flows from Canning's tongue, he possesses, in my opinion, in a far lower degree.

Canning, the hero of the day, now rose. If his predecessor might be compared to a dexterous and elegant boxer, Canning presented the image of a finished antique gladiator. All was noble, refined, simple;—then suddenly, at one splendid point, his eloquence burst forth like lightning—grand and all-subduing. A kind of languor and weakness, apparently the consequence of his late illness and of the load of business laid upon him, seemed somewhat to diminish his energy, but perhaps increased his influence over the feelings.

His speech was, in every point of view, the most complete, as well as the most irresistibly persuasive;—the crown and glory of the debate. Never shall I lose the impression which this, and that other celebrated speech of his on the affairs of Portugal, made upon me. . . .

On the following day the House of Lords was opened under the same remarkable circumstances as the House of Commons had been, though there are no men of talents equal to Brougham, nor, above all, to Canning. Lord Ellenborough rose first, and said that the late Ministers were accused of having resigned in consequence of a combination, and of having thus been guilty of the great offence of endeavouring to abridge the constitutional prerogative of the King to change his Ministers entirely at his own free will. For the preservation of their honour he must therefore claim for them to be heard fully in their own justification. Here I saw the great Wellington in a terrible strait. He is no orator, and was compelled, ' bongré, malgré, ' to enter upon his defence, like an accused person. He was considerably agitated; and this senate of his country, though composed of men whom individually, perhaps, he did not care for, appeared more imposing to him ' en masse ' than Napoleon and his hundred thousands. There was, however, something touching to me in seeing the hero of this century in so subdued a situation. He stammered much, interrupted and involved himself, but at length, with the help of his party, who at every stumbling-block gave him time to collect himself by means of noise and cheers, he brought the matter tolerably to this conclusion—that there was no ' conspiracy '. He occasionally said strong things—probably stronger than he meant, for he was evidently not master of his stuff. Among other things, the following words pleased me extremely. ' I am a soldier and no orator. I am utterly deficient in the talents requisite to play a part in this great assembly. I must be more than mad if I ever entertained the insane thought (of which I am accused) of becoming Prime Minister.' All the Lords who had resigned made their apology in turn, as well as they could. Old Lord Eldon tried the effect of tears, which he has always at hand on great occasions; but I did not see that they produced any corresponding emotion in the audience. He was answered by the new Peer and Minister, Lord Goderich, formerly Mr. Robinson, for himself and the Premier, who, being a commoner, cannot appear in the House of Lords, though he governs England, and is become too illustrious, as Mr. Canning, to exchange that name for a title.

The new peer's speech was a very good one, but the beginning excited an universal laugh. True to long habit, he addressed the speaker of the house as ' Sir '. He was so ' décontenancé ' at his blunder, that he put his hand to his forehead, and remained for a time speechless, but recovered his self-possession with the help of the friendly ' Hear, hear! '

. . . Lord Grey far excelled the rest in dignity of manner, a thing which English orators, almost without exception, either neglect or cannot acquire. The want of decorum, remarkable in the lower house, which is like a dirty coffee-house, and where many of the representatives of the people lie sprawling on the benches with their hats on, and talking all sorts of trifles while their colleagues are speaking, seldom appears here. The place and the deportment are, on the contrary, suited to the senate of a great nation.

When I question myself as to the total impression of this day, I must confess that it was at once elevating and melancholy;—the former when I fancied myself an Englishman, the latter when I felt that I was a German.

This twofold senate of the People of England, spite of all the defects and blemishes common to human nature which are blended in its composition, is yet something in the highest degree grand; and in contemplating its power and operation thus near at hand, one begins to understand why it is that the English nation is, as yet, the first on the face of the earth.

THE EDINBURGH REVIEW IS STARTED IN 1802

Its foundation in 1802 began a new period. A Whig journal and devoted to the cause of moderate reform, it was conservative in its literary policy. Its circulation quickly rose to more than ten thousand copies, and in 1815 one number sold fourteen thousand copies. It paid its contributors far more handsomely than had been the custom in the past.

Source: The Collected Works of the Reverend Sydney Smith, Longmans, 1839.

Further Reading: G. W. E. Russell, Sydney Smith, Macmillan, 1905.

(a)

'Among the first persons with whom I became acquainted [in Edinburgh] were Lord Jeffrey, Lord Murray (late Lord Advocate for Scotland), and Lord Brougham; all of them maintaining opinions upon political subjects a little too liberal for the dynasty of Dundas, then exercising supreme power over the northern division of the Island.

One day we happened to meet in the eighth or the ninth story or flat in Buccleugh Place, the elevated residence of the then Mr. Jeffrey. I proposed that we should set up a Review; this was acceded to with acclamation. I was appointed Editor, and remained long enough in Edinburgh to edit the first number of the *Edinburgh Review*. The motto I proposed for the Review was—

Tenui musam meditamur avena.
" We cultivate literature on a little oatmeal."

But this was too near the truth to be admitted, and so we took our present grave motto from Publius Syrus, of whom none of us had, I am sure, ever read a single line; and so began what has since turned out to be a very important and able journal. When I left Edinburgh, it fell into the stronger hands of Lord Jeffrey and Lord Brougham, and reached the highest point of popularity and success.'

The first number had a blue and buff colour (the colours being adopted by the Whigs from Fox's waistcoat) and was thus inscribed:

' THE EDINBURGH REVIEW

or

CRITICAL JOURNAL

FOR

Oct. 1802—Jan. 1803

To be continued quarterly.

———

Judex damnatur cum nocens absolvitur.
Publius Syrus.'

(b)

IN RETROSPECT: 1839

To appreciate the value of the *Edinburgh Review*, the state of England at the period when that journal began should be had in remembrance. The Catholics were not emancipated. The

Corporation and Test Acts were unrepealed. The Game-Laws were horribly oppressive; steel-traps and spring-guns were set all over the country; prisoners tried for their lives could have no counsel. Lord Eldon and the Court of Chancery pressed heavily on mankind. Libel was punished by the most cruel and vindictive imprisonments. The principles of Political Economy were little understood. The laws of debt and conspiracy were upon the worst footing. The enormous wickedness of the slave-trade was tolerated. A thousand evils were in existence, which the talents of good and able men have since lessened or removed; and these efforts have been not a little assisted by the honest boldness of the *Edinburgh Review*.

THE REFORM BILL

(*a*) *Source: The Greville Memoirs.*

March 7, 1831: . . . Nothing talked of, thought of, dreamt of, but Reform. Every creature one meets asks, What is said now? How will it go? What is the last news? What do you think? and so it is from morning till night, in the streets, in the clubs, and in private houses.

March 17, 1831 . . . The country *will* have it; there is a determination on the subject, and a unanimity perfectly marvellous, and no demonstration of the unfitness of any of its parts will be of any avail; some of its details may be corrected and amended, but substantially it must pass pretty much as it is.

(*b*) *Source: Life and Letters of Lord Macaulay*, 'Edinburgh Edition ', Longmans, 1897, vol. ix, pp. 204–6.

Thomas Babington Macaulay (1800–1859) was at this time M.P. for the pocket borough of Calne, which he had been offered by Lord Lansdowne, who was impressed by Macaulay's contributions to the *Edinburgh Review*.

The Bill referred to here is the First Reform Bill introduced in the House of Commons on March 1, 1831, and the scene described is the division on the second reading on March 23 at 3 a.m.

. . . Such a scene as the division of last Tuesday I never saw, and never expect to see again. If I should live fifty years, the impression of it will be as fresh and sharp in my mind as if it had just taken place. . . . The crowd overflowed the House in every part. When the strangers were cleared out, and the doors locked, we had six hundred and eight members present—more by fifty-five than ever were in a division before. The Ayes and Noes were like two volleys of cannon from opposite sides of a field of battle. When the opposition went out into the lobby, an operation which took up twenty minutes or more, we spread ourselves over the benches on both sides of the House: for there were many of us who had not been able to find a seat during the evening. When the doors were shut we began to speculate on our numbers. Everybody was desponding. ' We have lost it. We are only two hundred and eighty at most. I do not think we are two hundred and fifty. They are three hundred. Alderman Thompson has counted them. He says they are two hundred and ninety-nine.' This was the talk on our benches. I wonder that men who have been long in Parliament do not acquire a better coup d'oeil for numbers. The House, when only the Ayes were in it, looked to me a very fair House—much fuller than it generally is even on debates of considerable interest. I had no hope, however, of three hundred. As the tellers passed along our lowest row on the left hand side the interest was insupportable— two hundred and ninety-one—two hundred and ninety-two— we were all standing up and stretching forward, telling with the tellers. At three hundred there was a short cry of joy—at three hundred and two another—suppressed however in a moment: for we did not yet know what the hostile force might be. We knew, however, that we could not be severely beaten. The doors were thrown open, and in they came. Each of them, as he entered, brought some different report of their numbers. It must have been impossible, as you may conceive, in the lobby, crowded as they were, to form any exact estimate. First we heard that they were three hundred and three; then that number rose to three hundred and ten; then went down to three hundred and seven. . . . We were all breathless with anxiety, when Charles Wood, who stood near the door, jumped up on a bench and cried out, ' They are only three hundred and one '. We set up a shout that you might have heard to Charing Cross, waving our hats, stamping against the floor, and clapping our hands. The tellers scarcely got through the crowd; for the House was thronged

up to the table, and all the floor was fluctuating with heads like
the pit of a theatre. But you might have heard a pin drop as
Duncannon read the numbers. Then again the shouts broke out,
and many of us shed tears. I could scarcely refrain. And the
jaw of Peel fell; and the face of Twiss was as the face of a damned
soul; and Herries looked like Judas taking his necktie off for the
last operation. We shook hands, and clapped each other on the
back, and went out laughing, crying, and huzzaing into the lobby.
And no sooner were the outer doors opened than another shout
answered that within the House. All the passages, and the stairs
into the waiting-rooms, were thronged by people who had waited
till four in the morning to know the issue. We passed through a
narrow lane between two thick masses of them; and all the way
down they were shouting and waving their hats, till we got into
the open air. I called a cabriolet, and the first thing the driver
asked was, ' Is the Bill carried? ' ' Yes, by one '. ' Thank God
for it, Sir.' And away I rode to Gray's Inn. . . .

TRAVELLING BY COACH

Source: Travels of Carl Philipp Moritz in England in 1782, translated
from the German, by a lady. Reprint of English translation of 1795,
London, Humphrey Milford, 1924.

C. P. Moritz (1756–93) was born at Hameln of poor parents. His
childhood was unhappy, and friends provided for his education. He
read theology at Wittenberg and then taught at a *gymnasium* in Berlin.
He wrote copiously on language and psychology, visited Italy in
1786 and met Goethe in Rome.

Moritz spoke English well and had read much English literature,
especially Shakespeare and Milton. He liked the English and admired
their institutions—for example (op. cit., p. 113):

' It strikes a foreigner as something particular and unusual, when,
on passing through these fine English towns, he observes none of
those circumstances, by which the towns in Germany are distinguished
from the villages, no walls, no gates, no sentries, nor garrisons. No
stern examiner comes here to search and inspect us, or our baggage; no
imperious guard here demands a sight of our passports; perfectly free
and unmolested, we here walk through villages and towns, as unconcerned as we should through an house of our own.'

(*a*) By post-chaise from Dartmouth, where Moritz had landed, to
Greenwich. The same, p. 18.

Q

Our little party now separated, and got into two post-chaises, each of which hold three persons, though it must be owned three cannot sit quite so commodiously in these chaises as two; the hire of a post-chaise is a shilling for every English mile. They may be compared to our extra posts, because they are to be had at all times. But these carriages are very neat and lightly built, so that you hardly perceive their motion, as they roll along these firm smooth roads; they have windows in front, and on both sides. The horses are generally good, and the postillions particularly smart and active, and always ride on a full trot. The one we had wore his hair cut short, a round hat, and a brown jacket, of tolerable fine cloth, with a nosegay in his bosom. Now and then, when he drove very hard, he looked round and with a smile seemed to solicit our approbation. A thousand charming spots, and beautiful landscapes, on which my eye would long have dwelt with rapture, were now rapidly passed with the speed of an arrow.

(b) By coach from Leicester to London. The same, pp. 211–215.

I went up a long street [in Leicester] before I got to the inn, from which the post-coaches set out. I here learnt that the stage was to set out that evening for London, but that the inside was already full; some places were however still left on the outside. . .

Being obliged to bestir myself to get back to London . . . I determined to take a place as far as Northampton on the outside.

But this ride from Leicester to Northampton, I shall remember as long as I live.

The coach drove from the yard through a part of the house. The inside passengers got in, in the yard; but we on the outside were obliged to clamber up in the public street, because we should have had no room for our heads to pass under the gateway.

My companions on the top of the coach were a farmer, a young man very decently dressed, and a black-a-moor. The getting up alone was at the risk of one's life; and when I was up, I was obliged to sit just at the corner of the coach, with nothing to hold by but a sort of little handle fastened on the side. I sat nearest the wheel, and the moment that we set off, I fancied that I saw certain death await me. All I could do, was to take still faster hold of the handle, and to be more and more careful to preserve my balance.

The machine now rolled along with prodigious rapidity, over the stones through the town, and every moment we seemed to fly into the air; so that it was almost a miracle that we still stuck to the coach, and did not fall. We seemed to be thus on the wing, and to fly, as often as we passed through a village, or went down a hill.

At last the being continually in fear of my life became insupportable, and as we were going up a hill, and consequently proceeding rather slower than usual, I crept from the top of the coach, and got snug into the basket.

' O, sir, sir, you will be shaken to death! ' said the black; but I flattered myself he exaggerated the unpleasantness of my post.

As long as we went up hill, it was easy and pleasant. And, having had little or no sleep the night before, I was almost asleep among the trunks and the packages; but how was the case altered when we came to go down hill, then all the trunks and parcels began, as it were, to dance around me, and every thing in the basket seemed to be alive; and I every moment received from them such violent blows, that I thought my last hour was come. . . . I was obliged to suffer this torture nearly an hour, till we came to another hill again, when quite shaken to pieces, and badly bruised, I again crept to the top of the coach, and took possession of my former seat. . . .

About midnight we arrived at Harborough, where I could only rest myself a moment, before we were again called to set off, full drive, through a number of villages. . . . From Harborough to Leicester[1] I had a most dreadful journey; it rained incessantly; and, as before we had been covered with dust, we now were soaked with rain. My neighbour, the young man, who sat next to me in the middle, that my inconveniences might be complete, every now and then fell asleep; and, as when asleep, he perpetually bolted and rolled against me, with the whole weight of his body, more than once he was very near pushing me entirely off my seat.

We at last reached Northampton, where I immediately went

[1] A mistake of the translator; ' to Leicester ' should read ' to Northampton '.

to bed, and have slept almost till noon.   Tomorrow morning I intend to continue my journey to London in some other stage-coach.

London, 14th July, 1782.

The journey from Northampton to London I can again hardly call a journey; but rather a perpetual motion, or removal, from one place to another, in a close box: during your conveyance you may, perhaps, if you are in luck, converse with two or three people shut up along with you.

But I was not so fortunate; for my three travelling companions were all farmers, who slept so soundly, that even the hearty knocks of the head with which they often saluted each other, did not awake them.

Their faces, bloated and discoloured by their copious use of ale and brandy, looked, as they lay before me, like so many lumps of dead flesh. When now and then they woke, sheep, in which they all dealt, was the first and last topic of their conversation. One of the three, however, differed not a little from the other two: his face was sallow and thin, his eyes quite sunk and hollow, his long lank fingers hung quite loose, and as if detached from his hands. He was, in short, the picture of avarice and misanthropy. The former he certainly was; for at every stage he refused to give the coachman the accustomed perquisite, which every body else paid; and every farthing he was forced to part with, forced a G-d d--n, from his heart. As he sat in the coach, he seemed anxious to shun the light; and so shut up every window that he could come at, except, when now and then I opened them to take a slight view of the charms of the country through which we seemed to be flying, rather than driving.

A RAILWAY JOURNEY: 1837

Source: The Greville Memoirs.

Knowsley, July 18, 1837 . . . I started at five o'clock on Sunday evening [by coach from London] got to Birmingham at half-past five on Monday morning, and got upon the railroad at half-past seven. Nothing can be more comfortable than the vehicle in which I was put, a sort of chariot with two places, and there is nothing disagreeable about it but the occasional whiffs of stinking air which it is impossible to exclude altogether. The first sensation is a slight degree of nervousness and a feeling of being run away with, but a sense of security supervenes, and the velocity is delightful. Town after town, park and chateau one after another are left behind with the rapid variety of a moving panorama, and the continual bustle and animation of the changes and stoppages make the journey very entertaining. The train was very long and heads were continually popping out of the several carriages, attracted by well-known voices, and then came the greetings and exclamations of surprise, the ' Where are you going? ' and ' How on earth came you here? ' Considering the novelty of its establishment, there is very little embarrassment, and it certainly renders all other travelling irksome and tedious by comparison.

THE LIVERPOOL-MANCHESTER RAILWAY

This railway was opened in 1830. The promoters of the scheme had offered a prize for the best locomotive. It was won by Stephenson's *Rocket*.

Source: Record of a Girlhood, Frances Ann Kemble, Bentley, 1878, vol. ii.

Fanny Kemble, born 1809, was the daughter of Charles Kemble the actor. She went on the stage and had great success. She toured America with her father and married in 1834 a Southern planter, Pierce Butler, from whom she was divorced in 1848. She returned to England, and died in 1893.

My father knew several of the gentlemen most deeply interested in the undertaking [the Liverpool-Manchester railway], and Stephenson having proposed a trial trip as far as the fifteen-mile viaduct, they, with infinite kindness, invited him and permitted me to accompany them; allowing me, moreover, the place which I felt to be one of supreme honour, by the side of Stephenson. . . . He was a rather stern-featured man, with a dark and deeply-marked countenance; his speech was strongly inflected with his native Northumbrian accent.

From a letter dated Liverpool, August 26th (1830).

. . . . We were introduced to the little engine which was to

drag us along the rails. . . . This snorting little animal, which I
felt rather inclined to pat, was then harnessed to our carriage,
and, Mr. Stephenson having taken me on the bench of the engine
with him, we started at about ten miles an hour. The steam-horse
being ill-adapted for going up and down hill, the road was kept
at a certain level, and appeared sometimes to sink below the
surface of the earth, and sometimes to rise above it. Almost at
starting it was cut through the solid rock, which formed a wall
on either side of it, about sixty feet high. You can't imagine how
strange it seemed to be journeying on thus, without any visible
cause of progress other than the magical machine, with its
flying white breath and rhythmical, unvarying pace. . . . We
were to go only fifteen miles, that distance being sufficient to
show the speed of the engine. . . . After proceeding through
this rocky defile, we presently found ourselves raised upon
embankments ten or twelve feet high; we then came to a moss,
or swamp, of considerable extent, on which no human foot could
tread without sinking, and yet it bore the road which bore us.
This had been the great stumbling-block in the minds of the
committee of the House of Commons; but Mr. Stephenson has
succeeded in overcoming it. . . .

We had now come fifteen miles, and stopped where the road
traversed a wide and deep valley. Stephenson made me alight
and led me down to the bottom of this ravine, over which, in
order to keep his road level, he has thrown a magnificent viaduct
of nine arches, the middle one of which is seventy feet high,
through which we saw the whole of this beautiful little valley. . . .
We then rejoined the rest of the party, and the engine having
received its supply of water, the carriage was placed behind it,
for it cannot turn, and was set off at its utmost speed, thirty-five
miles an hour, swifter than a bird flies (for they tried the experiment with a snipe). You cannot conceive what that sensation of
cutting the air was; the motion is as smooth as possible, too.
I could either have read or written.

Four years have sufficed to bring this great undertaking to
an end. The railroad will be opened upon the 15th of next
month. The Duke of Wellington is coming down to be present
on the occasion. . . . The whole cost of the work (including the

engines and carriages) will have been eight hundred and thirty thousand pounds. . . .

From a letter dated Manchester, September 20th, 1830.

We started on Wednesday last, to the number of about eight hundred people, in carriages constructed as I before described to you. The most intense curiosity and excitement prevailed, and, though the weather was uncertain, enormous masses of densely packed people lined the road, shouting and waving hats and handkerchiefs as we flew by them. What with the sight and sound of these cheering multitudes and the tremendous velocity with which we were borne past them, my spirits rose to the true champagne height, and I never enjoyed anything so much as the first hour of our progress. I had been unluckily separated from my mother in the first distribution of places, but by an exchange of seats which she was enabled to make she rejoined me when I was at the height of my ecstacy, which was considerably damped by finding that she was frightened to death, and intent upon nothing but devising means of escaping from a situation which appeared to her to threaten with instant annihilation herself and all her travelling companions. While I was chewing the cud of this disappointment, which was rather bitter, as I had expected her to be as delighted as myself with our excursion, a man flew by us, calling out through a speaking-trumpet to stop the engine, for that somebody in the directors' carriage had sustained an injury. We were all stopped accordingly, and presently a hundred voices were heard exclaiming that Mr. Huskisson was killed; the confusion that ensued is indescribable; the calling out from carriage to carriage to ascertain the truth, the contrary reports which were sent back to us, the hundred questions eagerly uttered at once, and the repeated and urgent demands for surgical assistance, created a sudden turmoil that was quite sickening. At last we distinctly ascertained that the unfortunate man's thigh was broken. From Lady W——, who was in the duke's carriage, and within three yards of the spot where the accident happened, I had the following details, the horror of witnessing which we were spared through our situation behind the great carriage. The engine had stopped to take in a supply of water, and several of the gentlemen in the directors' carriage and jumped out to look about them. Lord W——, Count Batthyany, Count Matuscenitz, and Mr. Huskisson among the rest were standing talking in the middle of the road, when an engine on the other line, which was parading up and down merely to show its speed, was seen coming down upon them like lightning. The most active of those in peril sprang back into their seats; Lord W—— saved his life only by rushing behind the duke's carriage, and Count Matuscenitz had but just leaped into it, with the engine all but touching his heels as he did so; while poor Mr. Huskisson, less active from the effects of age and ill-health, bewildered, too, by the frantic cries of ' Stop the engine! Clear the track! ' that resounded on all sides, completely lost his head, looked helplessly to the right and left, and was instantaneously prostrated by the fatal machine, which dashed down like a thunderbolt upon him, and passed over his leg, smashing and mangling it in the most horrible way. (Lady W—— said she distinctly heard the crushing of the bone). So terrible was the effect of the appalling accident that, except that ghastly ' crushing' and poor Mrs. Huskisson's piercing shriek, not a sound was heard or a word uttered among the immediate spectators of the catastrophe. Lord W—— was the first to raise the poor sufferer, and calling to aid his surgical skill, which is considerable, he tied up the severed artery, and, for a time at least, prevented death by loss of blood. Mr. Huskisson was then placed in a carriage with his wife and Lord W——, and the engine, having been detached from the directors' carriage, conveyed them to Manchester. So great was the shock produced upon the whole party by this event, that the Duke of Wellington declared his intention not to proceed, but to return immediately to Liverpool. However, upon its being represented to him that the whole population of Manchester had turned out to witness the procession, and that a disappointment might give rise to riots and disturbances, he consented to go on, and gloomily enough the rest of the journey was accomplished.

[Huskisson died the same day.]

STEPHENSON ON SPEED

Son of a fireman at Wylam, near Newcastle, he was employed as engine-man at Willington Ballast Hill in 1802. He became engine-wright to the Killingsworth Colliery in 1812, and in 1815 designed safety lamps at the same time as Sir Humphrey Davy. He became engineer for the Stockton-Darlington railway which was opened in 1825, surveyed the proposed Manchester-Liverpool line which was opened in 1830 and won a prize with his ' Rocket ' in 1829. His fame was now established and in 1838 he became vice-president, mechanical section, of the British Association. He did his best to check the railway mania of 1844, and became the first president of the Institute of Mechanical Engineers in 1847. He visited Belgium and Spain and was knighted by Leopold I in 1835, but refused British honours. He died at Chesterfield in 1848.

Source: The Greville Memoirs.

Burghley, January 28,   1834.

. . . . Stephenson, the great engineer, told Lichfield that he had travelled on the Manchester and Liverpool railroad for many miles at the rate of a mile a minute, that his doubt was not how fast his engines could be made to go, but at what pace it would be proper to stop, that he could make them travel with greater speed than any bird can cleave the air, and that he had ascertained that 400 miles an hour was the extreme velocity which the human frame could endure, at which it could move and exist.

DOCTOR J. M. ROUTH (1755-1854)

Fellow of Magdalen College, Oxford, 1775, and President of Magdalen College from 1791 until his death in his hundredth year. Edited *Reliquiae Sacrae.* Descended on his mother's side from the family of Archbishop Laud, he directed that on his tombstone it should be recorded that he had lived and died ' attached to the Catholic Faith taught in the Church of England and averse from all papal and sectarian innovations '. A Whig in the sense that he accepted the Revolution of 1688 and rejected the doctrine of Passive Obedience, Routh was devoted to the High Church tradition. He linked the Oxford of Newman with that of Dr. Johnson whom he, as a young Fellow of Magdalen, had watched shambling up the steps of University College. The mother of one of his friends had seen Charles II walking with his spaniels in the Parks in 1665.

J. R. Green, the historian, who entered Magdalen College School, in 1846, said: ' We boys used to stand overawed as the old man passed by, the keen eyes looking out of the white drawn face, and feel as if we were looking at someone from another world '. Visitors would generally find him in his library of 16,000 books which he bequeathed on his death to Durham University. His massive and exact scholarship caused his advice to be often sought in Church matters: in particular he played a principal part in shaping the Episcopal Church in the United States. In 1837 Newman dedicated a book to him thus: *To Martin Joseph Routh, D.D., President of Magdalen College, who has been reserved to report to a forgetful generation what was the Theology of their Fathers.* In later years Newman wrote: ' Routh was civil to me as most were not, after I became a Roman Catholic '. It was to Dr. Burgon, the author of this extract, that Routh gave his celebrated advice: ' Since you care for the advice of an old man, Sir, you will find it a very good practice, Sir, always to verify your references.'

Source: Burgon: *Lives of Twelve Good Men* (1888), quoted in Macdonald: *Portraits in Prose*, Routledge, 1946.

Further Reading: R. D. Middleton, *Dr. Routh*, Oxford University Press, 1938. R. W. Church, *The Oxford Movement*, Macmillan, 1891.

Let me recall the occasion, the pretext rather, on which (Dec. 10th, 1846) I obtained my first interview with Dr. Routh. I had been charged with a book for him, and, having obtained his permission to bring it in person, presented myself at his gate. Moss received my name in a manner which showed me that I was expected. With a beating heart, I followed the man up the old-fashioned staircase—grim old Doctors in their wigs and robes, and bearded divines with little books in their hands, and college benefactors innumerable, eyeing me all the way from the walls, with terrible severity. My courage at last almost failed me; but retreat was impossible, for by this time we had reached the open door of the library—a room completely lined with books (the volumes in that room were reckoned at 5,000)—the shelves (which were of deal painted white) reaching from the floor to the ceiling; and the President was to be seen at the furthest extremity, his back to the window, with a blazing fire at his left. At the first intimation of my approach, I noticed that he slipped the book that he was reading into the drawer of the little table before him, and hastened to rise and come into the middle of the room to receive me. The refined courtesy which evidently was doing its best to persuade me not only that I was a welcome visitor but that I found the master of the house *entirely disengaged*, struck

me much. Most of all, however, was I astonished by his appearance. He wore such a wig as one only sees in old pictures:
cassock, gown, scarf and bands, shorts and buckles. And then
bow he did stoop! But besides immense intelligence, there was
a great deal of suavity as well as dignity in that venerable face.
And—' You have come to see a decrepit old man, sir! ' he said,
as he took me by the hand. Something fell from me about my
' veneration for so learned a Divine ', and my having ' long
coveted this honour '. ' You are very civil, sir, sit you down.'
And he placed me in the *arm*-chair, in which he told me he never
sat himself.

After a few civilities, he began to congratulate me on my
bachelor's gown, pointing to my sleeves. I learned to my astonishment that he supposed he was going to have an interview
with an undergraduate. He inquired after my standing in the
University—my late, my present college. 'And you are a fellow
of Oriel, sir? A very honourable college to belong to, sir. It
has produced many distinguished men. You know, sir, when you
marry, or take a living, you can always add to your name, " late
fellow ". I observe, sir, that Dr. Pusey always does so.' It was
impossible not to smile. My name (he thought) must be of French
origin—must be another form of *Burgoyne*. It soon became pain-
fully evident that he was only talking thus in order to relieve
me from the necessity of speaking, in case I should be utterly
at a loss for a topic. So, availing myself of a pause after he had
inquired about my intended pursuits, I leaned forward (for he
was more than slightly deaf) and remarked that perhaps he would
allow me to ask him a question. ' Eh, sir? ' ' I thought that
perhaps you would allow me to ask you a question about Divinity,
sir.' He told me (rather gravely) to go on. I explained that I
desired a few words of counsel, if he would condescend to give
me them—some directions as to the best way of pursuing the
study which he had himself cultivated with such signal success.
Aware that my request was almost as vague as the subject was
vast, and full of genuine consideration for the aged oracle, I
enlarged for a minute on the matter, chiefly in order to give him
time to adjust his thoughts before making reply. He inquired
what I had read? ' Eusebius, Hooker and Pearson, very care-

fully.' He nodded. The gravity which by this time his features had assumed was very striking. He lay back in his chair. His head sank forward on his chest, and he looked like one absorbed in thought. ' Yes—I think, sir ' (said he after a long pause which, besides raising my curiosity, rather alarmed me by the contrast it presented to his recent animated manner), ' I think, sir, were I you, sir—that I would—first of all—read the—the Gospel according to St. Matthew.' Here he paused. 'And after I had read the Gospel according to St. Matthew—I would—were I you, sir —go on to read—the Gospel according to St. Mark.' I looked at him anxiously to see whether he was serious. One glance was enough. He was giving me (but at a very slow rate) the outline of my future course. ' I think, sir, when I had read the Gospel according to St. Mark, I would go on, sir—to the Gospel according to—St. Luke, sir.' (Another pause, as if the reverend speaker were reconsidering the matter.) ' Well, sir, and when I had read those three gospels, sir, were I in your place, I would go on—yes, I would certainly go on to read the Gospel according to St. John.'

For an instant I had felt an inclination to laugh. But by this time a very different set of feelings came over me. Here was a theologian of ninety-one, who after surveying the entire field of sacred science, had come back to the starting-point, and had nothing better to advise me to read than—the Gospel! . . . It was time to go. Indeed the fire was so exceedingly hot that I could bear it no longer. My cap, which I had used for a screen, had been smoking for some time, and now curled and cracked. What annoyed me more, if possible, than the fire, was the President's canary, in a cage near his elbow. The wretched creature was quiet till we got upon Divinity; but the moment his master mentioned the Gospels, away it went into a paroxysm of song— scream, scream, scream—as if on purpose to make it impossible for me to hear what he said. If ever the President dropped his voice, the bird screamed the louder.

NEWMAN PREACHES AT OXFORD

John Henry Newman (1801–1890) was a scholar of Trinity and was elected in 1822 a Fellow of Oriel. The Oriel common-room had the reputation of being the most brilliant in Oxford. Unfriendly critics said that it ' stank of logic '. In 1828 he became Vicar of St. Mary's, the University Church. With Keble and Pusey, Newman became one of the leading figures in the Oxford Movement. His sermons at St. Mary's not only were famous but have remained so. This extract from J. A. Froude's *Short Studies on Great Subjects* (vol. iv) gives a singularly clear impression of the impact of Newman on an able young man whose subsequent intellectual development was to be very different from Newman's. Writing in 1881, Froude is able to paint vividly the leader from whom he now differed but of whose greatness he had no doubt.

Source: Froude, *Short Studies on Great Subjects*, iv, Longmans 1905, pp. 272–273, 278–279, 282–283, 283–286.

Further Reading: R. W. Church, *The Oxford Movement*, Macmillan, 1891. C. Dawson, *The Spirit of the Oxford Movement* (1934), Sheed and Ward. M. Ward, *The Young Mr. Newman* (1948), Sheed and Ward. L. Bouyer: *Newman* (1958) Burns and Oates.

When I entered at Oxford, John Henry Newman was beginning to be famous. The responsible authorities were watching him with anxiety; clever men were looking with interest and curiosity on the apparition among them of one of those persons of indisputable genius who was likely to make a mark upon his time. His appearance was striking. He was above the middle height, slight and spare. His head was large, his face remarkably like that of Julius Caesar. The forehead, the shape of the ears and the nose, were almost the same. The lines of the mouth were very peculiar, and I should say exactly the same. I have often thought of the resemblance, and believed that it extended to the temperament. In both there was an original force of character which refused to be moulded by force of circumstances, which was to make its own way, and become a power in the world; a clearness of intellectual perception, a disdain for conventionalities, a temper imperious and wilful, but along with it a most attaching gentleness, sweetness, singleness of heart and purpose. Both were formed by nature to command others, both had the faculty of attracting to themselves the passionate devotion of their friends and followers, and in both cases, too, perhaps the devotion was rather due to the personal ascendancy of the leader than to the cause which he represented. . . .

I had then never seen so impressive a person. I met him now and then in private; I attended his church and heard him preach

Sunday after Sunday; he is supposed to have been insidious, to have led his disciples on to conclusions to which he designed to bring them, while his purpose was carefully veiled. He was on the contrary the most transparent of men. He told us what he believed to be true. He did not know where it would carry him. No one who has ever risen to a great height in this world refuses to move till he knows where he is going. He is impelled in each step which he takes by a force within himself. He satisfies himself only that the step is a right one, and he leaves the rest to Providence. Newman's mind was world-wide. He was interested in everything which was going on in science, in politics, in literature. Nothing was too large for him, nothing too trivial, if it threw light upon the central question, what man really was, and what was his destiny. He was careless about his personal prospects. He had no ambition to make a career, or to rise to rank and power. Still less had pleasure any seductions for him. His natural temperament was bright and light; his senses, even the commonest, were exceptionally delicate. I was told that, though he rarely drank wine, he was trusted to choose the vintages for the college cellar. . . .

He, when we met him, spoke to us about subjects of the day, of literature, of public persons and incidents, of everything which was generally interesting. He seemed always to be better informed on common topics of conversation than anyone else who was present. He was never condescending with us, never didactic or authoritative; but what he said carried conviction along with it. When we were wrong he knew why we were wrong, and excused our mistakes to ourselves while he set us right. Perhaps his supreme merit as a talker was that he never tried to be witty or to say striking things. Ironical he could be, but not ill-natured. Not a malicious anecdote was ever heard from him. Prosy he could not be. He was lightness itself—the lightness of elastic strength—and he was interesting because he never talked for talking's sake, but because he had something real to say. . . .

Personal admiration, of course, inclined us to look to him as a guide in matters of religion. No one who heard his sermons in those days can ever forget them. They were seldom directly theological. We had theology enough and to spare from the select preachers before the university. Newman, taking some Scripture character for a text, spoke to us about ourselves, our temptations, our experiences. His illustrations were inexhaustible. He seemed to be addressing the most secret consciousness of each of us—as the eyes of a portrait appear to look at every person in a room. He never exaggerated; he was never unreal. A sermon from him was a poem, formed on a distinct idea, fascinating by its subtlety, welcome—how welcome!—from its sincerity, interesting from its originality, even to those who were careless of religion; and to others who wished to be religious, but had found religion dry and wearisome, it was like the springing of a fountain out of the rock. . . . These sermons were, I suppose, the records of Newman's own mental experience. They appear to me to be the outcome of continued meditation upon his fellow creatures and their position in this world; their awful responsibilities; the mystery of their nature, strangely mixed of good and evil, of strength and weakness. A tone, not of fear, but of infinite pity runs through them all, and along with it a resolution to look facts in the face; not to fly to evasive generalities about infinite mercy and benevolence, but to examine what revelation really has added to our knowledge, either of what we are or of what lies before us. . . . I recollect a sermon from him—I think in the year 1839—I have never read it since; I may not now remember the exact words, but the impression left is ineffaceable. . . . Newman described closely some of the incidents of our Lord's passion; he then paused. For a few moments there was a breathless silence. Then, in a low voice, of which the faintest vibration was audible in the farthest corner of St. Mary's, he said, ' Now, I bid you recollect that He to whom these things were done was Almighty God '. It was as if an electric stroke had gone through the church, as if every person present understood for the first time the meaning of what he had all his life been saying.

PRINCESS VICTORIA BECOMES QUEEN

Source: Queen Victoria's Journal in *Letters of Queen Victoria*, ed. A. C. Benson and Viscount Esher, Murray 1908, vol. i, pp. 75–6.

Further Reading: A. Ponsonby, *Queen Victoria*, Duckworth, 1933.

Tuesday, 20th June, 1837.

I was awoke at 6 o'clock by Mamma, who told me that the Archbishop of Canterbury and Lord Conyngham were here, and wished to see me. I got out of bed and went into my sitting-room (only in my dressing-gown) and *alone*, and saw them, Lord Conyngham (the Lord Chamberlain) then acquainted me that my poor Uncle, the King, was no more, and had expired at 12 minutes past 2 this morning, and consequently that I am *Queen*. Lord Conyngham knelt down and kissed my hand, at the same time delivering to me the official announcement of the poor King's demise. The Archbishop then told me that the Queen was desirous that he should come and tell me the details of the last moments of my poor good uncle; he said that he had directed his mind to religion, and had died in a perfectly happy, quiet state of mind, and was quite prepared for his death, . . . Lord Conyngham, whom I charged to express my feelings of condolence and sorrow to the poor Queen, returned directly to Windsor. I then went to my room and dressed.

Since it has pleased Providence to place me in this station, I shall do my utmost to fulfil my duty towards my country; I am very young and perhaps in many, though not in all things, inexperienced, but I am sure that very few have more real good-will and more real desire to do what is fit and right than I have.

QUEEN VICTORIA'S FIRST COUNCIL

William Lamb, 2nd Viscount Melbourne, (1779–1848).
Educated at Eton and Trinity College, Cambridge, he became member of parliament for Leominster in 1806, and for Portarlington in 1807. In 1812 he lost his seat because of his support for Catholic Emancipation. In 1816 he returned to parliament as member for Northampton, and for Hertfordshire in 1819. In 1827 he was Irish Secretary under Canning. In 1829 he succeeded his father in the peerage, and in 1830 he became Home Secretary under Grey. In 1833 he supported the Coercion Bill, and in 1834 he formed a ministry at the King's request, resigning in the same year. In 1835 he again became Prime Minister, advising the young Queen Victoria until 1841. Sydney Smith described him with some acuteness: 'he is nothing more than a sensible, honest man who means to do his duty to his Sovereign and to the country: instead of the ignorant man he pretends to be! . . . I am sorry to hurt any man's feelings, and to brush away the magnifi-

cent fabric of levity and gaiety he has reared; but I accuse our Minister of honesty and diligence.'

Source: The Greville Memoirs.

June 21, 1837. . . . The young Queen met the Council at Kensington Palace at eleven. Never was anything like the first impression she produced, or the chorus of praise and admiration which is raised about her manner and behaviour, and certainly not without justice. It was very extraordinary, and something far beyond what was looked for . . . the doors were thrown open and the Queen entered, accompanied by her two uncles who advanced to meet her. She bowed to the Lords, took her seat, and then read her speech in a clear, distinct, and audible voice, and without any appearance of fear or embarrassment. She was quite plainly dressed, and in mourning. After she had read her speech . . . the Privy Councillors were sworn, the two Royal Dukes first, by themselves; and as these two old men, her uncles, knelt before her, swearing allegiance and kissing her hand, I saw her blush up to the eyes, as if she felt the contrast between their civil and their natural relations, and this was the only sign of emotion which she evinced. Her manner to them was very graceful and engaging; she kissed them both, and rose from her chair and moved towards the Duke of Sussex, who was farthest from her and too infirm to reach her. . . . I particularly watched her when Melbourne and the Ministers and the Duke of Wellington and Peel approached her. She went through the whole ceremony, occasionally looking at Melbourne for instruction when she had any doubt what to do, which hardly ever occurred, and with perfect calmness and self-possession, but at the same time with a graceful modesty and propriety particularly interesting and ingratiating. When the business was done, she retired as she had entered. . . . [Peel] said how amazed he was at her manner and behaviour, at her apparent deep sense of her situation, her modesty, and at the same time her firmness. She appeared, in fact, to be awed, but not daunted, and afterwards the Duke of Wellington told me the same thing, and added that if she had been his own daughter he could not have desired to see her perform her part better.

R

THE CORONATION OF QUEEN VICTORIA

Source: Queen Victoria's Journal in *Letters of Queen Victoria*, ed.
A. C. Benson and Viscount Esher, 1908, vol. i, pp. 120–3.

Thursday, 28th June, 1838.

I was awoke at four o'clock by the guns in the Park, and
could not get much sleep afterwards on account of the noise of
the people, bands, etc. Got up at seven, feeling strong and well.
. . . I dressed, having taken a little breakfast before I dressed,
and a little after. . . . At 10 I got into the State Coach with the
Duchess of Sutherland and Lord Albemarle and we began our
Progress. . . . It was a fine day, and the crowds of people
exceeded what I have ever seen. . . . Their good humour and
excessive loyalty was beyond everything, and I really cannot say
how proud I feel to be the Queen of *such* a nation. I was alarmed
at times for fear that the people would be crushed and squeezed
on account of the tremendous rush and pressure.

I reached the Abbey amid deafening cheers at a little after half-
past eleven. [H.M. describes the ceremony, and then goes on.]
Then followed all the various things; and last (of those things)
the Crown being placed on my head—which was, I must own,
a most beautiful impressive moment; all the Peers and Peeresses
put on their coronets at the same moment.

My excellent Lord Melbourne, who stood very close to me
throughout the whole ceremony, was *completely* overcome at this
moment, and very much affected; he gave me *such* a kind, and I
may say *fatherly* look. The shouts, which were very great, the
drums, the trumpets, the firing of the guns, all at the same instant,
rendered the spectacle most imposing.

The Enthronisation and the Homage of, first, all the Bishops,
and then my Uncles, and lastly of all the Peers, in their respective
order was very fine. . . . Poor old Lord Rolle, who is 82, and
dreadfully infirm, in attempting to ascend the steps fell and rolled
quite down, but was not the least hurt; when he attempted to
re-ascend them I got up and advanced to the end of the steps, in
order to prevent another fall. When Lord Melbourne's turn to
do Homage came, there was loud cheering; they also cheered
Lord Grey and the Duke of Wellington. . . . I then again

descended from the throne and repaired with all the Peers bearing the Regalia, my Ladies and Train-bearers, to St. Edward's Chapel, as it is called; but which, as Lord Melbourne said, was more *un*like a Chapel than anything he had ever seen; for what was *called* an *Altar* was covered with sandwiches, bottles of wine, etc. The Archbishop came in and *ought* to have delivered the Orb to me, but I had already got it, and he (as usual) was *so* confused and puzzled and knew nothing, and—went away. Here we waited some minutes. Lord Melbourne took a glass of wine, for he seemed completely tired. The Procession being formed, I replaced my Crown (which I had taken off for a few minutes), took the Orb in my left hand and the Sceptre in my right, and thus *loaded*, proceeded through the Abbey—which resounded with cheers, to the first robing-room. . . . The Archbishop had (most awkwardly) put the ring on the wrong finger, and the consequence was that I had the greatest difficulty to take it off again, which I at last did with great pain. . . . At about half-past four I re-entered my carriage, the Crown on my head, and the Sceptre and Orb in my hands, and we proceeded the same way as we came—the crowds if possible having increased. The enthusiasm, affection, and loyalty were really touching, and I shall ever remember this day as the *Proudest* of my life!

SIR ROBERT PEEL: DISRAELI'S DESCRIPTION

He was the son of Sir Robert Peel, the great cotton magnate of Lancashire and a strong supporter of the younger Pitt. Educated at Harrow and Christ Church he gained a double first, being also the first man in history to achieve that honour. In 1809 he entered Parliament. Between 1812 and 1818 he was Chief Secretary for Ireland, and in 1817 he was returned as member for Oxford University. From 1822 to 1827 he was Home Secretary, and from 1828 to 1830 he was Leader of the House of Commons in the Duke of Wellington's administration. He opposed the Reform Bill. From December 1834 to April 1835 he was Prime Minister and Chancellor of the Exchequer. From 1841 to 1846 he was Prime Minister. He split the Tory party by the repeal of the Corn Laws. He died as a result of a fall from his horse. He has been described as the founder of conservatism.

Source: Disraeli, *Life of George Bentinck,* quoted in W. F. Monypenny and G. E. Buckle *Life of Benjamin Disraeli,* vol. i (2 vol. edn.) Murray, 1929, pp. 704–6.

As an orator Sir Robert Peel had perhaps the most available talent that has ever been brought to bear in the House of Commons. We have mentioned that both in exposition and in reply he was equally eminent. His statements were perspicuous, complete and dignified; when he combated the objections, or criticised the propositions of an opponent, he was adroit and acute; no speaker ever sustained a process of argumentation in a public assembly more lucidly, and none as debaters have united in so conspicuous a degree prudence with promptness. In the higher efforts of oratory he was not successful. His vocabulary was ample and never mean; but it was neither rich nor rare. His speeches will afford no sentiment of surpassing grandeur or beauty that will linger in the ears of coming generations. . . . In pathos he was quite deficient; when he attempted to touch the tender passions, it was painful. His face became distorted, like that of a woman who wants to cry but cannot succeed . . . he had no wit; but he had a keen sense of the ridiculous and an abundant vein of genuine humour. Notwithstanding his artificial reserve, he had a hearty and a merry laugh; and sometimes his mirth was uncontrollable. . . .

Sir Robert Peel was a very good-looking man. He was tall and, though of latter years he had become portly, had to the last a comely presence. Thirty years ago, when he was young and lithe, with curling brown hair, he had a very radiant expression of countenance. His brow was very distinguished, not so much for its intellectual development, although that was of a very high order, as for its remarkably frank expression, so different from his character in life. The expression of the brow might even be said to amount to beauty. The rest of the features did not, however, sustain this impression. The eye was not good; it was sly, and he had an awkward habit of looking askance. He had the fatal defect also of a long upper lip, and his mouth was compressed.

One cannot say of Sir Robert Peel, notwithstanding his unrivalled powers of despatching affairs, that he was the greatest minister that this country ever produced, because, twice placed at the helm, and on the second occasion with the court and the parliament equally devoted to him, he never could maintain himself in power. Nor, notwithstanding his consummate parliamentary tactics, can he be described as the greatest party leader that ever flourished among us, for he contrived to destroy the most compact, powerful and devoted party that ever followed a British statesman. Certainly, notwithstanding his great sway in debate, we cannot recognise him as our greatest orator, for in many of the supreme requisites of oratory he was singularly deficient. But what he really was, and what posterity will acknowledge him to have been, is the greatest member of parliament that ever lived.

THE INVENTION OF THE POWER LOOM

In the later decades of the eighteenth century there was some anxiety about the future of the textile industries. Inventors had developed machines which enormously increased the output of yarn. But, although Kay had produced his ' flying shuttle ' in 1733, no weaving machine had been invented; in fact such an invention was widely held to be an impossibility. Meanwhile, however, the weavers found great difficulty in keeping pace with the vast output of mechanically produced yarn. What would happen when Arkwright's patents expired and the quantity of yarn produced every year became vaster still? The weavers obviously could not cope with it, and yet to export yarn would merely encourage foreign competitors and perhaps ruin the British weaving trade. From this dilemma the textile industry was rescued by the brilliant invention of the Rev. Edmund Cartwright.

Edmund Cartwright (1743–1823) was educated at Wakefield Grammar School and University College, Oxford, and took Orders in the Church of England. He invented not only the power loom but a wool-combing machine in 1789 and a machine for making rope in 1792. He started a weaving factory at Doncaster in 1785 but lost money, and his creditors took over the factory, Cartwright composing a sonnet on this catastrophe. In 1793 he invented a reaping machine, and from 1800 to 1807 was employed by successive Dukes of Bedford as manager of an experimental farm. In 1809 Parliament voted him £10,000, and he bought a farm in Kent.

Source: E. Baines, *History of the Cotton Manufacture in Great Britain,* Fisher, 1835, pp. 229 et sqq. This is Cartwright's account of his invention.

Happening to be at Matlock in the summer of 1784, I fell in company with some gentlemen of Manchester, when the conversation turned on Arkwright's spinning machinery. One of the company observed, that as soon as Arkwright's patent expired so many mills would be erected, and so much cotton spun, that hands never could be found to weave it. To this observation I replied that Arkwright must then set his wits to work to invent a weaving mill. This brought on a conversation on the subject, in which the Manchester gentlemen unanimously agreed that the thing was impracticable, and in defence of their opinion, they adduced arguments which I certainly was incompetent to answer, or even to comprehend, being totally ignorant of the subject, having never at that time seen a person weave. I controverted, however, the impracticability of the thing by remarking that there had lately been exhibited in London an automaton figure which played at chess. Now you will not assert, gentlemen, said I, that it is more difficult to construct a machine that shall weave than one which shall make all the variety of moves which are required in that complicated game.

Some little time afterwards, a particular circumstance recalling this conversation to my mind, it struck me that, as in plain weaving, according to the conception I then had of the business, there could only be three movements which were to follow each other in succession, there would be little difficulty in producing and repeating them. Full of these ideas, I immediately employed a carpenter and smith to carry them into effect. As soon as the machine was finished I got a weaver to put in the warp, which was of such material as sail cloth is usually made of. To my great delight, a piece of cloth, such as it was, was the product. As I had never before turned my thoughts to anything mechanical, either in theory or practice, nor had ever seen a loom at work, or known anything of its construction, you will readily suppose that my first loom was a most rude piece of machinery. The warp was placed perpendicularly, the reed fell with the weight of at least half a hundredweight, and the springs which threw the shuttle were strong enough to have thrown a congreve rocket.[1] In short, it required the strength of two powerful men to work the machine at a slow rate, and only for a short time. Conceiving, in my great simplicity, that I had accomplished all that was required, I then secured what I thought a most valuable property by a patent, 4th of April, 1785.

---

[1] Sir Wm. Congreve (1772–1828) invented the war rockets named after him. They were first used in 1806 in an attack on Boulogne.

This being done, I then condescended to see how other people wove: and you will guess my astonishment when I compared their easy modes of operation with mine. Availing myself, however, of what I then saw, I made a loom, in its general principles nearly as they are now made. But it was not till the year 1787 that I completed my invention, when I took out my last weaving patent, August 1st of that year. . . .

THE EMPLOYMENT OF CHILDREN

The vexed problem of factory conditions illustrates at once the value and the danger of the evidence of the eyewitness. The following extracts should be read in conjunction with T. S. Ashton: 'The Standard of Life of the Workers in England, 1790–1830 ', and W. H. Hutt, 'The Factory System of the Early Nineteenth Century' which will be found as Part II of ed. Hayek, *Capitalism and the Historians*, Routledge, 1954. In brief, it seems to-day reasonably certain that much which contemporary evidence represented as normal was in fact exceptional; that many of the undoubted evils which were attributed by contemporaries to the conditions of factory life were in fact the consequences of quite other causes; and that the propositions that factory owners were normally inhumane men, and that factories were ' temples of Mammon' in which the children of the poor were habitually sacrificed to enrich their employers lack the support of historical scholarship. That there were crying evils is certain: their causes, incidence and consequences are more debatable.

(a) *Source: The Farington Diary*, by Joseph Farington, R.A., ed. Greig, Hutchinson, vol. i, 1922. Joseph Farington (1747–1821), who was a pupil of Richard Wilson, was the most influential member of the Royal Academy in his own day.

August 12, 1801. In the evening I walked to Cromford and saw the children coming from their work out of one of Mr. Arkwright's Manufactories. I was glad to see them look in general very healthy and many with fine, rosy complexions. These children had been at work from 6 or 7 o'clock this morning, and it was now near or about 7 in the evening. The time allowed them for resting is at 12 o'clock 40 minutes during which time they dine. One of them, a boy of 10 or 11 years of age, told me his wages were 3s. 6d. a week, and a little girl said her wages were 2s. 3d. a week

August 23.—We went to Church at Cromford where is a Chapel built about 3 years and ½ ago by Mr. Arkwright. On each side the organ a gallery in which about 50 boys were seated. These children are employed in Mr. Arkwright's work in the week-days, and on Sundays attend a school where they receive education. They came to Chapel in regular order and looked healthy and well and were decently clothed and clean. They were attended by an old man their school master. To this school girls also go for the same purpose, and alternately with the boys go to Church, the boys on one Sunday, the girls on the next following. Whichever are not at Chapel are at the school, to which they both go every Sunday both morning and afternoon. The whole plan appears to be such as to do Mr. Arkwright great credit.

EVIDENCE OF SAMUEL COULSON

(b) *Source:* Report of Committee on Factory Children's Labour, 1831–2.

At what time in the morning, in the brisk time, did these girls go to the mills?

In the brisk time, for about six weeks, they have gone at 3 o'clock in the morning, and ended at 10, or nearly half past at night.

What intervals were allowed for rest or refreshment during those nineteen hours of labour?

Breakfast a quarter of an hour, and dinner half an hour, and drinking a quarter of an hour.

Was any of that time taken up in cleaning the machinery?

They generally had to do what they call dry down; sometimes this took the whole of the time at breakfast or drinking, and they were to get their dinner or breakfast as they could; if not, it was brought home.

Had you not great difficulty in awakening your children to this excessive labour?

Yes, in the early time we had to take them up asleep and shake them when we got them on the floor to dress them, before we could get them off to their work. . . .

What was the length of time they could be in bed during those long hours?

It was near 11 o'clock before we could get them into bed after getting a little victuals. . . .

What time did you get them up in the morning?

In general me or my mistress got up at 2 o'clock to dress them.

So that they had not above four hours sleep at this time?

No they had not.

For how long together was it?

About six weeks it held; it was only done when the throng was very much on; it was not often that.

The common hours of labour were from 6 in the morning till half-past eight at night?

Yes.

With the same intervals for food?

Yes, just the same.

Were the children excessively fatigued by this labour?

Many time; we have cried often when we have given them the little victualling we had to give them; we had to shake them and they have fallen to sleep with the victuals in their mouths many a time.

Did this excessive term of labour occasion much cruelty also?

Yes, with being so very much fatigued the strap was very frequently used. . . .

What was the wages in the short hours?

Three shillings a week each.

When they wrought those very long hours what did they get?

Three shillings and sevenpence halfpenny.

DERBYSHIRE

(c) *Source: Report on the Physical and Moral Condition of the Children and Young Persons engaged in Mines and Manufactures. London 1843.*

In this district, the hours of work are commonly 14, and are sometimes extended to 16 out of 14, and the mines in general are most imperfectly drained and ventilated. . . .

Thomas Straw, aged seven, Ilkiston: They wouldn't let him sleep in the pit or stand still; he feels very tired when he comes out; gets his tea and goes to bed. John Hawkins, aged eight, Underwood: Is tired and glad to get home; never wants to play. Robert Blount, aged ten, Eastwood: He is always too tired to play, and is glad to get to bed; his back and legs ache; he had rather drive plough or go to school than work in a pit. John Bostock, aged seventeen, Babbington: Has often been made to work until he was so tired as to lie down on his road home until twelve o'clock, when his mother has come and led him home— has done so many times when he first went to the pits; he has sometimes been so fatigued that he could not eat his dinner, but has been beaten and made to work until night; he never thought of play, was always too anxious to get to bed.

John Leadbeater, aged eighteen, Babbington; Has two miles to go to the pit and must be there before six, and works until eight; he has often worked all night, and been made to work as usual the next day; has often been so tired that he has lain in bed all Sunday. He knows no work so bad as that of a pit lad.

John Beasley, collier, aged 49, Shipley. He has seen those (children) who could not get home without their father's assistance, and have fallen asleep before they could be got to bed; has known children of six years old sent to the pit, but thinks there are none at Shipley under seven or eight; in his opinion a boy is too weak to stand even the hours to drive between until he is eight or nine years old; the boys go down at six in the morning, and has known them kept down until nine or ten, until they are ' almost ready to exhaust '; the children and young persons work the same hours as the men; the children are obliged to work in the night if the waggon-road is out of repair, or the water coming on them; it happens sometimes two or three times in the week; they then go down at six p.m. to six a.m. and have from ten minutes to half an hour allowed for supper; when he was a boy he has worked 36 hours running many a time, and many more besides himself have done so.

North Durham and Northumberland—Mr. James Anderson handed in the following written evidence: 'The boys go too soon to work; I have seen boys at work not six years of age, and though their work is not hard, still they have long hours, so that when they come home they are quite spent. I have often seen them lying on the floor fast asleep; then they often fall down asleep in the pit, and have been killed. Not long ago a boy fell asleep, lay down on the way, and the waggons killed him. Another boy was killed; it was supposed he had fallen asleep when driving his waggon, and fallen off and was killed.'

GEORGE SMITH OF COALVILLE

(d) *Source: George Smith of Coalville*, by Edwin Hodder, Nisbet, 1896.

George Smith, helped by Robert Baker, a factory inspector, made great efforts to inform the public about the condition of children working, as he had worked in his childhood, in the brick yards. In 1871 Mundella introduced a Bill to ameliorate the condition of such children, and Lord Shaftesbury moved an Address to the Crown. The Bill was passed.

When a child of about seven years of age [i.e. in 1838] I was employed by a relative to assist him in making bricks. It is not my wish to say anything against him; but, like most of his class at that time, and like many even now [1871], he thought kicks and blows formed the best means of obtaining the maximum of work from a lad; and, as if these were not enough, excessively long hours of work were added.

At nine years of age my employment consisted in continually carrying about 40 lb. of clay upon my head from the clay heap to the table on which the bricks were made. When there was no clay I had to carry the same weight of bricks. This labour had to be performed, almost without intermission, for thirteen hours daily. Sometimes my labours were increased by my having to work all night at the kilns.

The result of the prolonged and severe labour to which I was subjected, combined with the cruel treatment experienced by me at the hands of the adult labourers, are shown in marks that are borne by me to this day. On one occasion I had to perform a very heavy amount of labour. After my customary day's work I had to carry 1,200 nine-inch bricks from the maker to the floors on which they are placed to harden. The total distance thus walked

by me that night was not less than fourteen miles, seven miles of
which I traversed with 11 lb. weight of clay in my arms, besides
lifting the unmade clay and carrying it some distance to the maker.
The total quantity of clay thus carried by me was 5½ tons. For
all this labour I received sixpence! The fatigue thus experienced
brought on a serious illness, which for several weeks prevented
me from resuming work.

CLIMBING BOYS

In 1803 a Society was founded to obtain the abolition of chimney
sweeping by climbing boys. An Act of 1788 had forbidden the use of
boys under eight for this purpose, but it was widely disregarded. As a
result of the Society's propaganda, a Select Committee was set up in
1817 to examine the whole question of climbing boys. But Bills to
better their lot did not succeed in Parliament until 1834, when an
Act was passed forbidding boys under ten to climb chimneys. In
1840 an Act forbade anyone under 21 to sweep chimneys by climbing
them. Both these Acts were disregarded by the master sweeps, and
not until Lord Salisbury's Chimney Sweepers Bill of 1875, which
provided for the registration of master sweeps with the local police,
was the problem solved.

(e) *Source:* Extracts from evidence given before a Select Committee
of the House of Commons in 1817 and a Royal Commission in 1864.

[In evidence, John Cook, a master sweep who had himself started
work as a climbing boy at the age of six, had just said that parents sold
their children to master sweeps for two or three pounds.]

Do you give more for children that are delicately formed, and
who therefore are better calculated for ascending small chimneys?
—The smaller they are the master generally likes them the better,
because they are generally more serviceable to them.

So that a small boy bears a better price than a full grown
boy?—Yes, if he is strong enough to do the duty, and is a hearty
looking boy of his age.

Is it not the practice of some masters to advertise themselves
as being in possession of small boys for the purpose of ascending
flues?—Almost every one has got it in their bills, that they keep
small boys for the register stoves, and such like as that; I do not

recollect ever seeing it in the newspapers, but they do it in their bills.

How do you ascertain the age of the boy when he is offered to you as an apprentice; do you take the parents' word for it? —The parents will often say that he is older than what he is.

Are you in the habit of getting any other evidence of their ages than the parents' own words?—No.

Are the boys ever washed?—Yes, I wash mine regularly; but some of the lower class are not washed for six months.

Do they receive any education?—Many do not.

Is it a general practice to attend divine worship?—Great numbers are neither washed nor attend on the Sunday.

Are not climbing boys subject to sores and bruises, and wounds and burns on their thighs and knees, in consequence of ascending chimneys?—Yes, because learning very fresh boys makes their knees and elbows very sore, but when they have properly learnt their trade these parts get very hard, and they very seldom get sore again unless they meet with an accident; sometimes they get burnt by chimneys partly on fire.

The committee understand, by use, that the extremities of the elbows and of the knees become as hard as the heel of the foot of a person who walks without shoes?—Yes, it does.

What time does it take before those parts get cartilaginous? —Six months.

Do you find many boys show great repugnance to go up at first?—Yes, most of them do.

And if they resist and reject, in what way do you force them up?—By telling them we must take them back again to their father and mother, and give them up again; and their parents are generally people who cannot maintain them.

So that they are afraid of going back to their parents for fear of being starved?—Yes; they go through a deal of hardship before they come to our trade.

Do you use any more violent means?—Sometimes a rod. When I was an apprentice, journeymen often used to keep a cat, made of rope, hard at each end and as thick as your thumb, in their pocket to flog the boys; and I think it is sometimes used now.

Have you ever known a journeyman ill-use any of the children?—Yes, for very little faults they will frequently kick them and smack them about; the boys are more afraid of them than of their masters.

You said that the elbows and knees of the boys, when they first begin the business, become very sore, and afterwards get callous; are those boys employed in sweeping chimneys during the soreness of those parts?—It depends upon the sort of master they have got; you must keep them a little at it, or they will never learn their business, even during the sores.

Is the skin broke generally?—Yes, it is. . . .

From evidence of B. M. Foster, Esq., a member of the Climbing Boys Committee.

One mode of teaching children to climb which I understand to be common, though I will not say universal, is to send a greater boy up the chimney after the lesser one, who has a pin in his hand, and if the little boy does not climb properly he sticks it in his feet.

Do you happen to know this of your own personal knowledge? —I have heard of it as a practice, and when I was at Norwich I made particular enquiry upon that subject. In the whole city of Norwich I could find only nine climbing boys, two of whom I questioned in many particulars; one was with respect to the manner in which they are taught to climb; they both agreed in that particular, that a larger boy was sent up behind them to prick their feet, if they did not climb properly. I purposely avoided mentioning about pricking them with pins, but asked them how they did it; they said that they thrust the pins into the soles of their feet.

From the evidence of Mr. Ruff, a master sweep at Nottingham, before a Royal Commission in 1864.

. . . No one knows the cruelty a boy has to undergo in learning. The flesh must be hardened. This must be done by rubbing it, chiefly on the elbows and knees, with the strongest brine, close by a hot fire. You must stand over them with a cane, or coax them by a promise of a half-penny, if they will stand a few more rubs. At first they will come back from their work streaming with blood, and the knees looking as if the caps had been pulled off. Then they must be rubbed with brine again!

AN ATTACK ON PUBLIC EXECUTIONS

Source: a Letter from Charles Dickens published in *The Times,* November 14, 1849. The execution seen by Dickens was that of George and Maria Manning for the murder of Patrick O'Connor, who lodged with them. Robbery was the motive for the murder.
The last public hanging in England was in 1868.

Sir,

I was a witness of the execution at Horsemonger-lane this morning. I went there with the intention of observing the crowd gathered to behold it, and I had excellent opportunities of doing so, at intervals all through the night, and continuously from daybreak until after the spectacle was over. . . . I believe that a sight so inconceivably awful as the wickedness and levity of the immense crowd collected at the execution this morning could be imagined by no man, and could be presented in no heathen land under the sun. The horrors of the gibbet and of the crime which brought the wretched murderers to it, faded in my mind before the atrocious bearing, looks and language, of the assembled spectators. When I came upon the scene at midnight, the *shrillness* of the cries and howls that were raised from time to time, denoting that they came from a concourse of boys and girls already assembled in the best places, made my blood run cold.
. . . When the day dawned, thieves, low prostitutes, ruffians, and vagabonds of every kind, flocked on to the ground, with every variety of offensive and foul behaviour. Fightings, faintings, whistlings, imitations of Punch, brutal jokes. tumultuous demonstrations of indecent delight when swooning women were dragged out of the crowd by the police with their dresses disordered, gave a new zest to the general entertainment. When the sun rose brightly—as it did—it gilded thousands upon thousands of upturned faces, so inexpressibly odious in their brutal mirth or callousness, that a man had cause to feel ashamed of the shape he wore, and to shrink from himself, as fashioned in the image of the Devil. When the two miserable creatures who

attracted all this ghastly sight about them were turned quivering into the air, there was no more emotion, no more pity, no more thought that two immortal souls had gone to judgement, no more restraint in any of the previous obscenities than if the name of Christ had never been heard in the world, and there were no belief among men but that they perished like the beasts.

. . . I am solemnly convinced that nothing that ingenuity could devise to be done in this city, in the same compass of time, could work such ruin as one public execution, and I stand astounded and appalled by the wickedness it exhibits. I do not believe that any community can prosper where such a scene of horror and demoralisation as was enacted this morning outside Horsemonger-lane Gaol is presented at the very doors of good citizens, and is passed by, unknown or forgotten. And when, in our prayers and thanksgiving for the season, we are humbly expressing before God our desire to remove the moral evils of the land, I would ask your readers to consider whether it is not a time to think of this one, and to root it out.

I am, Sir, your faithful servant,

Charles Dickens.

Devonshire Terrace, *Tuesday, Nov.* 13.

CHANGES FOR THE BETTER

Source: Collected Works of the Reverend Sydney Smith, Longmans, 1839. ' Modern Changes '.

Sydney Smith (1771–1845) educated at Winchester and New College. Took orders, 1794. Close friend of Jeffrey, Brougham and Horner. Started, with the assistance of the first two, the *Edinburgh Review*, 1802. A prominent wit amongst the Whigs at Holland House. Published the *Plymley Letters*, advocating Catholic Emancipation. Settled in his living of Foston-le-Clay in Yorkshire, at the instance of Archbishop Vernon-Harcourt (1757–1874) in 1808; Prebendary of Bristol, 1828; Canon of St. Paul's, 1831. A convinced supporter of Reform, but opposed the ballot. Probably the wittiest writer in defence of reform and of religious toleration in the history of England. This extract illustrates the frame of mind of the better type of English reformer in the first half of the century, and the way in which gas and steam were to such men symbolic of beneficial change.

Further Reading: G. W. E. Russell, *Sydney Smith*, Macmillan, 1905.

Sir Leslie Stephen, article on Sydney Smith in *Dictionary of National Biography*, 1898. Hesketh Pearson, *The Smith of Smiths*, Hamilton, 1934.

It is of some importance at what period a man is born. A young man, alive at this period, hardly knows to what improvements of human life he has been introduced; and I would bring before his notice the following eighteen changes which have taken place in England since I first began to breathe in it the breath of life—a period amounting now to nearly seventy-three years. Gas was unknown: I groped about the streets of London in all but the utter darkness of a twinkling oil lamp, under the protection of watchmen in their grand climacteric, and exposed to every species of depredation and insult.

I have been nine hours in sailing from Dover to Calais before the invention of steam. It took me nine hours to go from Taunton to Bath, before the invention of rail roads, and I now go in six hours from Taunton to London! In going from Taunton to Bath, I suffered between 10,000 and 12,000 severe contusions, before stone-breaking Macadam was born.

I paid £15 in a single year for repairs of carriage-springs on the pavement of London; and I now glide without noise or fracture, on wooden pavements.

I can walk, by the assistance of the police, from one end of London to the other, without molestation; or, if tired, get into a cheap and active cab, instead of those cottages on wheels, which the hackney coaches were at the beginning of my life.

I had no umbrella! They were little used, and very dear. There were no waterproof hats, and my hat has often been reduced by rains into its primitive pulp.

I could not keep my small clothes in their proper place, for braces were unknown. If I had the gout, there was no colchicum. If I was bilious, there was no calomel. If I was attacked by ague, there was no quinine. There were filthy coffee-houses instead of elegant clubs. Game could not be bought. Quarrels about Uncommuted Tithes were endless. The corruptions of Parliament, before Reform, infamous. There were no banks to receive the savings of the poor. The Poor Laws were gradually sapping the vitals of the country; and, whatever miseries I suffered, I had

s

no post to whisk my complaints for a single penny to the remotest corners of the empire; and yet, in spite of all these privations, I lived on quietly, and am now ashamed that I was not more discontented, and utterly surprised that all these changes and inventions did not occur two centuries ago.

I forgot to add that, as the basket of stage-coaches, in which luggage was then carried, had no springs, your clothes were rubbed all to pieces; and that even in the best society one third of the gentlemen at least were always drunk.

CHARTISM

The climax of the Chartist agitation came in 1848, when the Chartist leader, Feargus O'Connor, M.P., decided that the time had come to present a third petition to Parliament. Half a million Chartists would assemble on Kennington Common on Monday, April 10, and would march to Westminster. The Government entrusted the Duke of Wellington with the task of taking precautionary measures: troops were concentrated and special constables enrolled. But April 10 passed without bloodshed. O'Connor accepted the refusal of the authorities to allow the march to Westminster to take place, and advised his followers to return home. The famous petition was taken to Parliament in three cabs. It was found to contain not five million, but two million signatures, among them, apparently, were those of Queen Victoria, the Duke of Wellington, and ' Cheeks the Marine '.

(a) Source: The Greville Memoirs.

Further Reading: M. Hovell, *The Chartist Movement*, Manchester University Press, 1925. D. Williams, *John Frost: A Study in Chartism*, University of Wales Press, 1939.

April 6, 1848. . . . I saw the Duke in the morning at Apsley House in a prodigious state of excitement, said he had plenty of troops, and would answer for keeping everything quiet if the Government would only be firm and vigorous, and announce by a proclamation that the mob should not be permitted to occupy the town. He wanted to prevent *groups* from going into the Park and assembling there, but this would be impossible.

April 9, 1848. . . . All London is making preparations to encounter a Chartist row tomorrow: so much that it is either very sublime or very ridiculous. All the clerks and others in the different offices are ordered to be sworn in special constables, and to constitute themselves into garrisons. I went to the police office with all my clerks, messengers, etc., and we were all sworn. We are to pass the whole day at the office to-morrow, and I am to send down all my guns; in short, we are to take a warlike attitude. Colonel Harness, of the Railway Department, is our commander in chief; every gentleman in London is become a constable, and there is an organisation of some sort in every district.

April 13, 1848. Monday passed off with surprising quiet, and it was considered a most satisfactory demonstration on the part of the Government, and the peaceable and loyal part of the community. Enormous preparations were made, and a host of military, police, and special constables were ready if wanted; every gentleman in London was sworn, and during a great part of the day, while the police were reposing, they did duty. The Chartist movement was contemptible. . . .

In the morning (a very fine day) everybody was on the alert; the parks were closed; our office was fortified, a barricade of Council Registers were erected in the accessible room on the ground floor, and all our guns were taken down to be used in defence of the building. However, at about twelve o'clock crowds came streaming along Whitehall, going northward, and it was announced that all was over. The intended tragedy was rapidly changed into a ludicrous farce. . . .

(b) *Source:* Thomas Frost: *Forty Years Recollections*, Sampson Low, 1880, pp. 136 et sqq.

'There will be a fight,' observed one of my colleagues, looking grave, and speaking in a thoughtful tone. 'I trust not,' said I. 'If there must be, it will be a mistake if Kennington Common is made the battlefield. It is on the wrong side of the river.'

Notwithstanding the sinister apprehensions of many, my view prevailed with my immediate associates; and I have reason to believe that the vast majority of the tens of thousands who assembled on the following day went unarmed, at the risk of another Peterloo, rather than afford any pretext for a Whig Reign of Terror. . . .

It was impossible not to feel some degree of anxiety as to the end, and the feeling increased momentarily in intensity as I proceeded towards Kennington Common, and saw every road converging to that point thronged with working men, pouring in continuous stream towards the space which had been selected for the intended demonstration. Who could say whether it would be the Government or the directors of the movement whose resolution would falter at the last moment? Who knew whether the tens of thousands who were assembled on the Common would refuse to disperse. . . ?

I was standing near the van in which were the members of the Executive Council and many delegates of the National Convention, with the piled-up rolls of the petition, when I heard a cry of, ' They have got him! ' And a wild rush was made towards the western side of the Common. Looking in that direction, I saw the giant form of Feargus O'Connor—he and Wakley were the two tallest men in the House—towering above the throng, as he moved towards the road, accompanied by a courageous inspector of police. There was a cry repeated through the vast throng that O'Connor was arrested; a moment of breathless excitement, and then a partial rolling back of the mass of human forms that had suddenly impelled itself towards the road. The tumult subsided; but no one knew as yet what was the situation at that moment.

Presently O'Connor was seen returning, and his reappearance was hailed with a tremendous shout. He mounted the van, and in a few words explained the state of affairs to the anxious throng. He had had an interview with Sir Richard Mayne at the Horns Tavern, and concessions had been made on both sides. The Government had consented to allow the meeting to be held without molestation, and the honourable member for Nottingham had promised to use his influence with the masses for the purpose of inducing them to abandon the intended procession to the House of Commons with the petition. . . .

THE GREAT EXHIBITION

The opening of the Exhibition on Tuesday, May 1, 1851, was a personal triumph for the Prince Consort, who had worked tirelessly for the project against massive opposition. It was also a great triumph

for Paxton, the designer of the structure which *Punch* had christened
' The Crystal Palace '.

(*a*) *Source:* Letter from Lord Palmerston to Lord Normanby (ambassador in Paris), quoted in E. Ashley, *Life and Correspondence of Lord Palmerston*, Bentley, 1879, vol. ii, p. 178.

Further Reading: The Great Exhibition of 1851, compiled by C. H. Gibbs-Smith, H.M.S.O., 1950. C. Hobhouse, 1851 *and the Crystal Palace*, Murray, 1937.

C.G. [Carlton Gardens]:

May 2, 1851.

. . . . yesterday is the topic of thought and of word with everybody in London. It was indeed a glorious day for England; and the way in which the royal ceremony went off was calculated to inspire humility into the minds of the representatives of foreign Governments and to strike despair into the breasts of those, if any such there be, who may desire to excite confusion in this country. There must have been nearer a million than any other number of people who turned out to post themselves as they could to see some part of the show; and Mayne, the head of the police, told me he thought there were about thirty-four thousand in the glass building. The Queen, her husband, her eldest son and daughter, gave themselves in full confidence to this multitude, with no other guard than one of honour, and the accustomed supply of stick-handed constables, to assist the crowd in keeping order among themselves. Of course there were in reserve, in proper stations, ample means of repressing any disorder if any had been attempted; but nothing was brought out and shown beyond what I have mentioned; and it was impossible for the invited guests of a lady's drawing-room to have conducted themselves with more perfect propriety than did this sea of human beings.

The royal party were received with continued acclamation as they passed through the parks and round the Exhibition House; and it was also very interesting to witness the cordial greeting given to the Duke of Wellington. I was just behind him and Anglesey, within two of them, during the procession round the building, and he was accompanied by an incessant running fire of applause from the men and waving of handkerchiefs and kissing of hands from the women, who lined the pathway of march during the three-quarters of an hour that it took us to march round.

The building itself is far more worth seeing than anything in it, though many of its contents are worthy of admiration. You ought to contrive to run over to take a look at it before its final close.

Though this first day of the campaign has passed off so well, of course we shall have to keep a watchful eye during the whole four months upon those who might be disposed to take advantage, for purposes of mischief, of the congregation of foreigners in London; but with the means we have of making such people pay dearly for any such attempt, I do not entertain any apprehension as to the result of any schemes they may plan.

(b) *Source:* Earl of Bessborough, *The Diaries of Lady Charlotte Guest* (1833–1852), 1950, chapter xv, pp. 268–271.

Lady Charlotte Guest (1812–1895), was the daughter of Albermarle Bertie, ninth Earl of Lindsey. She married Sir Josiah John Guest, the famous ironmaster of Dowlais, Glamorgan. Helped by Carnhuanawc and Tegid, two scholarly Welsh clergymen, she translated the *Mabinogion* into English; and her famous collection of china is now in the Victoria and Albert Museum. She took an enlightened and energetic interest in the welfare of her husband's workmen and their families at Dowlais. Supremely and triumphantly the product of her epoch, she knits together the golden age of the Whig aristocracy with the splendours of the new industrial feudalism, and in her *Diary* the reader can watch it in all its strength and weakness. A woman of great energy and ability, she was able to help her husband considerably in the conduct of his business. She represents the *mulier fortis* of the age of Victoria.

Further Reading: Ed. G. M. Young, *Early Victorian England*, Oxford University Press, 2 vols. 1934.

April 30th

A large and pleasant party at Lady John Russell's. Everybody was talking of tomorrow's opening. Most people were going, but some few professed to treat it with contempt, and some had not thought it worth while to take season tickets, by which admission could be had. Some days before a great deal had been said about the dangers attendant on the ceremony. Some affirmed the whole edifice would tumble down, some that the noise of the cannons would shatter the glass, many that the crowd and rush at the doors would be intolerable, and not a few expected that riots and rebellions and conspiracies were suddenly to break out. Alarm however by this time seemed in great measure to be allayed, yet in my own case I felt very doubtful what to do about going there. . . . But Maria was so anxious to be present that for her sake I determined to see what could be done, and luckily for us we found that evening that Kitson being a Gentleman at Arms and having consequently the entrée, we could, by going in the same conveyance with him, be admitted without any trouble. . . .

May 1*st*

I was up next day very early. We took a hearty breakfast, i.e. Maria and I, and soon after 8 Mr. Kitson came. He had however to proceed first to the Palace for orders, so we waited till his return, which was in about an hour; I sat down quietly and wrote letters and notes. When he came back our carriage was at the door, he got into it with me and Maria and we proceeded. Having the Pass we had not to stop at all, but drove up at once to the Queen's (North) Entrance. When we left our house the line of carriages extended into the Haymarket, which seemed somewhat hopeless for many at least of the occupiers. We crossed this line in Piccadilly and drove on. We reached the building exactly at 10 o'clock, and our first business on entering was of course to look for places. Mr. Shelley came forward and offered us places not very far from the throne, at the back. They seemed the best that remained, and we were doubtful whether it might not be best to accept them, when Mr. Baldock saw our difficulty and good-naturedly motioned us to excellent seats which were vacant near him. These were the nearest to the throne of any in the North Transept, and raised a few feet from the floor. They were on the East side of the Transept, so that we commanded a complete and excellent view of the Western End of the Nave, and could see a good portion of the Eastern, by looking round the point. Of course our view of the Chair of State and of both transepts was perfect; we were just above the seats reserved for the Lord Mayor and Corporation of London, only being raised above them we had a finer coup d'oeil. Once seated and with so little trouble, the two hours from ten to twelve were most amusing. We saw all the officials, diplomats, Ambassadors and remarkable persons come in and group themselves, and we watched their various expedients for passing away the time. There was a hearty cheer for the Duke of Wellington when he arrived, and a tolerably good one for Lord John Russell. We were diverted by a Chinese gentleman in full costume who placed himself among the Diplomatic Corps, and held a long palaver to—I can hardly say with—the Duke of Wellington, and there were numberless little incidents besides, which filled up the time and made it anything but long and tedious. At length a rumour was heard that the Queen was in the building, and precisely as the clock struck twelve she issued from the waiting room which had been prepared for her, and accompanied by Prince Albert and the two eldest children, proceeded to her place amidst the uncontrolled enthusiasm of the multitudes of people. It was a noble sight; she stood on the raised dais, in front of the Chair of State on which she sat not, even for a moment. Her husband and her children were beside her, her Court immediately about her. Around her, the highest names of England, and thousands less renowned but no less loyal; and all this pomp and panoply were called together to do honour to the industry of millions, whose toils, erst scorned upon, seemed suddenly ennobled. It was a proud moment for our Queen, for England! While the nations of the earth were convulsed, she has called into existence this peaceful meeting, the most gigantic ever known, whether as regards the numbers assembled or the objects of the undertaking. I am lost in thronging thoughts, I cannot fitly express what I would say. But as the wife of the largest manufacturer in the world I could not but feel this to be a most impressive sight. Parts of the ceremony were to me most touching, and many times I found the tears starting from my eyes. I need not describe what any newspaper of the day will tell more accurately. I only know it was the most dazzling sight I ever beheld, grander even than Her coronation in our glorious Abbey. The masses were so wonderful, the whole intention and execution so stupendous!

When she had received and replied to the address, which, near as we were, was all but inaudible to us, and when the Archbishop had concluded his fine prayer, the procession formed to perambulate the building. She set forth amidst the loudest cheers, which accompanied her during all her progress. But it was a singular effect of the magnitude of the space, that from the time that she had reached about half the length of each end of the Nave, the cheer, though taken up quite heartily, was not to be heard where we sat. At first we thought they were receiving her in silence, but this the violent gesticulations, waving and handkerchiefs, etc., that we could discover among the distant audience, at once contradicted, and the fact was soon ascertained that the size of the edifice prevented any sound being heard beyond about one quarter of its space. The Queen remained in the building from twelve to one—glorious hour! Byron's notes to Childe Harold recurred to my mind: ' Oh, for one hour of Dundee! ' Surely Victoria's ' hour ' was the grandest ever recorded.

THE CRIMEAN WAR

The Crimean War was by no means the first war in which British troops had suffered great hardships, but it was the first in which there was a war correspondent to tell the British public about these hardships, and about the administrative chaos which made them far worse than they need have been. Russell, the special correspondent of *The Times*, wrote accounts which caused great indignation in England, and contributed largely to the fall of the Aberdeen government.

(*a*) *Source:* W. H. Russell, *The War*, Routledge, 1855, pp. 290-2.

Sir William Howard Russell (1821-1907) special correspondent of *The Times* in the Crimea, also reported on the Indian Mutiny, the Civil War in America, and the Franco-Prussian War.

Further Reading: Cecil Woodham-Smith: *The Reason Why*, Constable, 1953. Cecil Woodham-Smith: *Florence Nightingale*, Constable, 1950. S. H. F. Johnston: *British Soldiers*, Collins, 1934.

CONDITIONS AT THE FRONT

Before Sebastopol, December 4.

. . . . The whole plateau on which stands ' the camp before Sebastopol ' . . . is a vast black dreary wilderness of mud, dotted with little lochs of foul water, and seamed by dirty brownish and tawny-coloured streams running down to and along the ravines. On its surface everywhere are strewed the carcasses of horses and miserable animals torn by dogs and smothered in mud. Vultures sweep over the mounds in flocks; carrion crows and 'birds of prey obscene' hover over their prey, menace the hideous dogs who are feasting below, or sit in gloomy dyspepsia, with drooped head and drooping wing, on the remnants of their banquet.

It is over this ground, gained at last by great toil and exhaustion and loss of life on the part of the starving beasts of burden, that man and horse have to struggle from Balaclava for some four or five miles with the hay and corn, the meat, the biscuit, the pork, which form the subsistence of our army. Every day this toil must be undergone. . . . Horses drop exhausted on the road, and their loads are removed and added to the burdens of the struggling survivors; then, after a few efforts to get out of their Slough of Despond, the poor brutes succumb and lie down to die in their graves. Men wade and plunge about, and stumble through the mud, with muttered imprecations, or sit down on a projecting stone, exhausted, pictures of dirt and woe unutterable. Sometimes on the route the overworked and sickly soldier is seized with illness, and the sad aspect of a fellow-countryman dying before his eyes shocks every passer-by—the more because aid is all but hopeless and impossible. . . . The painful recollection which ever occurs to one is, what necessity is there for all the suffering and privation created by this imperfect state of our communications? Why should not roads have been made when we sat down before the place? Their formation would have saved many lives, and have spared our men much sickness and pain. Had there been the least foresight—nay, had there existed among us the ordinary instincts of self-preservation—we would have set the Turks to work at once while the weather was fine, and have constructed the roads which we are now trying to make under most disadvantageous conditions. The siege operations have been sometimes completely—sometimes partially —suspended, and the attack on Sebastopol has languished and declined. Neither guns nor ammunition could be brought up to the batteries.

The mortality amongst the Turks has now assumed all the

dimensions of a plague. Every sense was offended and shocked by the display, day after day, in the streets, of processions of men bearing half-covered corpses on litters at the busiest hour of the day. . . .

(b) *Source:* Russell—*The War*, pp. 303–304.

The thermometer, which was at 18° yesterday morning, rose to 33° last night, and it thawed for several hours towards morning, and the snow and ice are now giving way rapidly. The cavalry horses have suffered severely. At the present rate of mortality, the whole division, which musters about 500 horses, will be extinct in thirty days.

The 63rd Regiment had only seven men fit for duty yesterday. The 46th had only thirty men fit for duty at the same date. A strong company of the 90th have been reduced by the last week's severity to fourteen file in a few days, and that regiment though considered very healthy, lost fifty men by death in a fortnight. The Scots Fusilier Guards, who have had out from beginning to end 1562 men, now muster, including servants and corporals, 210 men on parade. Many other regiments have suffered in like proportion. As a matter of course, the men in this cold weather seek after ardent spirits with great avidity, and instances not a few—some of which I have witnessed—have taken place in which the men carrying out rum to the camp have broached the kegs when the eye of the officer in charge was off them, and have almost paid the penalty of their consequent drunkenness in the loss of life at night as they staggered across the waste of snow to the camp. The duty of the fatigue parties is, indeed, very trying. The men are provided with a stout pole for each couple, and a cask of rum, biscuits, or beef, is slung from it between them, and then they go off on a tramp of about five miles from the commissariat stores at Balaclava to the head-quarters. I have seen the officers dividing this labour with their men; and as I was coming in from the front on Saturday, I met a lad who could not long have joined in charge of a party of the 38th Regiment, who took the place of a tired man, and struggled along under his load, while the man at the other end of the pole exhausted the little breath he had left in appeals to his comrades, ' Boys! Boys!

won't you come and relieve the young officer?' Horses cannot do this work, for they cannot keep their legs, and now almost every 100 yards of the road is marked by a carcase. To give an idea of the loss we have sustained in this way, here is a fact. There is now on duty in Balaclava a party of orderlies, whose duty it is to go about and bury all offal and dead animals every day. On an average they have to inter the bodies of twelve horses each twenty-four hours, all of which have died within the town. It is really humiliating to our national pride, and distressing to our sense of what we might be, and ought to be, to see the French entering Balaclava with their neat wagons and clean-looking men, and stout horses, to aid our wretch-looking, pale, weakly soldiers and emaciated horses in carrying up ammunition.
. . . The arrangements at Balaclava are much better now than when I wrote about them some time ago. But let no one at home dream that our troops are in huts, or that they are well clad. It will be weeks ere the huts can be up at the camp. Some have been pitched close to the town for the artillery, and a few suits of warm clothing have been distributed. But hundreds of men have still to go into the trenches at night with no covering but their great coats and no protection for their feet but their regimental shoes. The trenches are two and three feet deep with mud, snow, and half-frozen slush. Many men when they take off their shoes are unable to get their swollen feet into them again, and they have been seen barefooted hopping along the camp, with the thermometer at twenty degrees, and the snow half-a-foot deep on the ground. Our fine patent stoves are wretched affairs. They are made of thin sheet iron, which cannot stand our fuel—charcoal. Besides, with charcoal they are mere poison manufactories, and they cannot be left alight in the tents at night. They answer well for drying the men's clothes at day. There are not many of them distributed as yet, however, so that, such as they are, the troops have not the advantage. On this, the 8th day of January, some of the Guards, of Her Majesty Queen Victoria's Household Brigade, are walking about in the snow *without soles to their shoes.*

THE BATTLE OF THE ALMA
Wednesday, September 20th, 1854

The storming of the heights of the Alma is one of the great achievements of the British army. The Russian command was certain that the position was impregnable.

Source: W. H. Russell, *The War*, Routledge, 1855, pp. 180–2.

Lord Raglan . . . gave orders for our whole line to advance. Up rose these serried masses, and passing through a fearful shower of round, case shot, and shell, they dashed into the Alma, and floundered through its waters, which were literally torn into foam by the deadly hail. At the other side of the river were a number of vineyards, and to our surprise they were occupied by Russian riflemen. Three of the staff were here shot down, but led by Lord Raglan in person, they advanced cheering on the men. And now came the turning point of the battle, in which Lord Raglan, by his sagacity and military skill, probably secured the victory at a smaller sacrifice than would otherwise have been the case. He dashed over the bridge, followed by his staff. From the road over it, under the Russian guns, he saw the state of action. The British line, which he had ordered to advance, was struggling through the river and up the heights in masses, firm indeed, but mowed down by the murderous fire of the batteries, and by grape, round shot, shell, canister, case shot, and musketry, from some of the guns of the central battery, and from an immense and compact mass of Russian infantry. Then commenced one of the most bloody and determined struggles in the annals of war. The 2nd Division, led by Sir de L. Evans in the most dashing manner, crossed the stream on the right. The 7th Fusiliers, led by Colonel Yea, were swept down by fifties. The 55th, 30th, and 95th, led by Brigadier Pennefather, who was in the thickest of the fight, cheering on his men, again and again were checked indeed, but never drew back in their onward progress, which was marked by a fierce roll of Minié musketry, and Brigadier Adams, with the 41st, 47th and 49th, bravely charged up the hill, and aided them in the battle. Sir George Brown, conspicuous on a grey horse, rode in front of his Light division, urging them with voice and gesture. Gallant fellows! they were worthy of such a gallant chief. The 7th, diminished by one-half, fell back to reform their columns lost for the time; the 23rd, with eight officers dead and four wounded, were still rushing to the front. . . . Down went Sir George in a cloud of dust in front of the battery. He was soon up and shouted, ' 23rd, I'm all right. Be sure I'll remember this day ', and led them on again, but in the shock produced by the fall of their chief, the gallant regiment suffered terribly, while paralysed for a moment. Meantime the Guards on the right of the Light Division, and the brigade of Highlanders, were storming the heights on the left. Their line was almost as regular as though they were in Hyde Park. Suddenly a tornado of round and grape rushed through from the terrible battery, and a roar of musketry from behind thinned their front ranks by dozens. . . . At this time an immense mass of Russian infantry were seen moving down towards the battery. They halted. It was the crisis of the day. Sharp, angular, and solid, they looked as if they were cut out of the solid rock. It was beyond all doubt that if our infantry, harassed and thinned as they were, got into the battery, they would have to encounter again a formidable fire, which they were but ill calculated to bear. Lord Raglan saw the difficulties of the situation. He asked if it would be possible to get a couple of guns to bear on these masses. The reply was ' Yes ', and an infantry officer . . . brought up two guns to fire on the Russian squares. The first shot missed, but the next, and the next, and the next cut through the ranks so cleanly, and so keenly, that a clear lane could be seen for a moment through the square. After a few rounds the columns of the square became broken, wavered to and fro, broke, and fled over the brow of the hill, leaving behind them six or seven distinct lines of dead, lying as close as possible to each other, marking the passage of the fatal messengers. This act relieved our infantry of a deadly incubus, and they continued their magnificent and fearful progress up the hill. . . . ' Highlanders,' said Sir C. Campbell, ere they came to the charge, ' I am going to ask a favour of you; it is, that you will act so as to justify me in asking permission of the Queen for you to wear a bonnet! Don't pull a trigger till you're within a yard of the Russians!' They charged, and well they obeyed their chieftain's wish; Sir Colin had his horse shot under him, but his men took the battery at a bound.

The Russians rushed out, and left multitudes of dead behind them. The Guards had stormed the right of the battery ere the Highlanders got into the left, and it is said the Scots Fusilier Guards were the first to enter. The Second and Light Division crowned the heights. The French turned the guns on the hill against the flying masses, which the cavalry in vain tried to cover. A few faint struggles from the scattered infantry, a few rounds of cannon and musketry, and the enemy fled to the south-east, leaving three generals, drums, three guns, 700 prisoners, and 4,000 wounded behind them. The battle of the Alma was won. It was won with a loss of nearly 3,000 killed and wounded on our side. The Russians' retreat was covered by their cavalry, but if we had had an adequate force, we could have captured many guns and multitudes of prisoners.

THE CHARGE OF THE LIGHT BRIGADE
Wednesday, October 25th, 1854
BATTLE OF BALACLAVA

(a) *Source:* Anonymous Eighth Hussar. *The Charge of the British Cavalry at Balaclava.* By one who was in it. Quoted Gilby, *Britain in Arms*, published Eyre and Spottiswoode 1953, pp. 195–6.

Further Reading: C. Woodham-Smith, *The Reason Why*, Constable, 1953.

The morning was clear and bright; in fact as beautiful a morning as you could wish to see. . . . And, says one of our men, ' Well, I'm damned if it isn't the Colonel; what do you say to the " old woman " now? '

The fact is, we had left him very ill, as we thought, in his tent, for he had been sadly troubled with gout and sickness; and suffering like the rest of us, besides being old for such exposure— and so, from one thing or another, he had got that name. But he was full of pluck, and when he knew that fighting was going on he came up to us, and we were pleased to see him too.

I saw, as he passed in front of us, that all at once his face expressed the greatest surprise and astonishment, and even anger, and, walking on, he broke out with, ' What's this? What's this? One, two, four, six, seven men *smoking!*—swords drawn, and seven men smoking!—why, the thing is inconceivable! I never heard of such a thing ... and no regiment except an " Irish" regiment would be guilty of it. Sergeant, advance and take these men's names.' All this time I heard strange dull noises thickening in the air.

I now saw the whole plain and the heights skirting the valley covered with Russian infantry and Cossacks, and some six-and-twenty grim-black muzzles pointed at us, which in a moment would be red-hot, and panting as the throats of famished wolves. This battery extended for perhaps a quarter of a mile right abreast of us, and as the mouths of the outer guns were slightly turned *in*, their range would meet together and cross in one common focus, which we at full gallop *must* have been in the very midst of.

Down the descending slope, over ground that seemed ploughed, we went like a rushing hurricane, with Lord Cardigan at our head, and he ' went in ' a regular ' buster '.

I felt, as I felt my horse beginning to bound under me, and gripping my sabre, which I had fastened to my wrist with a twisted silk handkerchief—I felt at that moment my blood thicken and crawl, as if my heart grew still and quiet like a lump of stone within me. I was a moment paralysed, but the snorting of the horse, the wild headlong gallop, the sight of the Russians before us, becoming more and more distinct, and the first horrible discharge with its still more horrible effects came upon us, and emptied saddles all about me. My heart now began to warm, to become hot, to dance again, and I had neither fear nor pity! I longed to be at the guns. I'm sure I set my teeth together as if I could have bitten a piece out of one.

(*b*) *Source: Henry Clifford, V.C.*, Michael Joseph, 1956, pp. 72-4.

From a letter of the Hon. Henry Clifford of the Rifle Brigade. He was awarded the Victoria Cross for gallantry at Inkerman.

I must tell you that but little confidence has been placed in the commanding powers of Lord Lucan commanding the Cavalry, and long and loud have been the feuds on public grounds, between his Lordship and Lord Cardigan (than whom, a braver soldier never held a sword) who commands the Light Brigade; and it was thought if a verbal order was sent to Lord L. it might be misunderstood, or not carried out. A written order was, therefore, sent from Lord Raglan by Captain Nolan,

General Airey's A.D.C. (formerly my brother A.D.C. in the Light Division) desiring his Lordship ' to charge! ' ' To charge what? ' said Lord Lucan very naturally. ' Here are your orders,' said poor Nolan, pointing to the paper, ' *and there* ', pointing to the Russian army, ' is the enemy ', and shouting ' Come on ' to the Light Brigade of Cavalry, he dashed forward. He was wrong, poor fellow, in doing so, he forgot his position, and his conduct was most insulting to Lord Lucan and Lord Cardigan, who at the head of his Brigade, pale with indignation, shouted to him to stop, that he should answer for his words and actions before Lord Raglan, but he was called to a higher tribunal, a shell struck him in the chest, and in a few minutes he was a mangled corpse. Lord Lucan then ordered the Light Brigade of Cavalry between 600 and 700 to charge the Russian Army, 30,000 strong. This is the explanation I heard afterwards.

From the commanding position in which I stood by the side of General Brite[1] we saw the Light Brigade of Cavalry moving forward at a trot, in face of the Russian army. ' Mon Dieu! ' said the fine old French general, ' Que vont-ils faire? ' They went steadily on, as Englishmen only go under heavy fire. Artillery in front, on the right and left. When some thousand yards from the foremost of the enemy, I saw shells bursting in the midst of the Squadrons and men and horses strewed the ground behind them; yet on they went, and the smoke of the murderous fire poured on them, hid them from my sight.

The tears ran down my face, and the din of musketry pouring in their murderous fire on the brave gallant fellows rang in my ears. ' Pauvre garçon ', said the old French general, patting me on the shoulder. ' Je suis vieux, j'ai vu des batailles, mais ceci est trop '. Then the smoke cleared away and I saw hundreds of our poor fellows lying on the ground, the Cossacks and Russian cavalry running them through as they lay, with their swords and lances.

Some time passed, I can't say how much, but it was *very* long, waiting to see if any would return. Horses without riders, galloped back in numbers, and men wounded on foot and men not hurt, but their horses killed, returned on foot, and then we

[1] 2nd in Command to the French General Bosquet.

T

saw a horse or a man fall, who wounded, had come as far home as he could and then fell and died.

At length about 30 horsemen dashed through a line of Cossacks, who had reformed to interrupt their retreat, and then another larger body came in sight from the middle of the smoke and dust. Two hundred men! They were all that returned of 600 odd that charged. I don't know the names of the officers who fell or were taken prisoner, but very few returned, and some are since dead of their wounds; one of the Officers of the 17th Lancers (his Regiment suffered most severely, I believe) told me they charged through a line of infantry, drove the gunners from their guns, but of course could not bring them away. Then through the line of Cavalry till they came to the Infantry when the handful that remained, turned about and recharged the same forces again. The Chasseurs d'Afrique also made a small charge, but when they came face to face with the Russian Infantry in square, with the exception of one or two Officers, they turned round and came back again.

THE CHARGE OF THE HEAVY BRIGADE
BATTLE OF BALACLAVA

(a) *Source:* W. H. Russell, *The War*, pp. 228–9.

Our eyes were, however, turned in a moment on our own cavalry. We saw Brigadier-General Scarlett ride along in front of his massive squadrons. The Russians—evidently corps d'elite —their light blue jackets embroidered with silver lace, were advancing on their left, at an easy gallop, towards the brow of the hill. A forest of lances glistened in their rear, and several squadrons of grey-coated dragoons moved up quickly to support them as they reached the summit. The instant they came in sight the trumpets of our cavalry gave out the warning blast which told us all that in another moment we should see the shock of battle beneath our very eyes. Lord Raglan, all his staff and escort, and groups of officers, the Zouaves, French generals and officers, and bodies of French infantry on the height, were spectators of the scene as though they were looking on the stage from the boxes of a theatre. Nearly everyone dismounted and sat down, and not a word was said. The Russians advanced down the hill at a slow canter, which they changed to a trot, and at last nearly halted. Their first line was at least double the length of ours—it was three times as deep. Behind them was a similar line, equally strong and compact. They evidently despised their insignificant looking enemy, but their time was come. The trumpets rang out again through the valley, and the Greys and Enniskilleners went right at the centre of the Russian cavalry. The space between them was only a few hundred yards; it was scarce enough to let the horses ' gather way ', nor had the men quite space sufficient for the full play of their sword arms. The Russian line brings forward each wing as our cavalry advance, and threatens to annihilate them as they pass on. Turning a little to the left, so as to meet the Russian right, the Greys rush on with a cheer that thrills to every heart—the wild shout of the Enniskilleners rises through the air at the same instant. As lightning flashes through a cloud, the Greys and Enniskilleners pierced through the dark masses of Russians. The shock was but for a moment. There was a clash of steel and a light play of sword-blades in the air, and then the Greys and the redcoats disappear in the midst of the shaken and quivering columns. In another moment we see them emerging and dashing on with diminished numbers, and in broken order, against the second line, which is advancing against them as fast as it can to retrieve the fortune of the charge. It was a terrible moment. ' God help them! they are lost! ' was the exclamation of more than one man, and the thought of many. With unabated fire the noble hearts dashed at their enemy. It was a fight of heroes. The first line of Russians, which had been smashed utterly by our charge, and had fled off at one flank and towards the centre, were coming back to swallow up our handful of men. By sheer steel and sheer courage Enniskillener and Scot were winning their desperate way right through the enemy's squadrons, and already grey horses and red coats had appeared right at the rear of the second mass, when, with irresistible force, like one bolt from a bow, the 1st Royals, the 4th Dragoon Guards, and the 5th Dragoon Guards rushed at the remnants of the first line of the enemy, went through it as though it were made of pasteboard, and, dashing on the second body of Russians as they were still disordered by the terrible assault of the Greys and their companions, put them to utter rout. This Russian horse in less than five minutes after it met our dragoons was flying with all its speed before a force certainly not half its strength. A cheer burst from every lip—in the enthusiasm, officers and men took off their caps and shouted with delight, and thus keeping up the scenic character of their position, they clapped their hands again and again. Lord Raglan at once despatched Lieutenant Curzon, Aide-de-camp, to convey his congratulations to Brigadier-General Scarlett. The gallant old officer's face beamed with pleasure when he received the message. ' I beg to thank his Lordship very sincerely,' was his reply.

LORD PALMERSTON

Educated at Harrow, Edinburgh and St. John's College, Cambridge, he entered Parliament as member for Newtown, Isle of Wight, in 1807. In the same year he became Junior Lord of the Admiralty in the Duke of Portland's administration. In 1809 he was Secretary at War. He was Foreign Secretary in Earl Grey's administration from 1830 to 1834, and from 1835 to 1841. In 1846 he again became Foreign Secretary in Lord John Russell's first administration, and resigned in 1851. He was Home Secretary from 1852 to 1855 in Lord Aberdeen's administration. In February 1855 he became Prime Minister, remaining in power until February 1858, and he returned to office in June 1859 until October 1865. Very varied judgements were formed on this ' versatile Victorian '. The Queen wrote: ' He had many valuable qualities, though many bad ones, and we had, God knows! terrible trouble with him about foreign affairs. Still, as Prime Minister, he managed affairs at home well and behaved to me well. But I *never* liked him. . . .' His Divorce Bill of 1857 may well, it has been suggested, seem more important one day than his famous speech on the theme ' Civis Romanus sum ' which so delighted the England of his day. His great virtue was that of generosity.

(*a*) *Source: Greville Memoirs.*

Further Reading: H. C. F. Bell, *Lord Palmerston*, Longmans, 1936. A. Cecil, *British Foreign Secretaries*, 1807–1916. Bell, 1927, ch. iv.

February 17, 1835. . . . His great fault is want of punctuality, and never keeping an engagement if it did not suit him, keeping everybody waiting for hours on his pleasure or caprice. This testimony is beyond suspicion, and it is confirmed by the opinions of his colleagues.

(b) *Source: Greville Memoirs.*

February 17, 1835. . . . The other night I met some clerks in the Foreign Office to whom the very name of Palmerston is hateful, but I was surprised to hear them (Mellish particularly, who can judge both from capacity and opportunity) give ample testimony to his abilities. They said that he wrote admirably, and could express himself perfectly in French, very sufficiently in Italian, and understood German; that his diligence and attention were unwearied—he read everything and wrote an immense quantity; that the foreign Ministers (who detest him) did him justice as an excellent man of business.

(c) *Source: Greville Memoirs.*

August 7, 1836. It is surprising to hear how Palmerston is spoken of by those who know him well officially—the Granvilles, for example. Lady Granville, a woman expert in judging, thinks his capacity first rate; that it approaches to greatness from his enlarged views, disdain of trivialities, resolution, decision, confidence, and above all his contempt of clamour and abuse.

(d) *Source: Greville Memoirs.*

September 23, 1839 . . . I said . . . that he was very able with his pen, but I did not know how he was in conference. He [Dedel—the Dutch minister] replied: 'Palmerston comes to any conference so fully and completely master of the subject of it in all the minutest details, that this capacity is a peculiar talent with him; it is so great, that he is apt sometimes to lose himself in the details.'

(e) *Source: Greville Memoirs.*

Lord Palmerston's conduct of the situation created by the ill-treatment of Don Pacifico in Greece, was made the occasion for a tremendous onslaught by the opposition on his foreign policy. In a great speech, on June 25, 1850, Palmerston triumphantly routed his attackers. The speech concluded with the famous sentence: 'As the Roman, in days of old, held himself free from indignity, when he could say " Civis Romanus sum ", so also a British subject, in whatever land he may be, shall feel confident that the watchful eye and the strong arm of England will protect him against injustice and wrong.'

London, July 1, 1850. . . . I rode with Lord Grey yesterday in the Park, when we talked over the debate and present state of affairs. He said that it was remarkable that this discussion, which was intended to damage Palmerston, had left him the most popular man in the country; that of this there could be no doubt. Bright had said that his vote had given great offence at Manchester, and that Cobden's vote and speech would probably cost him the West Riding at the next election; that amongst all the middle classes Palmerston was immensely popular. He spoke of Palmerston's speech as having been not only one of consummate ability, but quite successful as a reply, and he insisted that their side had much the best of the argument. I denied this, but acknowledged the ability of Palmerston and his success, though his speech was very answerable, if either Peel or Disraeli had chosen to reply to it, which neither of them would. It is beyond all contestation that this great battle, fought on two fields, has left the Government much stronger than before, and demonstrated the impossibility of any change, and it has incontestably immensely strengthened and improved Palmerston's position; in short, he is triumphant.

(f) *Source*: P. Grant, *A History of Factory Legislation*; quoted in E. Ashley, *Life of Lord Palmerston*, Bentley, 1879. Vol. i, pp. 460–2.

Grant was one of the two factory workers who had this interview with Palmerston in 1843.

. . . The pair made off for Carlton Gardens, the then residence of Lord Palmerston. . . . On presenting themselves at the door, the footman, in answer to their inquiry, said His Lordship was not at home. Their reply was, ' Not at home to visitors '. The man smiled, and was leaving, but they persisted. It was the last opportunity they might have before the division. . . . They urged the footman to take in their cards, but he refused, saying, ' It is more than my place is worth '. Whilst the altercation was going on, the noble lord happened to be passing from his dressing-room to the dining-room, and seeing the two at the door, inquired who and what they were. The servant at once handed him their cards, and returned, smiling, bringing with him the gladful news, ' His Lordship will see you '. They were at once ushered into the large dining-room. They found the member for Tiverton in excellent temper, and as lively as a cricket. Without ceremony the subject was entered into, detailing some of the hardships to which the factory children were subject. The statements at first appeared to puzzle the noble viscount, and after a short pause the veteran statesman said, ' Oh, the work of the children cannot be so hard as you represent it, as I am led to understand the machinery does all the work without the aid of the children, attention to the spindles only being required.' To carry conviction to a mind so strongly impressed with the ease and comfort of factory labour for a moment staggered the deputation, when a lucky expedient at once occurred to the writer, who, seeing a couple of large lounging chairs upon castors, called them to the rescue. Removing them into the centre of the large room, they were made to perform the operation of the ' spinning mule ', Mr. Haworth being placed, as it were, at the ' wheel handle ', and with arm and knee pushing them back to their destination, or to what is technically called the ' roller-beam ', whilst the writer performed the duties of the piecer, trotting from one side of the room to the other, following up the carriage, leaning over the imaginary advancing ' faller ', and piecing up the supposed broken ends. To complete the explanation of the mule, and to show the part the engine performed, they were about to explain by what power the carriage was caused to advance slowly, whilst the ' stretch ' was being made, and the yarn twisted. The noble lord at once caught the idea, and ringing the bell, the footman was ordered into the room and directed to run up one of the chairs slowly to its appointed place (or what is called the end of the stretch), whilst the noble lord catching hold of the other chair performed a similar office. Thus the imaginary spinning and piecing was carried on for several minutes. Lady Palmerston, who by this time had become impatient for her drive before dinner, entered the room, and appeared no little surprised to see her banqueting-room turned into a spinning-factory. Her Ladyship, however, appeared to enjoy the illustration. The veteran statesman, who appeared a little fatigued by performing the duties of ' Old Ned ' (the engine), with a significant look and shrug of the shoulders, said, ' Surely this must be an exaggeration of the labour of factory workers '. Mr. Haworth, who had come fresh from the wheel-handle in Bolton, and bearing indelible marks of the severity of his daily toil, exhibited the large ' segs ' upon his hands, at the same time pulling up his trousers, he said, ' Look at my knee, my lord ', pointing to the hard substance produced by ' putting up the carriage '. This victory over the mind of the great statesman appeared complete . . . and he hastily exclaimed, ' If what you have shown me, and what you have stated, be a fair illustration of the labour of factory people, and the statements you have made be a fair detail of the hardships to which they are subject, I can no longer withhold my support from your cause. . . . A promise which that great man ever afterwards kept, and on all occasions when the subject was before Parliament, he diligently performed by speaking and voting in favour of the ' poor factory child '.

THE INDIAN MUTINY

The mutiny of the native troops in the army of Bengal broke out at Meerut on May 10, 1857. From Meerut the mutinous Sepoys marched to Delhi, thirty-five miles away. Their arrival spread the mutiny to Delhi.

(a) At Delhi.

Source: Account by an English Officer in a Sepoy Regiment in Delhi, in Annual Register, vol. xcix (History), p. 251.

Further Reading: D. James, Lord Roberts, Hollis and Carter, 1954. Hesketh Pearson, Hero of Delhi, Collins, 1939.

I persuaded the Sepoys to let me take the regimental colour, and I took it outside, but on calling for my groom I found he had bolted with my horse. You may imagine my horror at this. I went back into the Quarter Guard and replaced the colour, but on coming out a trooper dismounted and took a deliberate shot at me, but, missing his aim, I walked up to him and blew his brains out. Another man was then taking aim at me, when he was bayoneted by a Sepoy of my company. The firing then became general, and I was compelled to run the gauntlet across the parade ground, and escaped unhurt miraculously, three bullets having passed through my hat, and one through the skirt of my coat. The whole of the houses in cantonments were burnt. Having gone as far as my weak state of health would permit, and being exhausted, I took refuge in a garden under some bushes. About half an hour after a band of robbers, looking out for plunder, detected me, robbed me of my rings, etc., and only left me my flannel waistcoat and socks. They then tore off the sleeve of my shirt, and with it attempted to strangle me. . . . They left me for dead, as I had become senseless. About one hour after I came to, and managed to stagger on about a mile without shoes, where I secreted myself in a hut until daybreak, when I resumed my dreary journey. . . .

(b) Events at Cawnpore, where British forces, commanded by General Sir Hugh Wheeler, were besieged by the forces of the Nana Sahib.

Source: Narrative of Mr. Shepherd of the Commissariat Department in *Annual Register*, vol. xcix (*History*), pp. 284–5.

We had but one well, in the middle of the intrenchment, and the enemy kept up their fire so incessantly both day and night, that it was as much as giving a man's life-blood to go and draw a bucket of water; and while there was any water left in the large jars usually kept in the verandah for the soldiers' use nobody ventured to the well; but after the second day the demand became so great that a Bheestie bag of water was with difficulty got for five rupees, and a bucket for a rupee, as most of the servants of officers and merchants had deserted, and it therefore became a matter of necessity for every person to get his own water, which was usually done during the night, when the enemy could not well direct their shots. . . .

There was no place to shelter the live cattle. Horses of private gentlemen, as also those of the 3rd Oude Battery, were obliged to be let loose. A few sheep and goats, as well as the bullocks kept for Commissariat purposes, were shot off, and in the course of five or six days no meat was to be got for the Europeans. They, however, now and again managed to get hold of a stray bullock or cow near the intrenchment at night, which served for a change. . . .

For the first four or five days of the outbreak, our artillery kept up a brisk firing, but after that it was considered inadvisable to exhaust our magazine, for the rebels took care to always keep well under cover, and we could not do much execution among them.

The heat was very great, and what with the fright, want of room, want of proper food and care, several ladies and soldiers' wives, as also children, died with great distress. Many officers and soldiers also were sun-struck, from exposure to the hot winds. The dead bodies of our people had to be thrown into a well outside the intrenchment, near the new unfinished barracks, and this work was generally done at the close of each day, as nobody could venture out during the day, on account of the shot and shell flying in all directions like a hail storm, our intrenchment was strewn with them. The distress was so great that none could offer a word of consolation to his friend, or attempt to minister to the wants of each other. I have seen the dead bodies of officers and tenderly-brought up young ladies of rank . . . put outside in the verandah in the rain, to await the time when the fatigue party usually went round to carry the dead to the well, as above, for there was scarcely room to shelter the living; the buildings were so sadly riddled that every safe corner available was considered a great object.

The enemy now commenced firing live shells well heated, with the intent of setting fire to the tents of officers in the compound, as also to the thatched barrack. . . . The tents therefore had all to be struck, as several had thus been burnt, and at last, on the 13th of June, the barrack also took fire; it was about 5 p.m., and that evening was one of unspeakable distress and trial, for all the wounded and sick were in it, also the families of the soldiers and drummers. The fire took on the south side of it, and the breeze being very strong the flames spread out so quickly that it was hard matter to remove the women and children, who were all in great confusion, so that the helpless wounded and sick could not be removed, and were all burnt down to ashes (about 40 or upwards in number). The whole of the medicines were also there, and shared the same fate.

It may easily be imagined that by this time our barracks were so perfectly riddled as to afford little or no shelter; yet the greater portion of the people preferred to remain in them than to be exposed to the heat of the sun outside, although a great many made themselves holds under the walls of the intrenchment, covered over with boxes, cots, etc. In these, with their wives and children, they were secure, at least, from the shots and shells of the enemy, though not so from the effects of the heat, and the mortality from apoplexy was considerable. At night, however, every person had to sleep out and take the watch in their turns. . . . Here the live shells kept them in perpetual dread, for nearly all night these shells were seen coming in the air and bursting in different places, often doing mischief. . . .

(c) On June 24th the Nana Sahib proposed to General Wheeler that if the stores and treasure were handed over, all the Europeans would be allowed to go in boats to Allahabad.

Source: Lieutenant Delafosse's Narrative in *Annual Register*, xcix (*History*), p. 287.

. . . we gave over our guns, etc., and marched out on the morning of the 27th of June, about 7 o'clock. We got down to the river and into the boats without being molested in the least; but no sooner were we in the boats, and had laid down our muskets, and had taken off our coats to work easier at the boats, than the cavalry gave the order to fire. Two guns that had been hidden were run out and opened on us immediately, while Sepoys came from all directions and kept up a fire. The men jumped out of the boats, and instead of trying to get the boats loose from their moorings swam to the first boat they saw loose. Only three boats got safe over to the opposite side of the River, but were met there by two field-pieces, guarded by a number of cavalry and infantry. Before these boats had got a mile down the stream half our small party were either killed or wounded and two of our boats had been swamped. We had now only one boat, crowded with wounded, and having on board more than she could carry. The two guns followed us the whole of the day, the infantry firing on us the whole of that night.

(d) Those who were not killed in the boats were taken back to Cawnpore as prisoners. The men were shot. An account of the shooting was later given by a native.

Source: *Annual Register*, xcix (*History*), p. 287.

Just as the Sepoys were going to fire, the padre called out to the Nana and requested leave to read prayers before they died. The Nana granted it. The padre's bonds were unloosed so far as to enable him to take a small book out of his pocket, from which he read; but all this time one of the Sahib-log,[1] who was shot in the arm and the leg, kept crying out to the Sepoys, ' If you mean to kill us, why don't you set about it quickly and get the work done? Why delay? ' After the padre had read a few prayers he shut the book, and the Sahib-log shook hands all round. Then the Sepoys fired. One Sahib rolled one way, one another, as they sat; but they were not dead, only wounded; so they went in and finished them off with swords.

(e) The Nana Sahib ordered the massacre of the imprisoned European women and children, on July 15, when the relieving force of General Havelock was a day's march from Cawnpore.

An officer of Havelock's force describes the scene where the massacre took place.

Source: Annual Register, xcix (History), p. 292.

I was directed to the house where all the poor miserable ladies had been murdered. It was along side the Cawnpore hotel, where the Nana lived. I never was more horrified. The place was one mass of blood. I am not exaggerating when I tell you that the soles of my boots were more than covered with the blood of these poor wretched creatures. Portions of their dresses, collars, children's socks, and ladies' round hats lay about, saturated with their blood; and in the sword-cuts on the wooden pillars of the room long dark hair was carried by the edge of the weapon, and there hung their tresses—a most painful sight! I have often wished since that I had never been there, but sometimes wish that every soldier was taken there that he might witness the barbarities our poor countrywomen had suffered. Their bodies were afterwards dragged out and thrown down a well outside the building where their limbs were to be seen sticking out in a mass of gory confusion.

(f) 855 officers and men, 153 civilian volunteers, 712 loyal native troops, and 1,280 non-combatants were besieged in the Residency at Lucknow for nearly five months.

Source: Day by Day at Lucknow. Mrs. Case. London, 1858, passim.

---

[1] People.

Monday, July 27th.

Last night, about nine o'clock, while we were reading Prayers, all undressed and ready for bed, we were suddenly stopped by heavy firing of musketry and cannon. It was preceded by a great shout, which we knew came from the enemy. At first we really thought for a moment they had got in. Mrs. Inglis knelt down and said a prayer. . . . The firing did not continue very long, and then succeeded a complete and death like silence, which was even more painful. It was frightful to hear the shells whizzing over our heads. Mrs. Inglis remained at the door for some time to see if any one might pass from whom she could hear what was really going on. I lay down and nearly fell asleep. A few minutes afterwards Colonel Inglis came in and told us that all was quiet, and that we might go to bed. So we finished reading our prayers, and did so. The night was afterwards quite quiet. . . . How sad and depressing all this is, day after day! Mrs. Need came before we were up this morning and told us that her husband had died in the night; and I have just heard that one of her children has got the cholera. . . . Colonel Inglis told us this morning at breakfast, that one of the enemy's mines had fallen in. They seem to think the attack last night was only a ruse to divert our attention from the mining. Mrs. Inglis went this evening to see Mrs. Cooper and there she heard that the enemy are mining just under the mess-room, close to where all the ladies are. It was first found out, I believe, by one of the ladies, who heard the noise when she was in her bath room, and called her husband to listen to the sound. But we are making a counter-mine there; so I hope we may get the best of it. The ladies are sadly frightened, and no wonder.

Tuesday, July 28th. . . . What a state to live in, never to know what these wretches are going to do! When our people were mining yesterday, they came close upon the enemy's mine, which they say was beautifully constructed, and a wax candle burning in it. They ran away as soon as they found we were near them; and in the evening we went in and blew the whole up, and completely destroyed it. As we heard the officers and men go by, they all seemed very much pleased with this affair.

Monday, August 3rd.

Still nothing heard of our relief, and the days appear months while this dreadful state of things is going on. . . . It is now said we have only provisions for twenty days more. What is to become of us if our relief does not arrive before that time! By some negligence six fine bullocks were smothered in the house yesterday —a great loss at such a time. The commissariat butcher came to ask for three of Colonel Inglis's goats this morning to kill them for food, which looks as if we are beginning to run short of meat. . . . It is dreadful to think we may be short of provisions. Every morning before she is dressed Mrs. Inglis weighs out everything for our own consumption with her own hands, and so good is her management that she is always able to give a little arrowroot or sugar to a sick child, and has two or three times succeeded in making little puddings for invalids without an egg and with but a very limited quantity of sugar. . . .

Thursday, August 6th.

Last night, while we were at prayers, a shell burst close to our door, just behind the punkah wallah. It struck into the ground with a great noise, and made us all rush to the door to see where it had fallen. Not many minutes afterwards a bullet came close to the ayah, and with a tremendous clatter broke a plate, which she had beside her. This also was just at our door. Several other shots were fired into our little courtyard. . . . This morning poor Mr. Studdy, of the 32nd, has had one of his arms taken off by a round shot in the Residency. I hear that he is likely to lose both, and that it is even doubtful if he will live. Poor young man! We were very sorry indeed to hear of this, he has behaved so well all through the siege. No news of any kind. It is now twelve days since we have heard anything from outside, and our relief was then supposed to be within three marches of us. To-morrow we and the servants are to be put on half rations. How dreadful it will be when they are obliged to commence that with the fighting men! . . .

Friday, August 7th. . . . Dr. Scott says, Mr. Studdy is going on well. His arm (the right one) was amputated, but he was able to bear it, and they do not think now, as was at first supposed,

that he had received a severe inward bruise. They gave him a bottle of champagne before the operation, as he was too weak for chloroform, and he bore it, poor fellow, without saying a word.[1]
. . .

Monday, August 10th. . . . About twelve p.m., as I was sitting at the table writing, Carry washing our things, and Mrs. Inglis working, we were suddenly alarmed by what appeared to us a great shaking of the earth, following by a *dreadful* noise, such as I never wish to hear again. It was indescribable, and sounded as if the whole earth was coming against us; it was a mine exploding without doing any harm. We thought it had been in the ladies' room, especially when we saw Mrs. Cooper, her nurse and children, and Mrs. Radclyffe with hers, all coming over to our room as fast as they could. Poor Mrs. C. was dreadfully frightened. We laid her on one of our couches, and gave her some wine. A fierce attack followed the explosion of the mine, and a round shot fell close to our door; half a yard nearer, and it must have been into the room. It sounded altogether very frightful, as these attacks always do. . . .

Wednesday, August 12th. A good deal of firing went on during the night. The enemy were as usual making an attack somewhere. The nights are dreadful; one looks forward so anxiously for the first ray of daylight. Then the day arrives with no news of our relief. One's heart sickens at all this delay, and knowing nothing of what is going on outside these gates.

They say that we might, with very great difficulty and pinching, as far as provisions go, hold out one month longer, but after that there will not be a hope for us; and now the natives have a report that the reinforcements will not be here for two months. . . . It is an awful time; and words could never make anyone understand all that we have undergone during now nearly three months (ever since the 17th of May). . . .

Tuesday, August 18th. This morning about six o'clock we were all roused by the explosion of one of the enemy's mines. Six drummers were buried in it; three have been got out, the

---

[1] He died on August 9th.

other three still remain. It is to be hoped that the poor fellows are dead; for they say it is impossible to extricate them, as the place is so completely under the enemy's fire. Two officers had a wonderful escape: one was in bed at the time, but they were both blown up in the air and came down again without being hurt.

Monday, August 24th. . . . So many children are sick now that one hears nearly every day of some one dying, and many children and grown up persons too are suffering from boils and eruptions on the skin.

Thursday, August 27th . . . heard of a ham being sold for £7, and a tin of soup sufficient only for one day's meal for £1 5s.! ! ! Money has ceased to be of any value, and people are giving unheard-of prices for stores of any kind—one dozen brandy, £20; one small box of vermicelli, £5; four small cakes of chocolate, £2 10s. ! ! !

[On August 28th a messenger arrived from General Havelock at Cawnpore, telling them to hold on, and promising relief in twenty to twenty-five days. The relieving force arrived on September 25th, but could only reinforce and partially revictual the garrison. Mrs. Case said 'everyone is depressed, and all feel that we are in fact *not relieved*.']

Saturday, October 24th. This morning, at breakfast, Colonel Inglis informed us that arrangements had been made that our provisions might last till the 1st of December, and in consequence our rations (with the exception of the meat) are to be reduced tomorrow.

Tuesday, November 10th. . . . Guns were heard in the distance and the ' Union Jack ' was seen flying from Allumbagh, which all seem to think means that Sir Colin Campbell has reached that place with his force. Mr. Kavanagh, the head clerk in Mr. Cooper's office, volunteered to go out last night to Allumbagh, and conduct our force into Lucknow. It was a most gallant act, and all were delighted when the signal agreed upon to announce his arrival (the hoisting a flag) was spied from the top of the Residency about twelve o'clock this morning. Mr.

Kavanagh went out about eight o'clock disguised as a native, with a man with him as a guide.

Tuesday, November 17th. . . . We were much surprised that last night passed off so quietly; indeed scarcely any firing was heard. Sir Colin's force was seen to advance very slowly, that is to say, artillery only were visible, *no infantry.* . . . About four o'clock, a sight we had not seen for a very long time caught our eyes; two officers, each leading a horse and coming into our court-yard inquiring for Colonel Inglis. We at once saw that they belonged to the advancing force, and we were told that one of them was Colonel Berkeley, the new Colonel of the 32nd . . . . When Colonel Inglis came to dinner he told us that Sir Colin Campbell's orders are that we are all to leave Lucknow tomorrow evening! Our consternation may be more easily imagined than described, and I think our faces when we looked at each other wore an expression of the most complete bewilderment. How all the wounded and sick people and women and children are to be got off in such a hurried manner, at only a few hours' notice, I cannot imagine.

[They left the Residency on Thursday, November 19th. ' Three short bits of road were dangerous, as the enemy could, from the top of a mosque, see people going along, and fire on them. At these places we had to take the children out of the carriage and have them carried—and all our party ran as fast as we could.']

THE YOUNG DISRAELI

The eldest son of Isaac D'Israeli, the author of *The Curiosities of Literature* and a convert from Judaism to Christianity. In 1827 he published his first novel *Vivian Grey,* and then travelled on the Continent and in Turkey and Egypt. In 1832 he was Radical candidate for High Wycombe. In 1837 he was returned to Parliament as the Conservative member for Maidstone. After representing Maidstone, he was successively member for Shrewsbury (1841) and for Buckinghamshire (1847). His first speech in the House was a conspicuous failure but, undaunted by ridicule, he concluded with the famous words ' the time will come when you will hear me '. When the Corn Laws were abolished, he bitterly attacked Peel. He was Chancellor of the Exchequer in the first Derby administration of 1852, in the second

U

Derby administration from February 1858 to June 1859, and in the third Derby administration in 1866. He became Prime Minister for the first time in February 1868, until the following December, and again from 1874 to 1880. In August 1876 he received a peerage. He died April 19th, 1881. Probably the best known of his novels are *Coningsby* (1844), *Sybil* (1845), *Tancred* (1847) and *Lothair* (1870).

Source: Both extracts are from *Pen and Ink Sketches of Poets, Preachers and Politicians,* 1846. Quoted Monypenny and Buckle, *Life of Benjamin Disraeli,* John Murray, 1929, vol. i.

(*a*) pp. 25–6.

This description was written when Disraeli was unsuccessfully contesting Taunton in 1835.

Never in my life had I been so struck by a face as I was by that of Disraeli. It was lividly pale, and from beneath two finely-arched eyebrows blazed out a pair of intensely black eyes. I never have seen such orbs in mortal sockets, either before or since. His physiognomy was strictly Jewish. Over a broad, high fore-head were ringlets of coal-black, glossy hair, which, combed away from his right temple, fell in luxuriant clusters or bunches over his left cheek and ear, which it entirely concealed from view. There was a sort of half-smile, half-sneer, playing about his beautifully-formed mouth, the upper lip of which was curved as we see it in the portraits of Byron. . . . He was very showily attired in a dark bottle-green frock-coat, a waistcoat of the most extravagant pattern, the front of which was almost covered with glittering chains, and in fancy-pattern pantaloons. He wore a plain black stock, but no collar was visible. Altogether he was the most intellectual-looking exquisite I had ever seen.

(*b*) pp. 288–9.

Disraeli was speaking at a banquet given by the Taunton Con-servatives after the election.

He commenced in a lisping, lackadaisical tone of voice. . . . He minced his phrases in apparently the most affected manner, and, whilst he was speaking, placed his hands in all imaginable positions: not because he felt awkward, and did not know, like a booby in a drawing-room, where to put them, but apparently for the purpose of exhibiting to the best advantage the glittering rings which decked his white and taper fingers. Now he would place his thumbs in the armholes of his waistcoat, and spread out his fingers on its flashing surface; then one set of digits would be released and he would lean affectedly on the table, supporting himself with his right hand; anon he would push aside the curls from his forehead. . . . But as he proceeded all traces of this dandyism and affectation were lost. With a rapidity of utterance perfectly astonishing he referred to past events and indulged in anticipations of the future. The Whigs were, of course, the objects of his unsparing satire, and his eloquent denunciations of them were applauded to the echo. In all he said he proved himself to be the finished orator. . . . His voice, at first so finical, gradually became full, musical, and sonorous, and with every varying sentiment was beautifully modulated.

DISRAELI AND GLADSTONE

Source: Henry Lucy, *Sixty Years in the Wilderness,* Murray, 1909, p. 349 et sqq.

Further Reading: D. C. Somervell, *Disraeli and Gladstone,* Faber, 1932.

Never in public life in either hemisphere were there confronted two men more diametrically opposed in manner and mode of thought than Disraeli and Gladstone. They had only one thing in common—genius. To each the other was an interesting, inexplicable puzzle. Here, again, there was difference in their method of contemplation. Gladstone, with his untamable energy, his rich verbosity, his susceptibility to religious and moral influences, rather amused Dizzy. When in fine frenzy rolling, whether championing the rights of nationalities or the privilege of minorities, Dizzy seated on the other side of the table, regarded him through his eyeglass with the air of one studying some strange animal recently imported. Gladstone was much more definite in his views about Disraeli. He rarely spoke or wrote of him in private relations. When he did there was only futile attempt to disguise his conviction that Dizzy was sorely lacking in principle.

·   ·   ·   ·   ·

In his prime, in a great debate when political parties were set in battle array, Gladstone's transcendent oratorical gifts had full

play. There was marked contrast in his manner of making a
speech and of answering a question addressed to him in his
Ministerial capacity. After purporting to make reply and taking
some ten minutes to do it, he sat down, frequently leaving his
interrogator and the House in a condition of dismayed bewilderment, hopelessly attempting to grope their way through the
intricacies of the sonorous sentences they had listened to. If, as
happened in expounding a bill or replying to a debate, he desired
to make himself understood, he had no equal.

His manner in speech-making was more strongly marked by
action than was that of his only rival, John Bright. He emphasised
points by smiting the open palm of his left hand with sledge-
hammer fist. Sometimes he, with gleaming eyes—' like a vulture's'
Mr. Lecky genially described them—pointed his forefinger
straight at his adversary. In the hottest moments he beat the
brass-bound Box with clamorous hand that occasionally drowned
the point he strove to make. Sometimes with both hands raised
above his head; often with left elbow leaning on the Box, right
hand with closed fist shaken at the head of an unoffending country
gentleman on the back bench opposite; anon, standing half a step
back from the Table, left hand hanging at his side, right uplifted,
so that he might with thumb-nail lightly touch the shining
crown of his head, he trampled his way through the argument he
assailed as an elephant in an hour of aggravation rages through a
jungle.

Disraeli lacked two qualities, failing which true eloquence is
impossible. He was never quite in earnest, and he was not
troubled by dominating conviction. Only on the rarest occasions
did he affect to be roused to righteous indignation, and then he
was rather amusing than impressive. He was endowed with a
lively fancy and cultivated the art of coining phrases, generally
personal in their bearing. When these were flashed forth he
delighted the House. . . .

When he rose to speak he rested his hands for a moment
on the Box—only for a moment, for he invariably endeavoured
to gain the ear of his audience by making a brilliant point in an
opening sentence. The attitude he found most conducive to
happy delivery was to stand balancing himself on heel and toe

with hands in his coat-tail pockets. In this pose, with head hung down as if he were mentally debating how best to express a thought just born to him, he slowly uttered the polished and poisoned sentences, over which he had spent laborious hours in the study. The merest tyro knew a moment beforehand when Disraeli was approaching what he regarded as the most effective opening for dropping the gem of phrase he made believe to have just dug up from an unvisited corner of his mind. He saw him lead up to it; he noted the disappearance of the hand in the direction of the coat-tail pocket, sometimes in search of a pocket-handkerchief brought out and shaken with careless air, most often to extend the coat-tails, whilst, with body gently rocked to and fro and an affected hesitancy of speech, the *bon mot* was flashed forth. . . .

DISRAELI AND THE QUEEN

Source: Monypenny and Buckle, vol. ii, p. 679 (1929 ed.). From a letter from Disraeli to Lady Bradford.

Further Reading: Hesketh Pearson: *Dizzy*, Methuen, 1952.

A. Cecil, *Queen Victoria and her Prime Ministers*, Eyre and Spottis-woode, 1953.

Longleat, Warminster, Aug. 7 (1874).

. . . . Osborne was lovely, its green shades refreshing after the fervent glare of the voyage, and its blue bay full of white sails. The Faery sent for me the instant I arrived. I can only describe my reception by telling you that I really thought she was going to embrace me. She was wreathed with smiles, and as she tattled, glided about the room like a bird. She told me it was ' all owing to my courage and tact ', and then she said, ' To think of your having the gout all the time! How you must have suffered! And you ought not to stand now. You shall have a chair! '

Only think of that! I remember that *feu* Lord Derby, after one of his severest illnesses, had an audience of Her Majesty, and he mentioned it to me, as a proof of the Queen's favour, that Her Majesty had remarked to him, ' how sorry she was she could not ask him to be seated.' The etiquette was so severe.

I remembered all this as she spoke, so I humbly declined the privilege, saying I was quite well, but would avail myself of her gracious kindness if I ever had another attack. . . .

THE PURCHASE OF THE SUEZ CANAL SHARES

It was on Disraeli's initiative that this purchase was made. It was financed by a loan from Rothschilds.

Source: Monypenny and Buckle, *Life of Benjamin Disraeli*, vol. ii pp. 783 et sqq. Murray, 1929.

To Queen Victoria.

Confidential, 2 Whitehall Gardens, Nov. 18, 1875.—Mr. Disraeli with his humble duty to your Majesty:

The Khedive, on the eve of bankruptcy, appears desirous of parting with his shares in the Suez Canal, and has communicated, confidentially, with General Stanton [the British Agent in Egypt]. There is a French company in negotiation with His Highness, but they purpose only to make an advance with complicated stipulations.

'Tis an affair of millions; about four at least; but would give the possessor an immense, not to say preponderating, influence in the management of the Canal.

It is vital to your Majesty's authority and power at this critical moment, that the Canal should belong to England, and I was so decided and absolute with Lord Derby on this head, that he ultimately adopted my views and brought the matter before the Cabinet yesterday. The Cabinet was unanimous in their decision, that the interest of the Khedive should, if possible, be obtained, and we telegraphed accordingly. . . .

The Khedive now says, that it is absolutely necessary that he should have between three and four millions sterling by the 30th of this month!

Scarcely breathing time! But the thing must be done.

To Queen Victoria.

2, Whitehall Gardens, Nov. 24, 1875—Mr. Disraeli with his humble duty to your Majesty:

It is just settled: you have it, Madam. The French Government has been out-generaled. They tried too much, offering loans at an usurious rate, and with conditions, which would virtually have given them the government of Egypt.

The Khedive, in despair and disgust, offered your Majesty's Government to purchase his shares outright. He never would listen to such a proposition before.

Four millions sterling! and almost immediately. There was only one firm that could do it—Rothschilds. They behaved admirably; advanced the money at a low rate, and the entire interest of the Khedive is now yours, Madam.

Yesterday the Cabinet sate four hours and more on this, and Mr. Disraeli has not had one moment's rest to-day; therefore this despatch must be pardoned, as his head is rather weak. He will tell the whole wondrous tale to-morrow.

DISRAELI IN THE HOUSE OF COMMONS

(a) *Source: Parliamentary Reminiscences and Reflections* 1868–1885, by Lord George Hamilton. pp. 143–4.

Disraeli was nearly always in the House, and he listened most attentively to the Under-Secretaries doing their work, and if you glided successfully over thin ice or counteracted a difficult attack, a quiet ' Hear, hear ', used to fall from his lips—a great encouragement to a young official. Gladstone once described him as the ' greatest master of Parliamentary sarcasm and irony for the past two centuries ', and the knowledge that at any moment, if provoked, he might have recourse to his armoury of inimitable satire kept many turbulent and self-advertising spirits quiet. Few people like being made to look ridiculous, especially if the ridicule becomes permanently plastered on their persons. Disraeli's extraordinary perception of human character made his phrases sting, because though they might be exaggerated, they were largely founded on what was seen to be truth. His description of Gladstone as coming down to the House ' with a countenance arranged for the occasion ', of Horsman as ' a very superior person ' . . . all clung to their victims, because whenever you looked at them Disraeli's epigram came back to you as being truly descriptive. . . .

(b) Disraeli is here speaking in a debate on Irish affairs in 1872. He is replying to Lord Hartington who has just brought in a second Coercion Bill. The extract illustrates Disraeli's presence of mind and rapidity of action at a moment of unpredictable disaster.

Source: Parliamentary Reminiscences and Reflections, 1868–1885, by Lord George Hamilton, John Murray, 1916, pp. 43–4.

Disraeli got up as soon as Lord Hartington finished, and he delivered a twenty minutes' speech of the most scathing invective and ridicule I ever heard. The House was worked up to a pitch of great excitement by this performance, for the speech was full of telling epigrams, namely: ' You have legalised confiscation . . . you have condoned high treason . . . you have emptied the gaols of Ireland . . . you cannot govern a single county in that country . . . you are making Government ridiculous.'

In the most effective part of his speech, Disraeli suddenly put up his right hand, in which was his handkerchief, to his mouth, and turning round to his neighbour, Lord John Manners, apparently asked him a question which he could not hear. 'What, what are you saying? ' Disraeli then said *sotto voce*: ' It is all right,' and he took up his speech at the exact word where he had left off, and finished it amidst uproarious applause from the whole Tory benches. The young men behind the Front Opposition Bench could not make out the purpose of this bit of by-play. Dining in the City two days afterwards, I sat next Alderman Lawrence, a well-known Radical Member of Parliament, who sat exactly opposite Disraeli in the House of Commons. He said to me: ' Your Chief is a wonderful fellow.' I replied: ' I am glad you think so.' He in return said: ' Would you like to know what happened the other night when he turned to John Manners? ' ' Very much ', said I. ' Well,' he added, ' in the best part of his speech and in the middle of a sentence his teeth fell out, and he caught them up with extraordinary rapidity in his right hand, turned round apparently to ask a question of his neighbour, put them in, and resumed his speech at the exact word where he had left it off.'

GLADSTONE

The son of Sir John Gladstone, a wealthy Liverpool merchant, he was educated at Eton and Christ Church, gaining a double first and a senior studentship. He entered Parliament in 1832 as member for

Newark, and soon distinguished himself. In 1839 Macaulay described him as ' the rising hope of those stern unbending Tories who follow, reluctantly and mutinously, a leader whose experience and eloquence are indispensable to them, but whose cautious temper and moderate opinions they abhor.' In 1834 he became Junior Lord of the Treasury in the first Peel administration and, in the next year, Under Secretary for the Colonies. In the second Peel administration (1846) he was Secretary for War and the Colonies. From 1852 to 1855 he was Chancellor of the Exchequer in the Aberdeen administration, and again in the first Palmerston administration from February 1855 to February 1858. In the second Palmerston administration and the second Russell administration from 1859 to 1866 he was yet again Chancellor of the Exchequer. In 1867 he succeeded Lord Russell as Leader of the Liberal Party. He was Prime Minister four times 1868 to 1874, 1880 to 1885, 1886, and from 1892 to 1894. He sat as member for Oxford University in 1847, moving to a Lancashire constituency in 1865, for Greenwich 1868–74 and 1874–80, for Leeds in 1874, and for Midlothian in 1880. In 1895 he withdrew from public life and was succeeded by Lord Rosebery.

(a) *Source:* Lord George Hamilton, *Parliamentary Reminiscences and Reflections* 1868–1885, John Murray, 1916, pp. 62–4.

Further Reading: P. Magnus, *Gladstone*, John Murray, 1954.

I doubt if there has ever been a man in politics during the last two centuries who combined such extraordinary physical and mental gifts. His knowledge was varied and great. His power of work and assimilation was amazing, his capacity to stand fatigue and long hours equally remarkable; he was endowed with unusual physical courage and unlimited assurance. For Parliamentary purposes he was unquestionably the most efficient and eloquent speaker of his generation, his voice, elocution, and gestures being almost faultless . . . with or without preparation Gladstone always spoke superbly well so far as the technique of speaking was concerned, and with an apparent conviction and a histrionic power that were most impressive. Without an effort he could always assume the attitude which most appealed to the sympathies of his audience, and his general pose was that of a very good man struggling with wickedly minded opponents. When I first got into the House of Commons, I was immensely struck by his personality, and though I did not agree with him it was a physical pleasure to me to hear him speak and argue; but, little by little, a suspicion was awakened, which grew and developed, as to how far all these protestations had their origin in high motives or principles, or were merely a part of his political baggage. As his Government became weaker his passionate appeals became stronger and more exalted, and then the conviction was slowly forced upon me that the main inspiration of his transcendental attitudes was to keep a majority in his lobby. His power of twisting the plain meaning of words and explaining away obvious facts was so extraordinary as to create the belief that whatever he wished he really did believe. For instance, he had two appointments to make under Statute—one legal, one clerical. The Statute laid down that the lawyer to be appointed must be a judge. Gladstone appointed his Attorney-General. The clerical statute laid down that an Oxford graduate must be appointed to the living of Ewelme: Gladstone selected a Cambridge man. What annoyed me was not the transgression of the Statutes, but the defence made for these transgressions. The original offences were forgivable, but the defence was unforgettable.

. . . If you believed in him, he became to you a Parliamentary Superman; if you suspected him or detected him in what you believed to be tricks, then dislike rapidly hardened into repulsion and wholesale distrust. So it came to pass that no statesman had as supporters a more devoted clientèle, or as antagonists more irreconcilable opponents. The latter group was constantly augmented by colleagues who left him on his not unfrequent abandonment of his previous principles, and their place was filled by political recruits representing the recently enfranchised and more advanced sections of political thought.

GLADSTONE IN 1852

(b) *Source:* Traill, *New Lucian*, 1884, pp. 305–6 quoted Morley, *W. E. Gladstone*, Macmillan, 1904, vol. iii, p. 91.

Sir, I can only tell you that, profoundly as I distrusted him, and lightly as on the whole I valued the external qualities of his eloquence, I have never listened to him even for a few minutes without ceasing to marvel at his influence over men. That white-hot face, stern as a Covenanter's yet mobile as a comedian's; those restless, flashing eyes; that wondrous voice, whose richness its northern burr enriched as the tang of the wood brings out the mellowness of a rare old wine; the masterly cadence of his elocution; the vivid energy of his attitudes; the fine animation of gestures;—sir, when I am assailed through eye and ear by this compacted phalanx of assailants, what wonder that the stormed outposts of the senses should spread the contagion of their own surrender through the main encampment of the mind, and that against my judgement, in contempt of my conscience, nay, in defiance of my very will, I should exclaim, ' This is indeed the voice of truth and wisdom. This man is honest and sagacious beyond his fellows. He must be believed, he must be obeyed.'

(c) *Source:* E. F. Benson, *As We Were.* Longmans 1930, pp. 108–9.

E. F. Benson (1867–1940) was the third son of Edward Benson, Archbishop of Canterbury.

Always there was this huge concentration of force; purpose at white heat roared like a furnace in every action of his life. When once he had convinced himself on any subject, it ceased to be his opinion, and became a cosmic truth, which it was the duty of every right-minded person to uphold . . . he was convinced, and said so, that the will of the English people was set on giving Home Rule to Ireland, and that he was the appointed instrument to accomplish their will for them: God gave him his health and vitality for that. Thus his conscience was invariably clear of personal ambition: he was working not for his own idea but for some great cause external to him. Never, so Mrs. Gladstone told my mother, did the estrangements and execrations of those who had been his friends cause him to say, ' I wish I had never done it! ' He might regret the bitterness he had aroused, but he never regretted those measures which had caused it.

This remorseless inflexibility was one of the reasons why in his official relation with the Queen he so often irritated her. He always paid her the most profound respect but his deference to her person did not include the slightest deference to her statecraft and nothing she said influenced him in the least when his mind was made up, for he knew he was right, whereas she, on those many occasions when their views differed, was equally certain that he was wrong. Though she maintained an impeccable impartiality in politics and would never attempt to resist the will of her people, she was a thorough Tory at heart, and regarded him as an enemy to Church and State, and thus an enemy to the throne, for he had disestablished the Irish Church and now he wanted to give Home Rule to Ireland. It was therefore with the most unfeigned pleasure that she saw the fall of his last ministry in 1894, and she commented on it privately to my father with remarkable frankness: this was perfectly correct on her part for he officially had no politics any more than she. ' Mr. Gladstone has gone out, disappeared all in a moment', she gleefully observed, ' his last two ministries have been failures, indeed his last three. Mr. Gladstone takes up one or two things, and then nothing else interests him. He cares nothing for foreign affairs which are always essential to England, knows nothing of foreign affairs, and is exceedingly distrusted on the Continent. They have thought he might abandon Egypt at any moment. He will not attend to any suggestion but his own mind's. He does not care what you say, does not attend. I have told him two or three facts of which he was quite ignorant of foreign tone and temper. It makes no difference. He only says " Is that so? Really!" ' Indeed it must have been most irritating, for the Queen had an unfailing fund of first-rate common sense, and her very long experience of foreign affairs made her a far more dispassionate observer than Gladstone on the war-path for an idea. Besides, she happened to be Queen of England, and it was surely reasonable that she should expect to be listened to.

A FRENCHMAN IN ENGLAND 1871

Source: Notes on England, H. Taine, Strahan, 1872.

H. Taine (1828–1893) French critic and historian. Visited England in 1858 and again in 1871.

(*a*) p. 9.

Sunday in London in the rain: the shops are shut, the streets almost deserted; the aspect is that of an immense and well-ordered cemetery. The few passers-by under their umbrellas, in the desert of squares and streets, have the look of uneasy spirits who have risen from their graves; it is appalling.

. . . The rain is small, compact, pitiless; looking at it one can see no reason why it should not continue to the end of all things; one's feet churn water, there is water everywhere, filthy water impregnated with an odour of soot. A yellow, dense fog fills the air, sweeps down to the ground. . . . After an hour's walk in the Strand especially, and in the rest of the city, one has the spleen, one meditates suicide.

(*b*) The Port of London. op. cit. pp. 6–7

Astonishment ends by turning into bewilderment. From Greenwich, the river is nothing but a street a mile broad and upwards, where ships ascend and descend between two rows of buildings, interminable rows of a dull red, in brick or tiles, bordered with great piles stuck in the mud for mooring vessels, which come here to unload or to load. Ever new magazines for copper, stone, coal, cordage and the rest; bales are always being piled up, sacks being hoisted, barrels being rolled, cranes are creaking, capstans sounding. . . . But that which carries the impression to its height, is the sight of the canals through which the docks communicate with the sea; they form cross-streets, and they are streets for ships; one suddenly perceives a line of them which is endless. . . . This is certainly one of the great spectacles of our planet. . . .

(*c*) Taine describes London in terms similar to those which might be used by a modern Englishman describing New York. op. cit. p. 16.

Enormous, enormous—this is the word which always recurs. . . . Paris is mediocre compared with these squares, these crescents, these circles and rows of monumental buildings of massive stone, with porticoes, with sculptured fronts, these spacious streets; there are sixty of them as vast as the Rue de la Paix; assuredly Napoleon III demolished and rebuilt Paris only because he had lived in London. In the Strand, in Piccadilly, in Regent Street, in the neighbourhood of London Bridge, in twenty places, there is a bustling crowd, a surging traffic, an amount of obstruction which our busiest and most frequented boulevard cannot parallel. Everything is on a large scale here; the clubs are palaces, the hotels are monuments; the river is an arm of the sea; the cabs go twice as fast; the boatmen and the omnibus-conductors condense a sentence into a word; words and gestures are economised; actions and time are turned to the utmost possible account; the human being produces and expends twice as much as among us.

(d) op. cit. p. 34.

. . . street boys abound—bare-footed, dirty, and turning wheels in order to get alms. On the stairs leading to the Thames they swarm, more pale-faced, more deformed, more repulsive than the scum of Paris; without question, the climate is worse, and the gin more deadly. Near them, leaning against the greasy walls, or inert on the steps, are men in astounding rags; it is impossible to imagine before seeing them how many layers of dirt an overcoat or a pair of trousers could hold; they dream or doze openmouthed, their faces are begrimed, dull, and sometimes streaked with red lines. It is in these localities that families have been discovered with no other bed than a heap of soot; they had slept there during several months. For a creature so wasted and jaded there is but one refuge—drunkenness. . . . A trader said to me, ' Look after your pockets, sir,' and a policeman warned me not to enter certain lanes.

(e) op. cit. p. 57.

. . . a skilful physician who prescribes for a Frenchman here does not give him more than half a dose; the English dose would be too strong for him, and would hurt him . . . the medicines here might be compounded for French horses. In like manner their common wines, port, sherry, very hot, very spiritous, are loaded with brandy in addition; this mixture deprives them of delicacy, yet if they were pure the English would consider them insipid; our Bordeaux wines and even our Burgundies are too light for them. Amongst the middle class, ale, stout, or porter are preferred, especially brandy and water, a kind of grog in which the half is spirit; to please them it is necessary that the beverage should be rough or fiery, their palate must be either scratched or scraped. The same impression is made on trying their cookery, which, excepting that of their very fine clubs, and of the ' Continental ' English, who keep a French or Italian cook, has no savour. I have purposely dined in twenty taverns, from the lowest to the highest, in London and elsewhere. I got large portions of fat meat and vegetables, without sauce; one is amply and wholesomely fed, but one has no pleasure in eating. In the best Liverpool eating-house they do not know how to dress a fowl. If you would tickle your palate there is a cruet filled with pickles, peppers, sauces, and Chili vinegar. I once inadvertently put two drops of it into my mouth. I might as well have swallowed a hot cinder. At Greenwich, having already partaken of plain Whitebait, I helped myself to some out of a second dish; it was devilled, and fitted for skinning the tongue.

THE MARQUESS OF SALISBURY

Lord Robert Cecil was sent to Eton where he was extremely unhappy: his father took him home for two years to Hatfield before he went up to Christ Church. In 1853 he entered Parliament as member for Stamford. As Lord Cranborne he was Secretary for India in the third Derby administration from June 1866 to March 1867. He succeeded as third Marquess of Salisbury in 1868. He was again Secretary for India in Disraeli's second administration from 1874 to 1878. He was Foreign Secretary 1878–1886, 1886–1892, 1895–1902. He died in 1903. Once when a friend commiserated with him on the double burden of the Premiership and the Foreign Office, he replied: ' I could do very well with two departments; in fact I have four—the Prime Ministership, the Foreign Office, the Queen, and Randolph Churchill.' In the Queen's view he was in the front rank of the ten prime ministers who had conducted the affairs of the country during her reign.

Source: Lord George Hamilton, *Parliamentary Reminiscences and Reflections* 1868–1885, John Murray, 1916, pp. 73–4.

Further Reading: A. L. Kennedy, *Salisbury* 1830–1903, John Murray, 1953. A. Cecil, *Queen Victoria and her Prime Ministers*, Eyre and Spottiswoode, 1953.

Lord Salisbury was then (1874) Secretary of State for India. He was in the zenith of his vigour. Those only who served under him, and whom he liked, can have any idea of his charm as a Chief, or the delight of working in subordination to him. His extraordinary quickness of apprehension spoiled one, for you rarely had to finish a sentence before he intervened with a remark anticipating your conclusion. He was a wonderfully concise draughtsman. Over and over again, when I brought him an answer to an embarrassing question which, with the aid of heads of departments, we had contrived to boil down to, say, two pages, he would reply, taking up his pen: 'A good answer; still, it might be put thus ', and reducing our long statement to two or three sentences, he would cover the ground more effectively than we had done with the long answer.

He could transact an enormous amount of business quickly and thoroughly, and he maintained an extraordinarily high literary level in all his writings, dispatches, and speeches. . . . Most courteous and considerate to his subordinates, he exacted from them in return full measure. Never ruffled or perturbed, he would give equally close attention to the most meticulous matter as to a big question of policy. . . .

It is curious how often private life contradicts and reverses the popular idea of big public men. In public life you could not find a trio of more sarcastic and stinging speakers than Salisbury, Disraeli and William Harcourt. I was intimately acquainted with all three, but, whatever they might say in public, I never knew any one of the three to do an unkind act intentionally, and, not only to their friends and associates, but even to their opponents when in trouble or distress, they were ever considerate and helpful.

THE CUP FINAL 1882

The Football Association was founded in 1863. In 1871 the F.A. Cup was instituted. To-day Association football has become a game which is played and watched across five continents, which involves the outlay of money in millions, and which draws the attention of even more millions of people. To the historian, Association football is not the least achievement of Victorian England.

The movement began in the public schools. They took the traditional mob scrimmage and fashioned it, according to their needs and opportunities, into a game of remarkable skill and still more remarkable potentialities. The origins of the dribbling game are to be found, in particular, in the cloisters of Westminster and Charterhouse; and on the fields of Eton, Winchester, Harrow, Shrewsbury and Lancing. From the schools it spread to the universities, and thence to London where the great amateur clubs organised the game and launched the English Cup. From London it spread to the industrial north and midlands, largely pioneered by public-school men. Muscular Christi-

anity laid the foundations of many of the great clubs of to-day:
Aston Villa sprang from a Methodist Sunday-school and Bishop
Auckland was launched by Oxford and Cambridge men reading for
Orders with Lightfoot. In the industrial north, and particularly in
Lancashire, there came an influx of Scotsmen, attracted by the high
wages and safe employment which a skilful footballer could command.
The greatest single factor in this surge of popular interest was the
competition for the F.A. Cup, started by men who were inspired by
the knock-out house-matches which had existed for many years at
Eton, Charterhouse, Westminster and Shrewsbury. The public
schools had returned the game, re-shaped and inspired, to the nation.

This extract illustrates both the first period and the transition to
the second period when industrial England is drawn into the movement:
Old Etonians and Blackburn Rovers. The Etonians win, but they win
for the last time. Lord Kinnaird will be one of the most famous
Presidents of the F.A., guiding and safeguarding the professional
football of the future. The famous Fergus Suter represents the Scottish
immigration. The memory of Arthur Dunn is perpetuated by the
Arthur Dunn Cup. Blackburn Rovers will dominate the next decade.
The development and fusion of tactics is also illustrated by the extract:
north-country heading, Clydeside dribbling and the Eton game. Even
if a Cup Final at the Oval appears to-day to be an odd conjuncture, the
crowd, already considered to be large, and the two special trains
clearly indicate the shape of things to come; even if a crowd of 200,000
for an international match at Rio de Janeiro in 1950 is still well over
the rim of the horizon.

Two things went unrecorded by the *Blackburn Times* (April 1st,
1882): the two M.P.s, confident of victory, had arranged a special
banquet for their team. The Cup was not on the table. And when the
final whistle went, Kinnaird, the Eton captain, conspicuous by his
red beard, celebrated the victory by standing on his head in front of
the Oval pavilion. But the future was with the Rovers.

Source: The Blackburn Times, April 1st, 1882 (abridged).

Further Reading: G. Green, *Soccer.* Phoenix, 1953, revised edit.
Pan Books, 1956.

With fine weather and the prospect of an exciting contest,
it was to be expected that a large number of persons would be
attracted to Kennington Oval, on Saturday afternoon, and the
expectation was realised, as the attendance was swollen to 6,000
about three o'clock. There was a considerable body of the
Rovers' supporters in attendance, the two special trains from East
Lancashire in the early hours of the morning having brought
about 700 persons, while 200 others had made the journey on the
previous day. Amongst them were many Blackburn gentlemen
and tradesmen, and, clustered on the grandstand in front of the

V

pavilion of the Surrey Cricket Club, they gave a hearty welcome to their Parliamentary representatives, Mr. W. E. Briggs and Mr. W. Coddington. Another well-known Blackburnian, Major-General Feilden, C.M.G., of Witton Park, lord of the manor, and junior member for the northern division of the county palatine, was also present to view the contest. The section of the ground in front of the pavilion, only once or twice previously used for football purposes, was enclosed for the match, and it was in splendid condition, as rain had not fallen there the previous day. The sunshine was not so glaring as to greatly dazzle the eyes of the players who had to face it, but during more than half the game a strong wind blew from goal to goal.

Some of the Old Etonians first appeared within the enclosure, and were soon followed by the main body of the Rovers, while the majority of the Eton men, followed by the two captains, did not leave the dressing room until some minutes later. The appearance of the Rovers was somewhat disappointing, for the familiar jerseys had been for the time discarded, and dark blue jerseys with white stripes donned in their stead. In the evening one member of the team jestingly attributed the result of the match to the change of jerseys, and affirmed that he had in one instance passed the ball to an opponent instead of to his partner. An alteration was requisite, however, as the jerseys of the opposing teams were similar in style and the Rovers, as the younger organisation, had to give way in the matter. There was a marked contrast in the style of play of the rival teams and to Blackburn spectators the game revealed features unusual in the north. While the Rovers worked their way towards their opponents' goal by passing, the Etonians did so by rushes, the player securing the ball at the start retaining possession of it until robbed or checked, and his partner bearing him company to render assistance when opposition appeared. The Etonians indulged in none of the dribbling or dodging which forms an interesting and pleasing part of the famous Lancashire team's play, reliance being placed instead on the weight and speed of the forwards. A still greater contrast was afforded in the kicking of the ball when running. While the Rovers sent the leather forward so little raised above the ground as almost to touch it in skimming along.

their opponents kicked the ball much higher, and springing up
at it while dashing along delivered the kick frequently with
both feet off the ground. The spring was made whether or not
an opponent was close to the ball when it bounded, and the
Rovers, unaccustomed to this practice, were badly kicked,
particularly towards the finish when the play was mainly in close
quarters. To the same fact was probably due the entire absence,
or nearly so, of the scrimmages almost on the goal-line that are
often seen on northern football fields, and while the Rovers
used heads, chests, and knees as well as feet in manipulating the
ball, the Old Boys relied entirely on kicking.

When the cheering which greeted the advent of the rival
captains had subsided, the toss for choice of goals was made, and
the Rovers' chief was unfortunate in losing. The Etonians chose
to play with the wind in their favour and the sun at their backs.
The ball was ' kicked off ' by Strachan at eight minutes past
three. A light touch to the left gave the leather to Brown, who
sent it forward, but it was instantly returned, and the Etonians
rushed along and in a few seconds Chevallier made a couple of
corner kicks but each was followed by a kick from the goal. Of
the Rovers forwards the right wing pair first became prominent.
Heading back the leather, J. Hargreaves, aided by Avery, made
a good run, but when the other goal was almost reached Macauley
intervened and sent it back again. Suter twice relieved his goal
cleverly, but Howorth was compelled to use his hands, and then
the besiegers had another corner kick, which like its predecessors,
proved fruitless. A free kick awarded for a handling of the ball
enabled Suter to place it well to the right wing forwards, and the
first kick from the corner flag for the Rovers was immediately
afterwards made by Douglas. The ball was missed by all the players
in the mouth of the goal, but was promptly sent in by the Rovers
captain. Kinnaird relieved his side, and Macauley made a run, in
which he was aided by Dunn, who passed to Anderson, and that
player by a side shot scored a goal at the end of the first eight
minutes' play.

Suter and McIntyre in turn interposed with good effect, and
enabled Strachan, Douglas, and Duckworth to make an attack
upon the Eton citadel. The leather was sent into the hands of

Rawlinson, who threw it away before he could be charged through the goal. A free kick from close to the goal enabled the Etonians to return to the attack, but they were unsuccessful, a tremendous kick from Macauley sending the ball some yards above the top bar. Subsequently the ball was thrown right into the mouth of goal by Anderson, and Howorth's charge was seriously imperilled for a time.

For a breach of rule, which forbids handling, a free kick was awarded against the Etonians in their quarters, but McIntyre missed the ball when it was lightly sent to him by Fred Hargreaves and, as the penalty, the opposing forwards rushed along the ground, and Dunn by a good kick sent the leather into the hands of Howorth.

Another rush was frustrated by McIntyre and Fred Hargreaves, and Avery secured possession of the ball. Foley interposed to bar his progress, and, jumping at the ball, gave Avery a tremendous kick on the thigh, which placed him ' hors de combat ' for some minutes, and partially disabled him during the remainder of the game.

Drs. Porteus and Morley attended him on the grass outside the bounds of play, and soon reported that no serious injury had been sustained.

Play was transferred to the Etonians' quarters, and kept there for a few minutes, during which J. Hargreaves, Avery, and Douglas appeared to advantage, but eventually the ball was again sent over the goal line. The ball, thrown in by Anderson, was headed back from the goal mouth by Suter just as the whistle sounded ' half-time '. Play this far had been remarkably fast, and, with the strong wind against them, the Rovers could not invade their opponents' territory very often, but their defence was good, and in the circumstances they had done exceedingly well to prevent the scoring of more than one goal against them.

With the score so low the Rovers' supporters hopefully awaited the result. At four minutes to four Goodhart started the ball from the centre, but he was instantly robbed by Strachan, who passed it to the left wing, along which it was taken by J. Hargreaves and Avery. Their progress was barred, and the

Etonian forwards returned, but a strong kick sent the ball considerably in advance of them, and Howorth ran out from the goal to kick the ball back. A free kick by Kinnaird was rendered of non-effect by the interposition of the head of Strachan, who played exceedingly well throughout, and the Eton quarters were again invaded.

Some combined play by the Etonian forwards enabled them to approach the Rovers' goal, but they were speedily driven back, and Douglas and Duckworth again came into prominence. The goalkeeper was forced to use his hands, but he had a place kick immediately afterwards, and Fred Hargreaves missing the ball, the Etonian forwards secured a chance which they promptly utilised, to break away, and Chevallier shot the leather behind the goal.

Macauley subsequently made a better attempt to score, but Howorth stopped the ball with his hands, while when Duckworth a few seconds later gave Douglas an opportunity he shot the leather over the bar of the Etonian citadel, and on a second attempt he sent it over the line. As the time for play gradually shortened, the supporters of the Rovers became less confident, and there were shouts from the grand stand of ' Play up Blackburn ', to which admirers of their opponents responded by cries of ' E-e-ton '. But there was ominous silence amongst the Lancashire spectators. For nearly twenty minutes before the close the Etonians were practically penned in their own quarters, and the Rovers were constantly striving to score, but only to be disappointed by seeing the ball go over the line, on the wrong side of the posts or to be stopped by the goalkeeper. All the shots were high, however, and there was no opportunity of judging of Rawlinson's power with his feet. The desperate struggle was continued until the referee's whistle signalled the expiration of time, and the Etonians were hailed the victors by one goal to none. Suter played magnificently, Strachan and Duckworth did remarkably well; McIntyre rendered good service; and the other members played well, but on the whole the team did not quite reach its most brilliant form. Of the Old Etonians the captain and Foley were best, while both backs played well; Rawlinson far exceeded expectations as goalkeeper and elicited many complimentary comments; and Macauley, Dunn, Novelli, and Anderson were the pick of the forward division.

The teams were composed as follows:

Rovers: R. Howorth, goal; H. McIntyre and F. Suter, backs; H. Sharples and F. W. Hargreaves (captain), half backs; J. Duckworth and J. Douglas, right wing; J. Hargreaves and G. Avery, left wing; T. Strachan and J. Brown, centre.

Old Etonians: J. F. P. Rawlinson, goal; T. H. French and P. J. de Paravicini, backs; Hon. A. F. Kinnaird (captain) and C. W. Foley, half backs; W. J. Anderson and J. B. Chevallier, right wing; P. C. Novelli and A. T. R. Dunn, left wing; R. H. Macauley and H. C. Goodhart, centre.

The umpires were Mr. C. H. R. Wollaston (Wanderers), and member of the committee of the Football Association; and Mr. C. Crump, president of the Birmingham Association; and the referee, Mr. J. C. Clegg, vice president of the Sheffield Association. All had been appointed by the Association committee.

THE DIAMOND JUBILEE
1897

(a) *Source:* Russell Thorndike, *Children of the Garter*, Rich and Cowan 1937, pp. 141–5.

An extract from the diary of the author who, at the time of the Jubilee, was a choir boy at Windsor.

On the twenty-second of June, Tuesday, we got up very early, and started from Windsor at 5.45 a.m., arriving in London about seven o'clock. Then we went from Waterloo to St. Paul's Cathedral. Then while we were waiting to get in, we sat on a stone near the railings and watched the men walking about in their robes and uniforms.

Then we got on to the lawn round St. Paul's, and we went and got our food, which we had left there the day before when we went to the rehearsal. The rehearsals were on the 18th and 21st.

Then we went down into St. Paul's Crypt and we ate a few sandwiches; then we went up and had some lemon squash mixed with water from a tap (I remember how we wondered if the water was all right, as it seemed to spring up from the graves in the churchyard).

Then, after looking round the Cathedral, which was very jolly, we descended to the Crypt again and put on our surplices. Then up again and sat in the nave watching the Bishops and Archbishops of all countries, and the Gentlemen of the Queen's Bodyguard carrying their axes studded all over with jewels.

One of them gave me his to hold, and went away for some time, and I began to wonder what I could do with it if he didn't come back. It would have looked very funny for a choir-boy to carry such a weapon. He happened to come back just as we were ordered to go out into our places on the steps, and I was asking Mr. Kempton, one of our basses, what on earth I should do with it. So he was only just in time.

Oh, it was a sight that we saw. The roads were all lined with Jack tars and soldiers. All the British troops were there, I should think. There were besides lots of soldiers of all regiments to play the band. . . .

Now I must tell you of some things that struck me about it all. The Queen was dressed in black silk with silver on it. She had a black bonnet made of lace, trimmed with white flowers and with an aigrette of diamonds. She carried a white lace sunshade, and she had a fan. Her parasol was up. Her horses looked exactly like a circus. Lord Roberts looked very well on his famous Arabian steed.

All the Princes looked very well on their chargers. The Queen looked very well indeed and ever so happy. Everybody looked very well. On the other hand, lots of people fainted in the crowds.

The Te Deum was most exciting, and made a grand noise with all the bands and the great choir. Sir George Martin conducted, and all the people joined in the singing of the Old Hundredth and ' God Save the Queen '. After the National Anthem the Archbishop of Canterbury called out, ' Three Cheers for the Queen '. . . .

After all this the Procession moved away and left us in peace to eat our dinner on the lawn in front of St. Paul's. It seemed funny to eat in a churchyard, but we were hungry all the same, and the graves didn't spoil our appetites one bit.

(*b*) *Source;* Queen Victoria's Journal in *Letters of Queen Victoria,* 3rd series 1886–1901, ed. Buckle. (Murray 1932), vol. iii.

22nd June. A never-to-be-forgotten day. No one ever, I believe, has met with such an ovation as was given to me, passing through those six miles of streets, including Constitution Hill. The crowds were quite indescribable, and their enthusiasm truly marvellous and deeply touching. The cheering was quite deafening, and every face seemed to be filled with real joy. I was much moved and gratified.

. . . At a quarter-past eleven, the others being seated in their carriages long before, and having preceded me a short distance, I started from the State entrance in an open State landau, drawn by eight creams, dear Alix[1], looking very pretty in lilac, and Lenchen[2] sitting opposite me. I felt a good deal agitated, and had been so all these days, for fear anything might be forgotten or go wrong. Bertie[3] and George C.[4] rode one on each side of the carriage, Arthur[5] (who had charge of the whole military arrangements) a little in the rear. My escort was formed from the 2nd Life Guards and officers of the native Indian regiments, these latter riding immediately in front of my carriage. Guard of Honour of Blue-jackets, the Guards, and the 2nd Surrey Regiment (Queen's) were mounted in the Quadrangle and outside the Palace.

Before leaving I touched an electric button, by which I started a message which was telegraphed throughout the whole Empire. It was the following: 'From my heart I thank my beloved people. May God bless them!' At this time the sun burst out. Vicky[6] was in the carriage nearest me, not being able to go in mine, as her rank as Empress prevented her sitting with her back to the horses, for I had to sit alone. Her carriage was drawn by four blacks, richly caparisoned in red. We went up Constitution Hill and Piccadilly, and there were seats right along

[1] The future Queen Alexandra.
[2] Princess Helena, wife of Prince Christian of Schleswig-Holstein.
[3] The Prince of Wales: the future King Edward VII (1901–1910).
[4] George, 2nd Duke of Cambridge (b. 1819; d. 1904), Grandson of George III (b. 1738, d. 1820).
[5] Arthur, Duke of Connaught (1850–1942).
[6] Princess Victoria, The Princess Royal: married the Emperor Frederick III of Germany. Died 1901.

the former, where my own servants and personal attendants, and members of the other Royal Households, the Chelsea Pensioners, and the children of the Duke of York's and Greenwich schools had seats. St. James's Street was beautifully decorated. . . . Trafalgar Square was very striking. . . . The denseness of the crowds was immense, but the order maintained wonderful. The streets in the Strand are now quite wide, but one misses Temple Bar. Here the Lord Mayor received me and presented the sword, which I touched. . . . As we neared St. Paul's the procession was often stopped, and the crowds broke out into singing *God Save the Queen*. . . .

In front of the Cathedral the scene was most impressive. All the Colonial troops, on foot, were drawn up round the Square. My carriage, surrounded by all the Royal Princes, was drawn up close to the steps, where the Clergy were assembled, the Bishops in rich copes, with their croziers, the Archbishop of Canterbury and the Bishop of London each holding a very fine one. A *Te Deum* was sung. . . .

I stopped in front of the Mansion House, where the Lady Mayoress presented me with a beautiful silver basket full of orchids. Here I took leave of the Lord Mayor. Both he and the Lady Mayoress were quite *émus*. We proceeded over London Bridge, where no spectators were allowed, only troops, and then along the Borough Road, where there is a very poor population, but just as enthusiastic and orderly as elsewhere. The decorations there were very pretty. . . . Crossed the river again over Westminster Bridge. . . . The heat during the last hour was very great, and poor Lord Howe, who was riding as Gold Stick, fainted and had a bad fall, but was not seriously hurt.

Got home at a quarter to two. . . . Had a quiet luncheon with Vicky, Beatrice,[1] and her three children. Troops continually passing by. Then rested and later had tea in the garden with Lenchen. There was a large dinner in the supper-room. . . . I walked into the Ball-room afterwards, and sat down in front of the dais. Felt very tired, but tried to speak to most of the Princes and Princesses. . . . In the morning I wore a dress of black silk

[1] Daughter of Queen Victoria: Married Prince Henry of Battenberg, who had died in January, 1896.

trimmed with panels of grey satin veiled with black net and steel embroideries, and some black lace, my lovely diamond chain, given me by my younger children, round my neck. My bonnet was trimmed with creamy white flowers, and white aigrette and some black lace. . . .

INDEX

Wade, George, field-marshal, 48
Wages, 101, 240–1, 244
Walcheren, 152–4
Walmer, 95, 183–4
Walpole, Horace, quoted, 49, 74–6, 88–9
Waterloo, battle of, 158–167, 169–70
Waterproof hats, 249
Watson, Richard, professor and bishop of Llandaff, 199–200
Wellington, Arthur Wellesley, 1st duke of, 180, 183–4, 185–6, 188, 210, 212, 222–4, 233, 256; and Canning, 188–90; and Castlereagh, 177–8; and Chartist Petition, 250; at Badajoz, 157–8; at Waterloo, 162, 165, 183;

after Waterloo, 166–8; during Peninsular War, 182–3; popularity of, 182–3, 184, 224, 224, 234, 253–4
Wesley, John, 40–2, 105–6
West Indies, 99, 169
Westminster, Abbey, 75, 180, 209, 234–5; Bridge, 158; elections, 203–6; Hall, 180–1, Palace of, 4, 59–61
Weymouth, 89–94
Wilkes, John, 88–9
William III, king, 1–2, 8
William IV, king, 208–9, 232
Wolfe, James, 64–5
Woodforde, Rev. James, diary of, quoted, 193–4, 199–200
Woolman, John, 99–101

DATE DUE

MAY 02 1985		

30 505 JOSTEN'S